WOODLAND CRI
FOR WILDLIFE:
a guide to creating new woodland for wildlife in Kent and East Sussex

by

David Blakesley

Dr David Blakesley, CEnv, MIEEM is an ecological consultant for Wildlife Landscapes, which specialises in habitat creation and wildlife surveys; david.blakesley@btinternet.com

Contributors

Dr Peter Buckley, MIEEM is Senior Lecturer in Forest Ecology at Imperial College at Wye

John Tucker is the Operations Director, Southern England, for The Woodland Trust

James Newmarch is a Landscape Architect for East Sussex County Council

Editor

Dr Neil Hipps is Business Development Manager for East Malling Research

emr

First published 2006

Disclaimer
The information presented in this book on behalf of East Malling Research is believed to be accurate and correct, but this cannot be guaranteed. Readers must take all appropriate steps to ensure health and safety of all users, and to follow their own health and safety policy. East Malling Research issues this book without responsibility for accidents or damage as a result of its use.

Citation
For bibliographic purposes, this book should be referred to as
Blakesley, David. 2006. Woodland Creation for Wildlife: a guide to creating new woodland for wildlife in Kent and East Sussex. East Malling Research, East Malling.

Published by
East Malling Research, New Road, East Malling, Kent, ME19 6BJ.
www.eastmallingresearch.com
Registered Charity No. 1102243

Designed by
NatureBureau, 36 Kingfisher Court, Hambridge Road, Newbury, RG14 5SJ

Photographs
All photographs © copyright David Blakesley, Wildlife Landscapes unless stated in the text

Photographic editing by
René Pop

Figures by
Valerie Alford, Simon Bell, Tharada Blakesley and Penny Greeves

Printed by
Information Press, Oxford

ISBN: 0-9553579-0-X   978-0-9553579-0-9

CONTENTS

Foreword   iv

Preface   v

Chapter 1
Introduction   1

    1.1   Why do we need to create more woodland?   1
    1.2   Woodland creation for wildlife – the scope of this guide   3

Chapter 2
Woodlands in the Kent and East Sussex Landscape   6

    2.1   Woodland history   6
    2.2   Regional landscape character   8
    2.3   Woodland types   13

Chapter 3
Woodland succession and wildlife   20

    3.1   Natural succession   20
    3.2   Succession in secondary woodland   22
    3.3   Flora of woodland rides, glades and open spaces   29
    3.4   Woodland birds   32
    3.5   Woodland bats   37
    3.6   Woodland invertebrates   39

Chapter 4
How to create new woodland for wildlife   46

    4.1   How to assess landscape character and survey wildlife habitats   46
    4.2   How to select trees and shrubs   60
    4.3   How to select herbs and grasses for rides and open spaces   75
    4.4   How to design a new wood   84
    4.5   How to plant and manage new woodland   97

Chapter 5
Case studies – new woods in Kent and East Sussex   111

    5.1   Comfort's Wood   112
    5.2   Chalket Farm Wood   117
    5.3   Cavalry Wood   120
    5.4   Runham Estate Woods   125
    5.5   Hastings Spine and Spur roadside   130
    5.6   Robertsbridge Bypass   136

References   140

Further reading   142

FOREWORD

Woodland provides a range of valuable habitats for wildlife, including high forest, woodland edge and grassland. Woodland wildlife continues to be threatened by damage to ancient woodland, despite the recognition that England is one of the least wooded countries in Europe. Historically, new woodland was planted for timber, but we now appreciate that it has important additional benefits, such as environmental services and wildlife conservation. Therefore, this book presents advice on how to create new woodland for wildlife, on agricultural land transport corridors in South East England, for local authorities, farmers, landowners, landscape architects, designers, developers, highway planners, nurseries, foresters, woodland owners, and conservation organisations.

The production of this book has been made possible primarily by INTERREG IIIa, an EC Community Initiative to promote cooperation between organisations within Kent and East Sussex in the UK, Picardie, Nord Pas-de-Calais in France and some other neighbouring regions in both countries. Matched funding was provided by the Highways Agency in the UK and the Councils of Nord Pas-de-Calais and Picardie in France.

Thus, it has been possible to bring together several organisations with excellent knowledge of woodland management, wildlife and biodiversity in South East England and northern France. East Malling Research is an independent provider of research and consultancy serving the landscape industries, that has expertise in environmental science, biodiversity and project management. Imperial College is one of the foremost academic institutions in the UK. Wildlife Landscapes has a proven track record in ecological assessment and habitat creation, both in the UK and overseas. East Sussex County Council manages large areas of woodland with a view to conserving and increasing biodiversity for the benefit of its constituents. The Woodland Trust is the UK's leading conservation charity dedicated to the protection of UK native woodland heritage. The Highways Agency has a roadside estate that extends to 30,000 ha and supports more than 25 million trees. Maintenance and improvement of biodiversity within this estate is a key priority. In France, the Centre Régional de la Propriété Forestière (CRPF) is in charge of the implementation of forest policy in privately owned woodlands. It has developed a large network of forest owners and timber growers and provides technical advice on woodland management. The regions of Nord Pas-de-Calais and Picardie contain woodland areas comparable to those found in Kent and East Sussex.

The practical experience of all of these organisations has been shared and supplemented by a comprehensive review of published literature on woodland creation and management, and natural succession. In addition, extensive surveys of woodlands in Kent and East Sussex by David Blakesley and Peter Buckley have provided real examples of woodland design and management. CRPF have produced several associated pamphlets.

Dr Neil Hipps,
Project Manager,
East Malling Research

PREFACE

This is a book about creating new native woodlands for wildlife, particularly on agricultural land and transport corridors. To design new woodland for wildlife, I believe that it is important to have some knowledge of how wildlife colonises a new habitat, and how this process can be accelerated. Consequently, the ecology of natural succession is introduced, together with a description of some of the more visible elements of woodland flora and fauna; birds, bats, insects and plants.

The core of this book describes how to create new native woodland for wildlife. This includes not only high forest – the traditional focus of the forester – but also shrubs of the woodland edge, and tall herbs and short turf of rides and open spaces. All provide important habitat for wildlife, but it is the woodland edge and open spaces which contribute most to biodiversity in the early life of a new wood. Descriptions of case study woodlands illustrate many of the issues raised in the earlier sections on woodland design and management practices. I am grateful to the owners of these woodlands for giving permission for the wildlife surveys reported in this book. I would also like to take this opportunity to thank Peter Buckley, for his invaluable assistance with vegetation surveys. Furthermore, extensive demonstration plots at The Woodland Trust's Victory Wood site in east Kent have been planted to demonstrate many of the design and management issues discussed in this book. I am especially grateful to John Tucker, Clive Steward and Toby Bancroft of The Woodland Trust for providing this opportunity.

There are a number of people who deserve special thanks. Firstly, without the constant support of Neil Hipps at East Malling Research, this book would not have been possible. I would like to thank Peter Buckley, James Newmarch and John Tucker for their contributions to the text; Neil Hipps for his editorial work; René Pop for editing the photographs; Valerie Alford, Simon Bell, Tharada Blakesley and Penny Greeves for their artwork; and Peter Creed for the design and layout. I am particularly indebted to Peter Buckley for his advice and constant support throughout the preparation of this book. Several other people have kindly read, and provided comments on part of the manuscript, including Steve Elliott, Richard Ferris, Rob Fuller, Keith Kirby, George Peterken, Tony Sangwine and Ian Willoughby.

David Blakesley
Wildlife Landscapes
Bearsted, Kent
2006

1 INTRODUCTION

1.1 Why do we need to create more woodland?

British woodlands enhance the character of our landscape and provide valuable habitat for wildlife. Ancient semi-natural woodlands in particular are rich in biodiversity. Although various vegetation classification systems enable us to group woodlands into distinct categories, their complex ecosystems ensure that, in some way, every ancient semi-natural wood is unique.

Despite the protection now afforded to ancient woodland, and other semi-natural habitats, it is still being damaged or lost today. Conservation and protection of these valuable habitats must be accompanied by efforts to reverse these losses by creating new woodland habitat for wildlife.

Woodland provides a range of habitats in addition to high forest and coppice, including: the scrub zone of the woodland edge; tall herb communities and short grassland of open areas; damp areas; and heathland. Many ancient woods have lost much of their structural diversity as management of coppice and rides has been neglected or abandoned. This threatens the conservation of fragments of species-rich open habitat (Peterken and Francis, 1999), which is particularly important in the context of a largely improved agricultural landscape. Early successional habitats and woodland edge are also threatened, as agriculture encroaches up to the very edge of woodlands. These habitats in particular are extremely important to wildlife in our historically fragmented and highly managed landscapes (Fuller and Warren, 1991).

Five year old woodland at White Horse Wood Country Park in the Kent Downs Area of Outstanding Natural Beauty.

The National Inventory of Woodland and Trees – England (Smith, 2001) showed that woodland covers 16–18% of the land area of Sussex. In contrast, the coverage in Kent is 10–12% of the land area. This is well below the average for counties in South East England, although Kent holds a significant proportion (6%) of ancient semi-natural woodland in the UK, with 20,347 ha (Kent Biodiversity Action Plan (BAP) Steering Group, 1997). The Kent Landcover Survey recently showed that despite this, woodland continues to disappear, with only 72% of woodland present in 1961 unchanged in 1999, the remainder being lost primarily to development, or conversion to grassland and arable. Fortunately these losses have been offset by woodland creation, such that the total area of woodland has remained largely unchanged. As considerable areas of land may come out of agriculture over the next 50 years or so, and with the introduction in July 2005 of the new English Woodland Grant Scheme, this trend of increasing woodland cover may continue. The old farm woodland grant schemes, initiated in 1992, were responsible for the planting of 42,314 ha of new woodland in England, primarily broadleaves on arable or improved land (Defra Farm Woodland Premium Scheme Statistics, 2004). Other factors which will influence the creation of new woodland in Kent in the coming years are the major pressures it faces from development; both as a gateway to Europe, with necessary transport links and infrastructure; and as a place to live and work, with major multi-sectoral developments such as the Thames Gateway, Kings Hill (West Malling), and the expansion of Ashford. This presents a major challenge to planners if the environment is to be protected and enhanced, both for wildlife and people.

There is considerable support amongst conservation agencies for woodland creation in the region. Increasing woodland cover for biodiversity is identified as a key aim by the Kent Countryside Strategy, the Kent Woodland Biodiversity Action Plan, the Sussex Habitat Action Plan and the 'Regional Biodiversity Framework Document – Sector Analysis'. All essentially see woodland creation as an opportunity to enhance biodiversity and the environment, both through the intrinsic wildlife value of new woodland, its ability to encourage the movement of flora and fauna and the maintenance of biodiversity within existing woodland sites. Small areas of new planting could greatly enhance the functional connectedness between woods and produce substantially larger habitat blocks (Sussex Biodiversity Partnership, 2001), creating more viable habitat for key species. The Sussex Wildlife Trust has identified the expansion of woodland blocks and the creation of narrow woodland corridors or shaws to link ancient woodlands as particularly valuable. The recreation of riverine woodlands, a habitat type missing from most of the English lowlands, is also highlighted. Furthermore, development of major new transport corridors is expected in Kent over the next two decades. This will require extensive tree and shrub-planting programmes, designed to safeguard woodland habitats and attract biodiversity.

At a national level, a recent policy statement on England's ancient and native woodland (Forestry Commission and Defra, 2005) states that the landscape context of woodland should be improved by "creating new native woodland to extend, link or complement existing woodland and other habitats". An ambitious programme for establishing new wildwoods is presented in a recent report produced for the Land Use Policy Group (Worrell et al., 2002). Extensive mosaics of new native woodland are envisaged through the expansion of existing ancient semi-natural woodland. This would result in a high level of tree cover at the landscape level. Several possible locations were reviewed, including the Sussex Weald.

Whether woodlands are planted for economic, environmental, social or cultural reasons – in rural areas or the urban fringe – they have the capacity to provide valuable habitats for wildlife. The England Forestry Strategy (Forestry Commission, 1998a) sets out four key programmes: rural development; economic regeneration; recreation, access and tourism; and environment and conservation. Here it is stated that the Government wants to maximise the quality of all benefits provided by woodlands, which includes meeting regional biodiversity objectives. The strategy clearly "embraces the role that woodlands can play in conserving and enhancing the character of our environment". The environment and conservation programme attaches special significance to the design and siting of new woodland to maximise environmental benefits, and to improve opportunities for species to move between ancient woods.

Climate change

Some of the predicted effects of climate change in the UK, the so-called UKCIP02 scenarios (Hulme et al., 2002) are already being felt: the UK climate will become warmer; higher summer temperatures will become more frequent and very cold winters increasingly rare; summers will be drier and winters wetter; snowfall will decrease; and precipitation will become heavier. What is impossible to predict is the severity of these changes, which vary between low and high emission scenarios. However, it is likely that changes will be most severe in the southern half of the UK. Some predictions of future species suitability have been made (Broadmeadow *et al.*, 2004, 2005) using Ecological Site Classification (Pyatt *et al.*, 2001); which suggest that beech and sessile oak, for example, will retreat north and westwards, being replaced in southern England by ash and pedunculate oak respectively.

Some practitioners have suggested that non-native tree species should be planted which will be most suited to the expected changes in climate. Predicting how climate change will affect woodland ecosystems is complex, so any attempts to incorporate climate change scenarios into woodland creation are fraught with difficulty. A precautionary principle should be applied at this stage, as it is too soon to design new woodlands in anticipation of climate change: planting non-native species would accelerate change. The adaptive genetic diversity present in the genomes of native trees and shrubs should not be underestimated. It is possible that many species will be more robust, and adaptable to climate change than is currently believed. Woodland ecosystems should be given an opportunity to develop and evolve as climate change takes place. Concentrating woodland creation in areas where there is already a high concentration of habitat may help the evolution and dispersal of some species in response to climate change, and buffer and extend the areas in which species exist.

1.2 Woodland creation for wildlife – the scope of this guide

This guide is written primarily for people interested in establishing new woodland by planting trees and shrubs, and managing their establishment to bring about rapid canopy closure and site capture. But this will not necessarily lead to woodland rich in wildlife. Studies such as those described in Chapter 5 of this book show that many new woods which have closed canopy are characterised by features which do not encourage the development of a diverse flora and fauna, resulting in woodland which is likely to remain impoverished for many decades. These features include:

- low tree and shrub species diversity
- poor vegetation structure in the high forest and woodland edge
- poorly designed and maintained rides and open spaces
- isolation from ancient, or long-established woodland
- woodland surrounded by farmland which acts as a barrier to the movement of many woodland species
- small size, with high edge to interior ratio.

This frequently mown ride looks attractive, but it represents a missed opportunity for wildlife, through its lack of plant species and structural diversity.

Tall herbs in a woodland ride can provide abundant nectar sources for insects.

There is a common misconception – even amongst some professionals – that new woodlands which have closed canopy are inevitably of low wildlife value and will remain so for decades to come. **This is certainly *not* the case**. New woodlands, including associated areas of shrubby woodland edge and scrub can support a rich variety of wildlife, providing they have been designed and managed appropriately. Knowledge of woodland wildlife, and its ecological requirements are crucial to successful woodland creation. Rare and threatened birds such as common nightingale, bullfinch and turtle dove; declining butterflies such as small copper and small heath; and specialist woodland vascular plants such as bluebell, black bryony and creeping soft-grass may be among the first colonists of new woodland in Kent and Sussex. Woodland rides and glades are becoming increasingly important in a wider countryside context too, with the loss of large areas of semi-natural habitat, including scrub, and unimproved grassland and wildflower-rich meadows from our modern agricultural landscapes. Woodland open spaces can offer a sanctuary for fragments of these habitats, protected from modern agricultural practices such as spraying and grassland reseeding. Even small fragments of habitat can become important reserves in their own right, supporting not just plants, but a rich diversity of grassland invertebrates too.

Woodland creation for wildlife often involves planting native woodland on land which has been without tree cover for a long period of time. The purpose of this book is to present advice on how to achieve this through the careful selection of a planting site, judicious choice of trees and shrubs, and appropriate design and management. The principles and practices described in this book include:

- landscape character assessment
- classifying woodland and grassland communities in the wider landscape
- selecting a suitable site(s), including an assessment of conservation value
- understanding succession, and the diversity of flora and fauna which might colonise new woodland
- selecting appropriate planting mixes of native plants, including trees, shrubs and grassland species for rides and open spaces
- sourcing local plant material
- woodland design
- managing woodland to accelerate wildlife colonisation.

Trees and shrubs vary enormously in the invertebrate fauna they support. Flowering phenology, for example, should be taken into account at the planning stage, to ensure the presence of flowers from spring through to autumn. Early summer is a particularly important time, when woodland supports large adult populations of invertebrates, and the numbers of feeding insectivorous birds and their young reach a peak. The attraction of these invertebrates *per se* will increase biodiversity, because insects attract insectivorous birds, and bats. These issues are explored in greater depth in Chapter 3.

Vegetation and foliage structure will determine the opportunities for breeding and feeding of a wide range of woodland fauna. Fruit-bearing shrubs will attract frugivorous birds, animals and invertebrates into new woodland. It is therefore important to ensure a resource of fruit throughout the year. Visitors such as winter thrushes enhance the biodiversity of woodland. Resident thrushes may also breed. Crucially, these species disperse seeds of other plants into new woodland.

Tim Loseby

If these issues are addressed when designing and managing new woodland, the resulting habitat will favour more rapid, and natural development of a complex woodland ecosystem. It is possible to achieve a closed canopy wood within 12–20 years of planting, with a diverse vegetation structure and rich diversity of wildlife, which is worthy of conservation. This is the premise upon which the guidelines on how to create new native woodland for wildlife, presented in Chapter 4, are based. Such woodland will be of benefit to wildlife and people within a generation, and each new woodland planted will be unique.

Natural regeneration

If an area of farmland is abandoned without any modification to the landscape or soil, it may take up to 50 years or more to become woodland, and several centuries to be classified as old growth (see Section 3.2). Even after several hundred years, its specialist and obligate shade flora is likely to be poor. However, natural regeneration may result in habitat patterns and mosaics that would not readily occur with more 'traditional' tree planting. These habitats could be highly beneficial to a wide range of wildlife.Natural regeneration is most likely to be successful on land close to native woodland. On larger sites, such areas could be set aside for natural regeneration, to complement more extensive areas of tree planting.

2 WOODLANDS IN THE KENT AND EAST SUSSEX LANDSCAPE

2.1 Woodland history

Woodland is the natural vegetation over much of the British Isles. Twelve thousand years ago, when Britain was in the grip of the last ice age, there were no trees at all. The southern edge of the ice sheet was bordered by tundra, which included what is now Kent and Sussex. As the climate warmed and the ice retreated, the landscape changed dramatically. Trees 'migrated' northwards across the British Isles from their southern refugia. Pollen records show that the earliest forest was composed of aspen, birch and sallow. More trees followed: Scots pine, oak, alder, lime and elm enriched the developing forest ecosystems. The migration of trees, plants and animals continued until the flooding of the English Channel around 5500BC, which restricted further colonisation. This can be appreciated from the disparity in bird diversity between British and continental European woodland. Many species never made it at all. At least 25 species of birds present in continental woodlands are absent from the British Isles.

Ancient woodland at Marline Valley Woods SSSI in the East Sussex High Weald.

The Atlantic Period 5500–3100BC, marked a period of relative stability for our mature woodland ecosystems. Most of the British Isles were covered by a huge expanse of pristine, primary forest, the so called 'wildwood' (Rackham, 1990). Only saltmarshes, coastal dunes and mountain tops were likely to have remained as permanently open country. Pollen records tell us a lot about the species composition of the forest (Huntley and Birks, 1983). Most of southern England was dominated by lime woodland. Within this, the second most dominant tree species – oaks, ash, elm, alder, Scots pine or hazel varied with locality, creating a patchwork of different lime woodland types. Limewoods are now extremely rare in South East England, but fragments can still be found today, including Farningham Woods in north Kent, and Clowes Wood north of Canterbury, both of which hold populations of small-leaved lime. Large-leaved lime occurs in woodland on the scarp slopes of the Western Sussex Downs. The disappearance of lime during the Atlantic Period was probably caused by human activity through forest clearance (Turner, 1962), although declining temperatures are believed to have been a major factor in its failure to recover, as this reduced fertility.

Even as the ecosystems of the wildwood matured, Mesolithic people were probably having an influence on its structure, by clearing trees around their settlements. What we know for certain is that during the Neolithic period, about 4,000 years ago, the destruction of the wildwood began in earnest. Coppicing, the extraction of timber, and agriculture opened up the wildwood, threatening populations of old growth species, whilst creating opportunities for colonization by the flora and fauna we find in woodland open spaces and the wider countryside today. It is a sobering thought as we try to persuade other countries to protect their tropical forests, that by the Middle Ages at the latest, the conversion was complete… no natural wildwood remained. No one can be sure exactly when the wildwood disappeared, although most was cleared during the Bronze and Iron ages. Oliver Rackham has suggested that on Cambridgeshire boulder clay, the last vestiges may have survived until Anglo-Saxon times. The wildwood of southern England, dominated by lime, has now been replaced by oakwoods, ashwoods and so on.

This has left 21st century Britain one of the least wooded temperate countries in the world. The destruction of the forests also saw substantial losses of biodiversity. Whilst some mammals such as aurochs disappeared in the Bronze Age, others became extinct much more recently. Brown bear and beaver survived into the Dark Ages, whilst lynx, wolf and capercaillie (later re-introduced) became extinct as recently as the mid to late 18th century. There is now some interest in 'wildwood' creation projects which include the introduction of some of these enigmatic mammals.

From the pollen record we have learnt much about the trees and shrubs of the wildwood. In contrast, we know far less about its structure. There is some debate amongst countryside historians about open space in the wildwood, and hence the origin of certain species found in today's woodland rides, glades and the wider open countryside. Did these species originate primarily along river margins, and in tree fall gaps maintained by grazing herbivores in the high forest – the so called 'gap-dynamic model', or was the wildwood an altogether more open landscape? Could parts of it have resembled the woodland pasture grazed by large herbivores, found in the New Forest as it is today? This has been suggested by the work of Francis Vera, described in his book *Grazing Ecology and Forest History* (2000). English Nature recently commissioned a review of the nature and current state of the debate on Vera's hypothesis, and its relevance to future conservation practice of using large herbivores in reserve management (Hodder *et al.*, 2005). This comprehensive report concluded that, whilst there may have been open areas resembling modern wood-pasture, the majority of the

Chalk grassland open space in ancient woodland at Yocklett's Bank, in the Kent Downs Area of Outstanding Natural Beauty.

wildwood would have been closed high forest with temporary and permanent glades. Crucial to this view is the absence of any pollen data to support the notion of an open canopy forest as envisaged by Vera.

What is termed ancient woodland today, is woodland which predates 1600AD. Some of this will have been continuously wooded since the time when the wildwood became fragmented. Secondary ancient woodland may, at some point in the more distant past, have lost its woodland cover to agriculture: this may be indistinguishable from continuously wooded land. 'Recent secondary' woodland refers to woodland which has been planted since medieval times (i.e. post 1600AD). If we use the term 'natural' to describe the wildwood which developed without any human interference, then the term 'semi-natural' (first used by Tansley in 1939 to describe remnants of original forest) can be applied to present day ancient woodland. This assumes that the influence of people on woodland is not viewed as wholly natural.

2.2   Regional landscape character

A brief geology of the region

Most of Kent and East Sussex, and parts of West Sussex, Surrey, Greater London and east Hampshire form part of a larger, distinctive geographic region in South East England known as the Weald. This is a region defined by an encircling chalk escarpment of soft limestone, formed during the Cretaceous period, on top of previous sedimentary layers of, respectively, Upper Greensand, Gault Clay, Lower Greensand, Weald Clay and finally the Hastings beds. All these layers were subsequently uplifted into a dome or anticline, the centre of which was later eroded, revealing a succession of concentric geologies that form the basis of the modern landscape.

Working inwards from the chalk rim of the North, Western and South Downs is the parallel escarpment of the Lower Greensand, separated from the chalk by narrow belts of Upper Greensand (mainly in western part of the Weald) and Gault Clay. Beyond this is the wide expanse of Weald Clay, forming the lower Weald, and finally, at the core of the region, are the Hastings beds of the High Weald, the latter comprised of the Tunbridge Wells and Ashdown sands, inter-bedded with Wadhurst clay.

Outside the envelope of the Weald, where the chalk strata descend into steep downfolds, are more recent, Tertiary era deposits of sands, clays, and pebble beds forming part of the Paleocene and Eocene series. These include the Thanet sands and the Woolwich, Reading and Blackheath Beds in north Kent and the Bagshot, Bracklesham and Barton Beds in Surrey, above which are exposures of London Clay. Finally, in places the parent geology is covered with thin surface drift of alluvium, wind-blown brickearth and the remnants of Tertiary sands. On the Downs this occurs as deposits of soliflucted chalk in footslope positions and dry valleys (Coombe Deposits), and on the plateaux as a complex of weathered chalk (Clay-with-Flints), together with Tertiary and wind-blown material (Plateau Drift), incorporated under periglacial conditions.

Regional landscape character

The Countryside Agency (Swanwick, 2002) defines landscape character as:

...the distinct and recognisable pattern of elements that occurs consistently in a particular type of landscape, and how these are perceived by people. It reflects particular combinations of geology, landform, soils, vegetation, land use and human settlement. It creates the particular sense of place of different areas of the landscape.

Landscape character assessment is used as a tool to inform planning and landscape management decisions, attempting to ensure that landscape change occurs in a considered way, respectful of the character of an area. Scale is important in landscape character assessment. There are three main levels:

- national and regional scale – represented by The Character of England work of the Countryside Commission and English Nature
- local authority scale, whether at county, district or unitary authority level – represented by the Landscape Assessment of Kent (Kent County Council, 2004) which identifies 114 local character areas, and the East Sussex Landscape Assessment
- local scale, where smaller areas are considered. In Kent and East Sussex, landscape character assessments have been carried out for Areas of Outstanding Natural Beauty, and for individual towns and villages.

In the late 1990s, the then Countryside Commission and English Nature combined to produce the Character of England map. In Kent and Sussex, nine character areas relevant to the region are included (Figure 2.1).

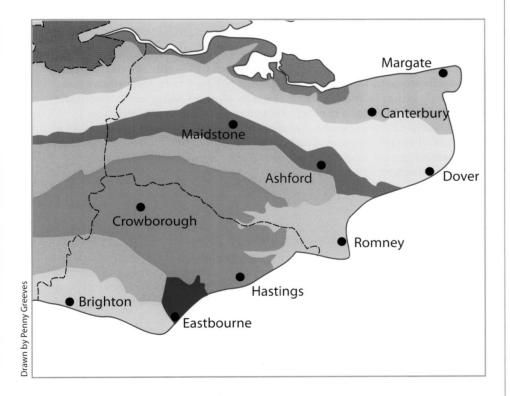

Drawn by Penny Greeves

Figure 2.1 Landscape character areas in Kent and East Sussex.

- 81: Greater Thames Estuary
- 113: North Kent Plain
- 119: North Downs
- 120: Wealden Greensand
- 121: Low Weald
- 122: High Weald
- 123: Romney Marshes
- 124: Pevensey Levels
- 125: South Downs

The contribution of woodland to landscape character in Kent and East Sussex

Kent and East Sussex are amongst the most wooded counties in England. The contribution that woodland makes to landscape character in the different character areas, as defined by The Character of England, is very variable. The presence or absence of woodland is an important influence on landscape character, creating a sense of place and reinforcing local identity. It provides pattern, texture and colour, enclosure and shelter, while enhancing remoteness and/or tranquillity. It has the capacity to absorb housing and industrial development, and associated roads and other infrastructure into the landscape, providing a setting and screening. It can emphasise a sense of history, and have cultural associations. From a functional point of view it can increase biodiversity and provide opportunities for recreation and economic activity.

81   Greater Thames Estuary

This flat, predominantly coastal landscape has few trees and almost no woodland, except on higher ground and in association with settlements. Some scrub is found associated with roads and railway lines. There has been much loss of tree cover in recent years due to Dutch elm disease.

> **Opportunities for the creation of new woodland features are restricted mainly to the screening of new and existing building development and roads using scrubby species appropriate to the location. Larger growing species are appropriate on higher ground.**

113   North Kent Plain

The underlying geology of the North Kent Plain is the chalk that outcrops mainly in Thanet, although most of the region is overlain by Eocene strata, including the Thanet sands and the Woolwich, Reading and Blackheath Beds, as well as the London Clay. This is a predominantly agricultural landscape with high quality soils and an open, low and gently undulating nature. Generally, wooded features are limited to shelterbelt planting of poplar and alder and scattered small woodlands. Significant woodland is confined to the west of the area, notably near the Blean, where the largest continuous woodland in Kent is found on heavy London clay. Commonly found species include sweet chestnut, sessile oak, hornbeam and beech.

> **Opportunities for the creation of new woodland features exist generally on agricultural land, especially adjacent to new roads and railway lines currently either in the planning stage or already being built. Woodland creation would reduce their landscape impact. Further landscape enhancement through woodland planting could be used to reduce the impact of new housing and industrial development. There are also many opportunities for woodland creation in the Blean to link fragments of existing ancient woodland.**

119   North Downs

South of the North Kent Plain, the ridge of the North Downs forms a geologically distinct region based on the chalk, giving rise to shallow, rendzina soils on the steeper scarp slopes. However, on the plateaux and much of the shallower dip slopes, the chalk is covered by superficial drift and on the footslopes with periglacial downwash (Coombe Rock) deposits, creating contrasting sequences of highly calcareous and acidic soils. This is

View from Bulltown Corner looking west across the Wye: Stour Valley local character area to the distant North Downs.

a landscape of rolling downland, relatively unspoilt and undeveloped due to the steep slopes, where some high-quality, species-rich chalk grassland still remains. Woodland is confined to areas of the plateaux on higher ground, some dip slopes, and valley sides. On thin chalk soils, chalk scrub with juniper and box occurs in a few localities, together with 'hangers' of beech and yew woodland. On the heavier Clay-with-Flints and Plateau Drift, oak-hornbeam woods have been replaced in many places by sweet chestnut, and, more recently, conifer plantations. Where arable agriculture does not predominate, the calcareous Coombe deposits are occasionally wooded with ash, field maple and beech, along with hawthorn scrub and increasing amounts of sycamore regeneration.

Opportunities for woodland planting are restricted by the importance of the open character of much of this area and the potential for the restoration of high quality chalk grassland. Enhancement of the wooded character of many scarp

120   Wealden Greensand

The escarpment of the Wealden Greensand character area includes not only the Upper and Lower Greensand, but also the Gault and Atherfield Clays, forming a complex of several different soil types across the region. This is an intimate landscape of diverse character, with scattered villages linked by winding lanes. Generally it is a very wooded landscape with both ancient woodland and conifer plantations. In Kent it becomes progressively less wooded further east and becomes increasingly an agricultural landscape with occasional large towns. The type and character of the woodland varies depending upon soils. Gault Clay in particular is associated with poorly drained, heavy soils on which the woodland survivors are generally pedunculate oak with hazel. In contrast the acid, sandy soils of the Upper and parts of the Lower Greensand support sessile oakwood, birch and sweet chestnut, while ash-dominated woodland is found on the base-rich soils associated with the Hythe Beds of the Lower Greensand. Parkland is also well represented in this region, for example at Knole and Hatch Parks in Kent and Petworth and Parham in Sussex.

Additional tree and woodland planting could be accommodated throughout the area, taking care to match existing character. New transport corridors and other developments can be assimilated into the landscape with sensitive planting.

BELOW LEFT **View across two character areas and five local character areas, from Trosley Country Park in the Luddesdown: West Kent Downs local character area.**

BELOW RIGHT **Spring cutting of sweet chestnut coppice in the Mereworth Woodlands local character area exposes bluebells and other woodland flowers.**

121   Low Weald

The Low Weald character area is a predominantly low-lying, gently undulating region dominated by wet, heavy clay soils formed from Weald Clay. Essentially rural in character, the landscape is small-scale and intimate, with a mix of fields and woods. Because of the poor drainage, a high density of ancient semi-natural woodland has survived, linked by a network of pre-enclosure hedges and shaws. The area contains much lowland beech and yew, but also significant patches of mixed deciduous coppice woodland of ash, hornbeam and field maple with oak standards, much of which has suffered from management neglect in recent decades. Wet woodland occurs along rivers such as the Wey, Mole, Arun, Adur, Ouse, Eden, Medway, Len, Teise and Beult. Ham Street Woods in Kent and Plashett Park Wood in East Sussex are good examples of mixed deciduous woodland in the Low Weald, and pasture woodlands are represented by The Mens and Ebernoe Common in West Sussex.

There are opportunities to create additional areas of woodland and hedgerows, as long as these would help to integrate existing and proposed developments within the area.

122 High Weald

The High Weald geology is complex, consisting of Lower Cretaceous clays and sandstones that give rise to a rolling landform of ridges and valleys. Some of the rivers and streams are deeply incised in steep, ravine-like valleys that are referred to as gills. This is a one of the most densely wooded areas in England, with ancient woodland, sweet chestnut coppice and conifer plantations, well connected by hedges. Intermingled with the woods is a close patchwork of small fields, hedges, shaws and sunken lanes. The main species are oak, ash, hornbeam, sweet chestnut, birch, field maple, holly and wild cherry. Scots pine is widely naturalised on the acid, free draining sands, and much hornbeam and sweet chestnut is grown as coppice, often with oak standards.

Gill woodland in Marline Valley Woods SSSI in the East Sussex High Weald.

Opportunities exist to extend broadleaved woodland into areas where this has been lost and neglected, to replace conifer plantations, and to restore the connectivity between blocks of woodland.

123   Romney Marshes

This is a very flat, open and predominantly agricultural landscape of reclaimed marshland with drainage dykes and occasional villages. Few trees exist apart from around settlements on slightly higher ground, and in isolated situations elsewhere. Willows predominate, with scrub species such as hawthorn and blackthorn.

Trees and woodland are not an important part of the character of this landscape, so opportunities for new planting are restricted.

124   Pevensey Levels

Like the Romney Marshes, this is another open landscape of mainly reclaimed marshland with isolated settlements and occasional lanes. Trees, woodland and hedges are scarce and restricted to occasional lines of hawthorn and willow along ditches or hedges alongside lanes and paths. More trees are found on the slightly higher ground where the settlements are.

> **As trees and woodland are not an important part of the character of the landscape, opportunities for planting are again restricted to the edges of settlements and farms.**

125   South Downs

In contrast to the North Downs which they resemble geologically, the South Downs are less well wooded, with fewer forestry plantations, although they have some of the best examples of yew woodland in the region. The rolling chalk downland meets the sea around Seaford and Eastbourne in sheer cliffs. Compared with West Sussex, the Downs landscape of East Sussex tends to be very open, with woodland confined to a few slopes, although a notable large area of woodland is Friston Forest, planted after the Second World War. Woods and parklands are a feature of the base of the Downs. Principal species include beech, ash, whitebeam, sycamore and yew, along with hawthorn and chalk shrubs such as privet and wayfaring-tree. Around the villages, holm oak, Corsican pine, horse chestnut and lime are commonly found.

> **Opportunities for new woodland planting are restricted to slopes and valleys where appropriate to the local character, and to enhance the setting of settlements and farms.**

2.3   Woodland types

Each character area contains several types of woodland, some of which have been listed as priority habitats in the UK Habitat Action Plan (HMSO, 1995), while others are more of local significance. Of the priority habitats listed, the nine character areas contain lowland beech and yew woods, wet woods, and lowland wood pastures (Table 2.1). These various woodland communities are broadly described by the pan-European Nature Information System (EUNIS) and the National Vegetation Classification (NVC). Together, the character areas contain a substantial proportion of the lowland beech forest within its original native distribution zone in Britain, most notably on the North Downs and in the Low Weald. A woodland type unique to Britain and Ireland, pure yew woodland, is also present on the chalk of the North and South Downs. Wet woodland, mainly dominated by alder, occurs in river valleys, including the humid ravines or gills of Sussex and on seasonally waterlogged soils. There are also some notable parklands present within the greater Weald region containing ancient, pollard trees within semi-natural grassland or heathland habitats.

Of lower conservation priority, but still of national significance and important for wildlife, are the very extensive areas of lowland mixed deciduous woodland present across the region. These include oak-hornbeam woods and acid oakwoods, typical of the Blean in east Kent, but also ash-dominated woods on more base-rich soils in parts of the Weald. On the chalk of the North Downs, box woodland survives in a few places. Taking the region as a whole, a high proportion (c.38%) of all semi-natural woodland has been converted to plantations over the past 70 years, while extensive new plantations have been established on heathland and chalk downland habitats during a period dating from the 1930s until the late

1970s More recently, over the past 25 years, small areas of farm woodlands have been planted on ex-arable and improved pasture land.

Woodland community types in Kent and East Sussex

Many woodland classification systems co-exist in Britain, but the most widely used currently is the National Vegetation Classification (NVC). This describes twenty-five main communities, most of which have two or more sub-community variants (Rodwell, 1991). Eight of these have a mainly northern distribution or are not found in the study region, and a further five are successional scrub communities, leaving twelve main woodland communities to consider (Figure 2.2), whose distribution can be inferred from soil associations present (Figure 2.3). For woods occurring on wet or waterlogged soils, the main types break down into alder, or willow dominated canopies, forming groups W5–7 and W1–2 respectively, the gradient between them being moderated by nutrient-rich or nutrient-poor conditions.

Figure 2.2 National Vegetation Classification overview, showing the main woodland communities in relation to soil type and their regional distribution in Britain. Examples of the woodland community types shown in colour are present in the study region. (After Whitbread and Kirby, 1992)

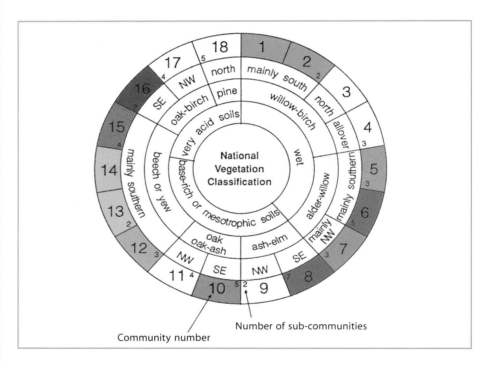

Figure 2.3 Map of Kent showing the potential distribution of different woodland communities based on soil associations present, and cross-referenced to sample woods (mainly Sites of Special Scientific Interest) for which detailed NVC information is available.

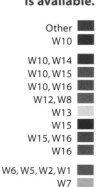

Other
W10
W10, W14
W10, W15
W10, W16
W12, W8
W13
W15
W15, W16
W16
W6, W5, W2, W1
W7

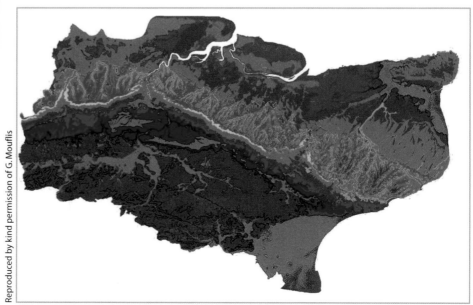

Table 2.1 Key woodland habitats present in six of the well-wooded character areas in the study region, showing Biodiversity Action Plan (BAP) priority types and associated woodland communities described in the NVC.
✓ areas of this woodland present in the region; ✓✓ extensive areas present

Woodland habitats	European woodland equivalent[1]	NVC type[2]	North Kent Plain	North Downs	Wealden Greensand	High Weald	Low Weald	South Downs
Priority BAP habitats								
Lowland beech and yew woods	G1.6	W12, 14, 15		✓✓extensive	✓	✓	✓✓extensive	✓
Yew woods – extensive stands	G3.9	W13						✓
Wet woodland – mainly alder	G1.1, G1.2	W5–7, W1–2			✓river valleys	✓gill woods	✓	
Lowland wood pastures and parklands	84.4 Bocage, 84.5 Parkland	W10, 14–16			✓	✓		
Other (broad) habitats								
Lowland mixed deciduous woodland	G1, G1.A, G1.B, G1.8	W10, W16, W8	✓✓	✓✓extensive	✓	✓	✓	✓*
Box woodland				✓				
Plantations, mainly conifer			✓✓extensive		✓	✓occasional		✓

[1] EUNIS (European Nature Information System) Classification
* includes large-leaved lime)

[2]W1–2: grey willow-common marsh-bedstraw; grey willow-downy birch-common reed
W5–7: alder-greater tussock-sedge; alder-nettle; alder-ash-yellow pimpernel
W8: ash-field maple-dog's mercury
W10: pedunculate oak-bracken-bramble
W12–15: beech-dog's mercury; yew; beech-bramble; beech-wavy hair-grass
W16: oak spp.-birch spp.-wavy hair-grass

On drier sites the woodland types break down into combinations of ash, oak and beech woods. Three community types are distinguished by the constant presence of beech in the canopy, which can tolerate a range of soil conditions ranging from calcareous to acidic (W12–15). Similar in composition to W12, but lacking beech, is yew woodland (W13), found on calcareous sites. Elsewhere, soil acidity levels determine whether mixed-deciduous or oak-birch communities predominate. On base-rich soils (rich in a range of basic cations), ash is a prominent canopy species, accompanied by field maple, hazel, and shrubs which grow on calcareous soils (rich in calcium but low in other cations); forming W8 woodland communities. On more acid soils the proportion of pedunculate oak increases, sometimes with birch, sweet chestnut and hornbeam, more typical of W10 woodland. In very acidic conditions pedunculate oak is replaced by sessile oak with abundant birch and rowan (W16). Individual communities are described for the priority BAP habitats in the following section.

Lowland beech and yew woodland

In the late 1980s the Nature Conservancy Council estimated that up to 30,000 ha of all ancient semi-natural and recent woodland of this woodland type was present in the South East Region, comprising calcareous, neutral-basic and acid types.

Calcareous beech and yew woodland, corresponding to NVC plant community W12 (beech-dog's mercury) woodland form perhaps 40% of the habitat type. These high forest stands occur on the chalk scarps of the North and South Downs and are dominated by beech, ash, sycamore, yew and whitebeam, with oak less common than in other beechwood types. At Rook Clift on the South Downs, coppiced large-leaved lime occurs, and almost pure stands of yew are found in places, corresponding to W13 of the NVC, with good examples occurring at Kingley Vale in East Sussex and Westfield Wood in Kent. Uncommon species in the understorey of calcareous beech and yew woods include box, coralroot bitter-cress and bird's-nest orchid.

On neutral-slightly acidic and usually heavier soils, comprising about 45% of the habitat, the beech canopy contains higher proportions of oaks and often merges with typical oak forest communities. Bramble is a characteristic component of the ground vegetation, with the rare violet helleborine sometimes present, forming beech-bramble woodland (W14). Holly and yew are occasionally present in the shrub layer. This type is common in both the High and Low Weald, occurring as high forest, wood-pasture or abandoned coppice.

Acidic beech woodland covers a smaller area of the south-eastern lowland beechwoods (the remaining 15%), but is typical of the well drained sands of the High Weald. Sites have low pH (3.5 to 4.5) and wavy hair-grass is common on the ground, giving rise to beech-wavy hair-grass woodland (W15). Oak is a common canopy associate, as is holly and sometimes yew in the shrub layer. This type also forms a large percentage of the lowland wood-pasture sites in England.

Wet woodlands

Wet woodlands in the region occur on seasonally wet soils, along river valleys, in floodplains and on fens, mires and bogs. Sadly they are now extremely rare in Kent and East Sussex. Alder, birch and willows are the predominant species, merging into oak, ash or beech communities and forming mosaics with them on drier soil types. Several of these woods are dominated by alder and have a previous history of coppice management, forming alder-greater tussock-sedge woodland (W5), alder-nettle woodland (W6), and alder-ash-yellow pimpernel woodland (W7). Elsewhere alder is replaced by grey willow-common marsh-bedstraw (W1) and grey willow-downy birch-common reed woodland (W2), and on drier parts of the flood plain, gives way to ash-field maple-dog's mercury woodland (W8).

A notable type of wet woodland occurs in the steep valleys or gills of the High Weald, which cut through the sandstone and clay strata: examples are Brenchley Wood and Hunstead Wood in Kent. The high humidity allows an Atlantic-type flora to develop, more characteristic of western Britain, which is rich in ferns, mosses and liverworts. Dead wood habitats on wet substrates also support a variety of localised invertebrates such as the Biodiversity Action Plan priority species *Melanopion minimum* (a weevil), jumping weevil (*Rhynchaenus testaceus*) and *Lipsothix* spp. (craneflies) – one specialist, *L. nigristigma*, is associated with wet wood in log jams in streams. Wet woodland also provides cover and breeding sites for otters, and may contain relict plant species more typical of formerly open wetlands on the site such as marsh fern (*Thelypteris palustris*).

Wet alder woodland in the River Len valley in the Wealden Greensand character area.

Lowland wood-pasture and parkland

Wood pasture and parkland habitats are historic sites distinguished by their structure of large, open grown trees, often pollarded, within a matrix of unimproved grazed grasslands or heathlands. In vegetation terms they can represent several vegetation types, but are most closely allied with NVC communities such as oak-bracken-bramble woodland (W10), beech-bramble woodland (W14), beech-wavy hair-grass woodland (W15) and oak-birch-wavy hair-grass woodland (W16), together with the surrounding non-woodland vegetation communities.

A key habitat feature is the distinctive saproxylic fauna (living in rotten wood, water-filled cavities on live trees, and sap runs) and epiphytic flora (which derive physical support from their host) associated with the ancient trees, which are also important for hole-nesting birds and bats. They are important in southern England, where they are relatively abundant, and are of national and European importance. In the Low Weald; the Mens and Ebernoe Common in West Sussex are notable examples, although these are currently under-grazed. On the acid Greensands, well-known sites include Knole and Hatch Park in Kent; Parham and Petworth in Sussex; and in the High Weald, Eridge Park.

Lowland mixed deciduous woodland

This is a very broad category comprising both ash and oak woods, representing the gradient between base-rich and more acid soils. Most are of coppice origin and small-scale, typical of the enclosed landscape pattern of parts of Kent and Sussex. The main vegetation types on base-rich substrates are the ash-field maple-dog's mercury woods (W8), for example at the base of the Downs or on the Hythe beds. These merge into oakwoods (W10) and finally, and less extensively, into acid oak-birch-wavy hair-grass woodland (W16). The latter type is common in parts of the Blean, for example in Church Wood and Ellenden Wood in Kent. The Blean is notable for coppice woodland supporting the rare heath fritillary butterfly, the bonfire beetle (*Acritus homeopathicus*) and a healthy population of common nightingales. This type of acid sessile oak woodland, analogous to the *Stellario-Carpinetum* forest (old oak woody on sandy plains) of Annex 1 of the EC Habitats Directive, also occurs outside the North Kent Plain on parts of the Wealden Greensand, for example at Toys Hill in Kent and on the High Weald sandstone at Nap Wood in East Sussex.

Blean Wood in east Kent, within the North Kent Plain character area.

By comparison, W10 types are found more universally in all of the character areas, especially on the North Downs and on the heavier clay soils, for example on the Gault and Weald Clays of the Low Weald. Chiddingfold Forest and Plashett Park Wood in Sussex and Ham Street Woods in Kent, and West Dean Woods on the South Downs are good examples of such oak-hazel woods. All three types – W8, W10 and W16 – form mosaics with other woodland types, in particular lowland beech and yew woodland. However, many have lost their semi-natural character and diversity of canopy species as a result of conversion to sweet chestnut or pure hornbeam coppice in the past, or more recently to conifer plantations.

Scrub

Scrub is a complex ecosystem: some types are temporary ecosystems in the successional series from open ground to mature woodland, known as seral stages; others form more stable habitats in their own right. The conservation value of scrub can be remarkably high, but it is frequently underrated. The NVC describes five scrub types, and two under-scrub communities. The most common types in lowland Britain are hawthorn-ivy scrub (W21) and bramble-Yorkshire-fog underscrub (W24). Blackthorn-bramble (W22) is also widespread and common. Bramble-Yorkshire-fog scrub, which frequently occurs on abandoned farmland often develops into hawthorn-ivy scrub on neutral or base-rich soils, and to gorse-bramble scrub (W23) on acid soils. Gorse scrub may occur on patches of acidic soil in areas of largely neutral or calcareous soil. On deeper, moist and richer neutral soils, blackthorn scrub may dominate. A mosaic may develop with patches of hawthorn and blackthorn scrub interspersed with bramble-Yorkshire-fog.

Recent secondary woodland and farm woodlands

Private landowners in Britain have for many decades received grant assistance from the state (the Forestry Commission) for planting and managing new woodland areas. Since a major revision of the Woodland Grant Schemes in 1988, the private sector has responded positively, mainly by planting small parcels of woodland on less profitable corners of their estates. The new arrangements were accompanied by the launch of The Farm Woodland Scheme (FWS) in England, jointly by the Forestry Commission and the Ministry of Agriculture, Fisheries and Food (MAFF),

Closed canopy farm woodland after 12 years.

later undergoing modification in 1992 when it was re-launched as the Farm Woodland Premium Scheme (FWPS). This scheme differed from its predecessors in that, besides receiving planting grants, annual payments were made to farmers on planting improved agricultural land in compensation for the income forgone. At its inception the scheme had broad aims: diverting land from agricultural production; boosting rural employment; contributing to farm income; and encouraging a greater interest in timber production on farms. Enhancing the landscape, providing new habitats and increasing biodiversity gradually assumed greater importance (MAFF 1988, 1998).

A study of the 110 participants entering the FWPS in Kent and East Sussex over a three-year period between 1992 and July 1995 found that new planting areas (a total of 480 ha) were generally small-scale, averaging 4.3 ha per holding, which in turn were dispersed as several smaller individual blocks (mean 1.7 ha). The uptake was greatest on holdings of 100–200 ha, but there was no strong relationship between the area planted and the total area farmed (Fraser and Buckley, 2000). The main farm business types concerned were arable crops, followed by cattle and sheep; 67% of participants considered the land taken for planting to be of 'average agricultural quality' compared with the rest of their holdings.

The new woodland areas showed a remarkably consistent pattern: nearly all were native broadleaved mixtures consisting of 2–4 main species (oak, ash, beech and wild cherry being particularly common), planted intimately or in segregated groups. Several schemes had 'edge-mixes' of shrubs planted along the margins and, in the bigger planting blocks, broad rides were left, reflecting grant scheme rules allowing for 20% open space and 10% shrub planting. A recent review of the Woodland Grant Scheme in Kent found that 520 ha of new woodland had been established during the period 1995–2001 in 383 separate blocks, an average of 1.36 ha per block (Coney, personal communication).

3 WOODLAND SUCCESSION AND WILDLIFE

A basic understanding of woodland ecology and woodland natural history will help the practitioner to improve the wildlife value of new woodland, through more informed species choices; better layout and design; and more enlightened approaches to management. This section provides an introduction to this topic, with a discussion of natural succession, and a description of some of the key groups of species which can be found in young woodland, including birds, bats, butterflies and plants. These groups represent highly visible elements of the woodland flora and fauna and clearly illustrate the potential conservation value of new woodland.

3.1 Natural succession

Woodland succession is essentially a series of more or less predictable changes in ecosystem structure and composition over time, known as seral stages, which result in a relatively stable, mature ecosystem. Succession from bare rock or sand dunes – which have not supported an ecological community before – to woodland, is termed primary succession, although it is difficult to find examples of this in today's British landscape. Succession on an area of cleared land such as farmland is called secondary succession. Each seral stage is accompanied by: different communities of plants and animals; increasing biomass; and an increase in biodiversity. In the British Isles, the cool temperate climate leads to deciduous forest. Recognisable stages include:

- establishment of saplings which are yet to close canopy
- thicket with closed canopy and heavy shading of the field layer
- maturing trees, leading to opening of the canopy and some tree/shrub regeneration
- mature woodland with relatively little dead wood
- managed coppice under man's influence
- old growth, with some very large, mature trees and standing/fallen dead trees.

Regeneration in ancient woodland usually involves colonisation of relatively small areas, such as a tree-fall gap. When such a gap is created, trees and shrubs will regenerate from seed, root-suckers and coppice. Regeneration will be fast, because of vegetative reproduction and the availability of seed in the immediate vicinity. Saplings may already be present in the understorey, ready to take advantage of any break in the canopy. Before canopy closure, ground vegetation will peak through invasion by species of open spaces. Catastrophic disturbances, such as those caused by the storm of 1987, may open up much larger areas of woodlands. There are several sites in Kent and Sussex which provide excellent examples of succession in a local context, for example Larkey Valley Wood in the Stour Valley, and Westfield Wood on the Kent Downs. In these woods, rapid natural regeneration has created interesting new habitat. Vegetative reproduction has a major role, together with germination of woodland herbs from the local (short-lived) seed bank. Saplings act as bird perches, which will increase the numbers of bird dispersed seeds. Maturing trees produce seed themselves. Canopy closure brings about natural thinning, which results initially in a stratified, but even aged stand which casts a heavy shade. After some 50 years or so, the vigour of the canopy declines, and light begins to penetrate to the understorey. This allows a secondary flush of saplings to reach for new light gaps, so diversifying the canopy (Oliver, 1981). Oliver Rackham's extensive studies in the ancient woods of Cambridgeshire make interesting reading (Rackham, 2003). Other long-term studies in ancient woods include Lady Park Wood in the Forest of Dean (Peterken and Mountford, 1995) and Denny Wood in the New Forest (Mountford *et al.*, 1999).

Characteristics of ancient woodland plants

The first modern reference to ancient woodland vascular plants (AWVPs) or 'indicator species' was Peterken's studies of Lincolnshire woods in the 1970s. He identified species which seemed to be particularly associated with ancient woodland (Peterken and Game, 1984; Peterken and Francis, 1999). Rose and Hornby later compiled a list of some 120 AWVPs which showed a strong affinity for ancient woods in southern counties (Rose, 1999): Joyce Pitt produced a similar list for Kent. Key characteristics of such species include:

- poor dispersal, sometimes linked to other ancient woodland specialists such as ants
- many have a short-lived seed bank
- poor ability to compete with vigorous weeds in sunlight
- adaptation to stress of woodland shade, including low light and low nutrient levels
- reliance on vegetative propagation through expansion and fragmentation of the plant by rhizomes, stolons or suckers.

Species which expand readily by vegetative propagation only colonise new woodland if they are already present, or can colonise initially by seed. In some cases, vegetative expansion may help the initial colonisation phase, particularly if it is difficult for seedlings to readily establish. In tree-fall gaps in established woodlands for example, wood anemone relies on vegetative persistence to survive. In these more stressful environments, seedling survival is likely to be poor.

Rose (1999) reported that Kent had a large number of 'high-scoring' woods, in terms of diversity of AWVPs. These tend to be larger woods which cover a range of soil types, often on the dip (gentle) slope of the North Downs, such as Ellenden Wood in the Blean. In contrast, woodland on the Weald of Kent and Sussex has a much lower diversity, due to the highly acidic sands and clays of the area. Some AWVPs can also be found in secondary woodland, and sometimes outside woodland altogether, particularly where trees are planted adjacent to ancient woodland. This is encouraging for woodland creation. Wood spurge is an example of an AWVP in Kent which also grows outside woodland on chalk. In the woodland of central

Lady orchid is a plant of ancient semi-natural woodland which is unlikely to colonise new woods.

Lincolnshire, the proportion of records of AWVPs in secondary woods varies from 0%, for specialists such as common cow-wheat, wood vetch and herb-Paris, to about 40% in the case of species such as moschatel, slender St John's-wort and sanicle (all AWVPs in the South East) (Peterken, 2000). Rose contends that as the number of AWVPs in a site increases, so too does the probability that it is an ancient wood, although there can be some overlap. A note of caution: AWVPs in one region, may not be 'indicators' in another. For example, golden-rod, wood club-rush and marsh violet are all indicators of ancient woodland in the South East, but not in East Anglia.

3.2 Succession in secondary woodland

Secondary woodland succession follows a different course to succession in ancient woodland, as natural colonisation by a wide diversity of species is restricted. Managed plantations and coppice for example, are usually truncated in terms of tree age, size, dead wood build up etc. Secondary woods are often isolated from sources of colonisers. However, where plantations on ancient woodland sites (PAWS) have been cleared for woodland restoration, succession may follow a pattern which is similar in some aspects to natural succession following a catastrophic disturbance in ancient woodland. This will ultimately depend on how badly damaged the site was following clearance and introduction of plantation species.

Studies of the biodiversity of older secondary woods can help us to understand more about natural succession on farmland, and the likely future development of woodland planted today. We must, of course take into account the features of the landscape when older secondary woods were planted, and how this might have differed quite dramatically from what we see today. Planting may have taken place on heathland, marshland or unimproved grassland; and there may have been considerable movement of farm traffic between the woodland and nearby unimproved habitats.

In contrast to succession within treefall gaps, the early stages of succession on abandoned agricultural land may last for several decades and there may be considerable variation from site to site. Here, there is unlikely to be any remnants of a woodland seed bank, ground vegetation, shrub layer, underwood or mature trees. The soil profile will have been altered considerably following years of fertiliser application, drainage and movement of heavy machinery. Factors which limit woodland regeneration include:

- lack of seed bank
- lack of seed sources or absence of nearby suckering species
- lack of seed dispersers
- unsuitable microclimate and soil conditions for colonisation and establishment of woodland plants
- dominance by highly competitive herbaceous weeds
- browsing by deer or domesticated animals.

At some point however, the site will be colonised by light, windblown pioneers such as birches and willows, and bird dispersed hawthorn. Ash and sycamore have heavier seeds, and may only be dispersed a few hundred metres. Oak and beech, whose seed is distributed several kilometres by birds such as Eurasian jays, can also be early colonisers. The classic long-term colonisation experiment at Broadbalk Wilderness, Rothamsted on ex-arable loamy brown earths, went through a phase of weeds, followed by false oat-grass (*Arrhenatherum*) grassland and scrub, reaching a thicket stage only after 30 years (Brenchley and Adam, 1915; Tansley, 1939). In a companion plot, Geescroft, on heavier clay soils, Yorkshire-fog-tufted hair-grass (*Holcus-Deschampsia*) grassland established first, and the invasion of shrubs and trees was even slower. After 70 years, the woodland here consisted largely of ash, oak and small-leaved elm (Harmer *et al.*, 2001). There are many other examples of secondary succession across the British Isles, although none as well recorded as the Rothamsted plots. These include birchwood regeneration on southern English heathland, the ashwoods of Derbyshire, beech woodland in the Chilterns, and fen woodland in the Fens.

Scrub can be excellent for wildlife, although often overlooked by ecologists and conservationists, being viewed simply as a successional stage in woodland development, rather than a habitat in its own right. Consequently the marked decline in areas of valuable scrub have not received the level of attention attracted by other vulnerable habitats, such as ancient woodland and unimproved grassland. There are a number of areas in the UK, including the North Downs in Kent, where extremely biodiversity-rich scrub can be found. This type of scrub often exists as a metastable habitat, i.e. it is dynamic, but stable, forming part of the transition zone (ecotone) between grassland and woodland.

Scrub on the North Downs escarpment at Trosley, a valuable wildlife habitat.

Succession in ash-field maple-dog's mercury woodland (NVC W8): an example

Drawn by Tharada Blakesley

Figure 3.1 Succession from grassland to W8 woodland, through bramble-Yorkshire-fog underscrub, and hawthorn-ivy scrub communities.

On ex-agricultural land, it is difficult to predict what the exact course of succession might be: quite diverse communities have been seen to lead to ash-field maple-dog's mercury woodland (Rodwell, 1991). Mesotrophic false oat-grass (*Arrhenatherum*) sub-communities (MG1) or calcareous downy oat-grass (*Avenula pubescens*) grassland (CG6) develop on well drained soils. Less base-rich soils may develop into oak-bracken-bramble (W10) woodland. Wetter, heavier soils may be invaded by Yorkshire-fog-tufted hair-grass (*Holcus-Deschampsia*) (MG9) or Yorkshire-fog-soft rush (*Holco-Juncetum*) grassland (MG10). In southern England, these grasslands may be invaded directly by the major trees of ash-field maple-dog's mercury or oak woodland (W10), or there may be an intervening seral scrub stage, usually resulting in a hawthorn-ivy scrub. Bramble-Yorkshire-fog underscrub often forms a fringe between grassland and scrub: it survives in many woodlands as fringes along a woodland edge, often with bramble-Yorkshire-fog underscrub and a false oat-grass ground layer (Figure 3.1). This knowledge is useful when designing a new ash-field maple type woodland (see Section 4.2) and indicates that one cannot be too precious when prescribing species mixes for ex-agricultural sites.

Harmer *et al.* (2001) analysed all records for the Broadbalk and Geescroft Wilderness, including recent observations of their own made in 1995 and 1998. This fascinating study illustrates clearly the process of succession through to mature ash-field maple-dog's mercury woodland on land abandoned in 1883. Of 100 herbs and 20 grasses recorded in Broadbalk over the study period, only 20 remained in 1995. Five of these were initially present, the rest being shade bearing plants which subsequently colonised. Bluebell and lesser celendine were among eight species which colonised in the past 50 years or so. In Geescroft, 30 species of grasses and herbs were found in 1998, the most frequent being bluebell and ground-ivy. In both woods, many of the shade species were still restricted to the margins. Harmer comments that the flora now is typical of many small woods on abandoned farmland in eastern England: it was most diverse just before canopy closure.

What is particularly interesting about both woods is that there has been a substantial turnover of shade species since canopy closure, which limits overall colonisation. At Broadbalk for example, 13 shade species have died out, six from the initial flora of the site and seven early colonists, including normally aggressive colonists such as hogweed, bracken, sanicle and sweet violet. Other shade plants which colonised the adjacent meadow at Broadbalk, notably barren strawberry and goldilocks buttercup, failed to colonise the wood. In the woodlands of Lincolnshire, Peterken (2000) found that the number of ancient woodland vascular plants (AWVPs) in secondary woods ranged from 0 to 22: 21 secondary woods contained 10 or more AWVPs, which exceeded six of the ancient woods investigated. He concluded that the 'relatively' rich woodland vascular flora in these woods was due to their close proximity to ancient woodland, which offers further encouragement to practitioners of woodland creation.

An interesting study carried out by Peterken (1981) on the composition of ash-maple woodland (Peterken stand type 2A: synonymous with ash-field maple-dog's mercury woodland) in Cambridgeshire on calcareous boulder clay compared woodland of different ages: from recent woodland planted in the last 100 years or so, through to the undisturbed ancient woodland of Hayley Wood. The secondary woods were recognisably related to ash-maple woodland, the youngest of which held a mixture of rapid colonists including ash, hawthorn, wayfaring-tree and elder. Field maple and Midland hawthorn only appeared in woods planted in the 17th–18th centuries, whilst oak and hazel were only present in ancient woodland, and secondary woods more than 500 years old.

Secondary woodland seed bank

We know relatively little about the composition of the seed bank in secondary woodland. Where it occurs in close proximity to ancient woodland, it is not clear to what extent the seed bank may be influenced by its neighbour. In ancient woodland, the seed bank mostly consists of light demanding, early successional species, so there is often a poor correlation between the seed bank and the actual ground vegetation. These light demanding species are usually not able to establish large populations in a stressful, shady woodland environment, unless there is a light gap, created by a tree falling, for example. Such an opportunity allows seed to germinate, and replenish the seed bank. In contrast, many shade-tolerant ancient woodland species produce small numbers of short-lived seeds, which do not become incorporated into the seed bank for any length of time: only a few, such as wood-sedge, broad-leaved willowherb and wood spurge are likely to be permanent components of the seed bank. Studies in Belgium have shown that as secondary woodland ages beyond 50 years, the number of forest species in the seed bank will increase, but reach only low densities (Hermy *et al.*, 1999).

In secondary woodland, even after 50 years, there may still be a sizeable density of early successional species in the seed bank. Consequently soil disturbance should be avoided in such habitat (Bossuyt *et al.*, 2002), although it is generally believed that if forests remain undisturbed for 50 years or more, most of these seeds will begin to lose their viability, and the seed bank will decline steadily thereafter. However, there is no early replacement with ancient woodland plants: even after 100 years or more, these may still be undetectable in the secondary woodland seed bank, irrespective of the proximity of ancient woodland, although large seeded forest species may disperse across short distances (Bossuyt *et al.*, 2002).

Colonisation by herbs

In the years following canopy closure, some shade-tolerant species may be found in new woodland, but there will be very few specialist ancient woodland species amongst them and few of the intimate mixes of species which typify ancient woodland. For these plants to establish in new woodland – in the absence of a seed bank – there must be both a source of seed nearby, and a high probability of that seed reaching the site. To assess whether colonisation is likely to take place, we need to consider: the dispersal distance of seed; the area of the new wood; and the ratio of core area to edge habitat. If seed does arrive, the site must have sufficient undisturbed core areas suitable for establishment. A species may establish small colonies in discrete parts of a wood, which may be defined by quite sharp edges. Hermy *et al.* (1999) identified 132 target species for the restoration of European deciduous forests, which constitute approximately 20% of the forest flora. Each species was representative of ancient forest (equivalent to our AWVPs). They exhibit low colonisation ability, but survive well where they occur, despite having almost no persistent seed bank (Thompson *et al.*, 1997). These species also have a low sexual reproductive capacity –

Lords-and-ladies is one of the faster colonising woodland species, which can be found in new woods.

reproducing vegetatively – and generally possess short distance seed dispersal mechanisms. Twenty six percent of these ancient forest plants are ant dispersed or have no special seed morphology enhancing dispersal. A further 27% are animal-dispersed and only 11% are dispersed easily by wind (Honnay *et al.*, 2002). Distance from ancient forest source populations is significant: a decrease in cover of forest species occurs with increasing distance. Species which are ingested by birds or animals may be dispersed over greater distances than species relying on wind or ants (Matlack, 1994).

The size of woodland plots will also influence species richness, probably due to habitat diversity and age structure rather than the area *per se* within a wood. Consequently, relatively small woods of 2-3 ha, even those isolated from ancient forest, can support a diverse flora, providing they include diverse habitat. This is a fact which should be very encouraging to designers of new woodland in the UK. The ratio of edge to core woodland interior is also important in succession of the herb layer. If a wood has an irregular shape, the length of its edge will be greater, which could be a disadvantage in a small wood, because of the penetration into the central area of edge species and habitat. It will however favour species of the woodland edge.

Because of the relative immobility of many ancient woodland species, it is worthwhile incorporating species-rich hedgerows into a new planting design, especially those which are remnants of former ancient woodland. Other useful 'semi-woodland' habitats include ditches, old lanes, stream banks and riparian woodland. Such an approach may lead to the incorporation of several ancient woodland species into the ground flora of a new wood. The rate of colonisation, even from such a fringe is unpredictable: few studies have been carried out on colonisation rates of ancient woodland species.

When new woodland is planted immediately adjacent to ancient woodland, or another source of woodland species, the main issues which govern whether a species is able to colonise the wood successfully are dispersal, and establishment, which can only take place if the habitat is suitable (Verheyen and Hermey, 2001). Species may be limited by: dispersal and establishment, e.g. oxlip and yellow archangel; or just establishment, e.g. herb-Paris and Solomon's-seal. Even introduction of these species into new woodland might be problematic. However, species limited mainly by dispersal, e.g. wood anemone, tufted hair-grass; or by neither factor e.g. wood avens, lesser celendine, ground-ivy, ground-elder, bugle, moschatel, wood-sorrel, represent a group which may respond positively, albeit very slowly to introduction.

Colonisation of new woods by yellow archangel is limited by dispersal.

Surveys by the author in new woods planted within a few metres of ancient woodland in Kent and East Sussex have identified several colonising ancient woodland vascular plants, including moschatel, pendulous sedge, remote sedge, pignut, enchanter's-nightshade, bluebell, three-nerved sandwort, common spotted-orchid, black bryony and wood speedwell.

Species more likely to colonise new woodland once canopy closure has taken place, include those with an efficient dispersal mechanism, some shade tolerance and an ability to thrive on fertile soils with elevated levels of phosphate and other nutrients. Agricultural soils are characterised by acidification which is countered by liming, loss of calcium and magnesium cations with time, and increased phosphate from fertilisation, which can persist for many decades. Soil phosphate is largely immobile and total phosphate is stable in reforested land, which seems to represent a major barrier for colonisation by ancient woodland species (Keersmaeker *et al.*, 2004; Honnay *et al.*, 1999). Very little is known about how long phosphate levels take to decline once no more is added. Agricultural soils are also characterised by poorer soil structure and compaction. Few studies have tried to relate changes in the chemical and physical characteristics of the soil to the ability of forest species to germinate and establish. It seems likely that competition from vigorous, fast colonising herbs such as nettle, against which forest specues are unable to compete, is more likely to inhibit colonisation than soil conditions *per se*. Once canopy closure has taken place, the competitive advantage of nettle is much reduced, and there is an opportunity for colonisation by woodland species. This effect can clearly be seen in many new woods in Kent and Sussex. However, vigorous weeds may

TOP LEFT **Ropes of black bryony berries attract frugivorous birds to new woodland in autumn.**

TOP RIGHT **Pendulous sedge is an ancient woodland plant which has been recorded in several new woods in Kent and East Sussex.**

BOTTOM LEFT **Bluebells occur sporadically in new woods planted adjacent to ancient woodland.**

BOTTOM RIGHT **Ramsons have been found along the edge of new woods planted within a few metres of a source population.**

still remain in the seed bank, and continue to threaten the colonisation of vulnerable shade species. Older secondary woods which exhibit some diversity of shade flora may have been planted close to ancient woodland habitat, such as a hedgerow, which is no longer present today. Care must therefore be exercised when predicting natural colonisation of herbs based on studies of older woodlands, because source populations of plants may be absent in the modern landscape.

Table 3.1 Examples of potential semi-shade colonists of new woodland in Kent and East Sussex

		Ellenberg light score
Species occurring in partial shade		
Ground-elder	*Aegopodium podagraria*	6
Garlic mustard	*Alliaria petiolata*	5
Cow parsley	*Anthriscus sylvestris*	6
Lesser burdock	*Arctium minus*	6
False oat-grass	*Arrhenatherum elatius*	7
White bryony	*Bryonia dioica*	7
Rosebay willowherb	*Chamerion angustifolium*	6
Spear thistle	*Cirsium vulgare*	7
Cock's-foot	*Dactylis glomerata*	7
Common hemp-nettle	*Galeopsis tetrahit*	7
Cleavers	*Galium aparine*	6
Hogweed	*Heracleum sphondylium*	7
White dead-nettle	*Lamium album*	7
Nipplewort	*Lapsana communis*	6
Field forget-me-not	*Myosotis arvensis*	7
Annual meadow-grass	*Poa annua*	7
Creeping cinquefoil	*Potentilla reptans*	7
Broad-leaved dock	*Rumex obtusifolius*	7
Bittersweet	*Solanum dulcamara*	7
Common chickweed	*Stellaria media*	7
Dandelion	*Taraxacum officinale*	7
Upright hedge-parsley	*Torilis japonica*	7
Ivy-leaved speedwell	*Veronica hederifolia*	6
Faster colonising woodland species		
Lords-and-ladies	*Arum maculatum*	4
False brome	*Brachypodium sylvaticum*	6
Hairy-brome	*Bromus ramosus*	6
Enchanter's-nightshade	*Circaea lutetiana*	4
Narrow buckler-fern	*Dryopteris carthusiana*	6
Broad buckler-fern	*Dryopteris dilatata*	5
Male-fern	*Dryopteris filix-mas*	5
Broad-leaved willowherb	*Epilobium montanum*	6
Giant fescue	*Festuca gigantea*	5
Herb-robert	*Geranium robertianum*	5
Wood avens	*Geum urbanum*	4
Ground ivy	*Glechoma hederacea*	6
Ivy	*Hedera helix*	4
Common twayblade	*Listera ovata*	6
Honeysuckle	*Lonicera periclymenum*	5
Three-nerved sandwort	*Moehringia trinervia*	4
Dewberry	*Rubus caesius*	7
Brambles	*Rubus fruticosus* agg.	6
Raspberry	*Rubus ideaus*	6
Wood dock	*Rumex sanguineus*	5
Sanicle	*Sanicula europaea*	4
Red campion	*Silene dioica*	5
Hedge woundwort	*Stachys sylvatica*	6
Black bryony	*Tamus communis*	6
Common nettle	*Urtica dioica*	6
Sweet violet	*Viola odorata*	5

Ellenberg light scores:
1 = Plants in deep shade; 2 = Between 1 and 3; 3 = Shade plants; 4 = Between 3 and 5; 5 = Semi-shade plants; 6 = Between 5 and 7; 7 = Generally well lit places; 8 = Between 7 and 9; 9 = Full light plants

Based on our current knowledge, a list has been drawn up of potential colonists of new woodland in Kent and East Sussex (Table 3.1), which includes: shade-bearing species typically found in woodland margins, hedges and waste ground; and species characteristic of ancient woodland communities which are relatively fast colonisers. In each case, Ellenberg light scores are presented, based on values recalibrated for the British situation (Hill *et al.*, 1999).

3.3 Flora of woodland rides, glades and open spaces

Wild angelica is very attractive to insects and can be found in the open spaces of new woodland.

The vegetation of open areas in ancient woodland, and secondary woods planted on semi-natural habitats, is characterised by a mixture of woodland edge species and species of open, semi-natural habitats such as grassland and heathland. Rides in woodlands planted more recently, on agricultural land, are more likely to resemble false oat-grass grassland (MG1), which is known as 'rank grassland', and has a low botanical conservation value. Peterken and Francis (1999) found that in 362 woods in central Lincolnshire, 60% of all woodland species recorded were associated with open space. Although most of the specialised species associated with semi-natural habitats such as unimproved grassland and heathland were absent, healthy populations of formerly common grassland species were found.

Species-rich unimproved neutral grassland in Marline Valley Woods SSSI in East Sussex.

Species found in new woodland rides and roadside verges in Kent and Sussex include:

TOP LEFT **Bristly oxtongue**
TOP CENTRE **Teasel**
TOP RIGHT **Marsh thistle**
MIDDLE LEFT **Meadowsweet**
MIDDLE RIGHT **Lesser celandine**
BOTTOM LEFT **Germander speedwell**
BOTTOM RIGHT **Greater stitchwort**

Most unimproved neutral grassland occurring in Kent and Sussex is the crested dog's-tail-common knapweed type (MG5). Neutral grassland is often described as 'mesotrophic', which means it is neither very acid nor very alkaline. Species-richness depends on soil fertility and disturbance: the richest swards develop on ground which is intermediate in fertility, where vigorous competitors establish poorly. This situation is maintained by grazing and mowing, both of which prevent the build up of fertility, and the establishment of dominant competitive weeds. Just 531 ha of unimproved, and 453 ha of species-rich semi-improved grassland remain in Kent. Both are valuable habitats of county importance. The most recent estimate for unimproved grassland in Sussex is approximately 480 ha in East Sussex, and 380 ha in West Sussex. Most of this is located in the Low and High Weald character areas. These are areas of extremely high conservation value and

are the equivalent of ancient woodlands, as they may have been managed by grazing and hay cutting for many hundreds of years. They are species-rich, containing many rare and endangered grassland specialists, and may also be important habitat for fungi such as waxcaps (Griffith *et al.*, 2004). The rarity of this grassland emphasises the importance of utilising woodland open spaces to develop diverse swards to support this threatened habitat. Furthermore, these areas must be managed, to avoid succession to trees.

Most improved agricultural land has been fertilised to some extent, and with the cessation of grazing and mowing, a reversion to a species-poor grassland is inevitable unless grassland mixes are sown (see Section 4.3). Some of the potential colonists of open ground in new woodland are listed in Table 3.2.

Table 3.2 Examples of potential colonists of open ground in new woodland in Kent and East Sussex. Note most also occur in partial shade

		Ellenberg light score
Species of generally well lit places		
Creeping bent	*Agrostis stolonifera*	7
Wild angelica	*Angelica sylvestris*	7
False oat-grass	*Arrhenatherum elatius*	7
Glaucous sedge	*Carex flacca*	7
Common knapweed	*Centaurea nigra*	7
Common mouse-ear	*Cerastium fontanum*	7
Creeping thistle	*Cirsium arvense*	8
Marsh thistle	*Cirsium palustre*	7
Cock's-foot	*Dactylis glomerata*	7
Common couch	*Elytrigia repens*	7
Great willowherb	*Epilobium hirsutem*	7
Hoary willowherb	*Epilobium parviflorum*	7
Field horsetail	*Equisetum arvense*	7
Cut-leaved crane's-bill	*Geranium dissectum*	7
Hogweed	*Heracleum sphondylium*	7
Yorkshire-fog	*Holcus lanatus*	7
Perforate St John's-wort	*Hypericum perforatum*	7
Compact rush	*Juncus conglomeratus*	7
Soft-rush	*Juncus effusus*	7
Meadow vetchling	*Lathyrus pratensis*	7
Perennial rye-grass	*Lolium perenne*	8
Common bird's-foot-trefoil	*Lotus corniculatus*	7
Greater bird's-foot-trefoil	*Lotus pedunculatus*	7
Bristly oxtongue	*Picris echioides*	7
Ribwort plantain	*Plantago lanceolata*	7
Greater plantain	*Plantago major*	7
Annual meadow-grass	*Poa annua*	7
Smooth meadow-grass	*Poa pratensis*	7
Rough Meadow-grass	*Poa trivialis*	7
Creeping cinquefoil	*Potentilla reptans*	7
Selfheal	*Prunella vulgaris*	7
Common fleabane	*Pulicaria dysenterica*	7
Meadow buttercup	*Ranunculus acris*	8
Creeping buttercup	*Ranunculus repens*	6
Curled dock	*Rumex crispus*	8
Wood dock	*Rumex sanguineus*	7
Hoary ragwort	*Senecio erucifolius*	7
Common ragwort	*Senecio jacobaea*	7
Lesser stitchwort	*Stellaria graminea*	7
Dandelion	*Taraxacum officinale*	7
Red clover	*Trifolim pratense*	7
White clover	*Trifolium repens*	7
Thyme-leaved speedwell	*Veronica serpyllifolia*	7
Tufted vetch	*Vicia cracca*	7
Common vetch	*Vicia sativa*	7

Ellenberg light scores:
1 = Plants in deep shade; 2 = Between 1 and 3; 3 = Shade plants; 4 = Between 3 and 5; 5 = Semi-shade plants; 6 = Between 5 and 7; 7 = Generally well lit places; 8 = Between 7 and 9; 9 = Full light plants

Blackcap is a woodland species commonly found in new woods.

René Pop

3.4   Woodland birds

Woodland supports a rich diversity of birds in Britain, more than any other habitat. Compared to natural grassland for example, woodland has a far more pronounced three-dimensional structure which provides many niches for birds to nest and feed. An abundance of insects through the summer months provides food for: breeding birds; roving flocks of adults and juveniles during the vital post-fledging period; and birds preparing for autumn migration. Trees and shrubs can yield bumper crops of seed for finch flocks; alder seed can be heavily used by siskins, goldfinches, common chaffinches and redpolls; beech mast by common chaffinches and bramblings; and acorns by Eurasian jays. Fleshy fruits attract starlings, wood pigeons, thrushes and warblers. Other species which feed in the wider countryside such as rooks and grey herons use woodland for nesting. In the winter months, woods can hold large roosts of starlings, finches and thrushes. Lowland woods and scrub in southern England have the richest bird communities in the British Isles, with several species, such as turtle dove and common nightingale largely restricted to this region. Soils in the south tend to be richer, which may encourage a greater abundance of plant and insect food for woodland birds.

Great spotted woodpecker, a bird of mature woodland is a frequent visitor to new woodlands.

Bird diversity in mature woodland

A study of the abundance and frequency of breeding woodland birds carried out in 240 woods (Fuller, 1982) showed some species to be widespread and very common at that time. Wood pigeon, wren, blackbird, song thrush, robin, dunnock, willow warbler, blue tit, great tit, starling and common chaffinch form a core of woodland species which occur in the vast majority of woodland, at the highest abundance. Species which are similarly widespread, but present in lower numbers, include: treecreeper, mistle thrush, great spotted woodpecker, tawny owl and crows.

Tim Loseby

Other species, such as common nightingale and wood warbler occur in only a few woodlands in low numbers. New woodland that has closed canopy, would be expected to provide habitat for those species which are both frequent and abundant, but they might also support species of lower abundance such as bullfinch and Eurasian jay, or rarer species such as common nightingale and lesser whitethroat.

Sixty-five species breed regularly in the woodland of Kent and East Sussex (Tables 3.3 and 3.4), the majority of them in closed-canopy woodland. Just over one third of closed canopy woodland species breed in holes, which severely limits the potential colonisation of new woodland by these species. Woodland birds are primarily insectivorous in the breeding season, although some will take fruit in the autumn and winter. Most frugivores and granivores such as wood pigeon, finches and buntings also feed on invertebrates during the breeding season. Consequently an abundant source of insects is essential for the diets of most woodland breeding birds.

In late summer and autumn, flocks of tits, which often include warblers, goldcrests and treecreepers range through the woodland and scrub of Kent and Sussex. Large family parties of long-tailed tits are particularly noticeable at this time of year. The diet of many of these species may shift from invertebrates, to predominately seeds and fruits in the autumn. Sites which are particularly rich in food resources may attract birds which were not resident during the breeding season. Consequently, new woodland with abundant sources of seed and fruit will be of benefit to a much larger community than simply those birds which bred within it. This may lead to an increase in overall numbers of birds before the departure of summer migrants, and the onset of winter. The numbers of birds remains relatively stable through the winter months in mature woodland, but the departure of migrants coupled with some dispersal of resident birds into the surrounding countryside may deplete the bird community of new woodland. New woodland with plenty of fleshy fruiting shrubs should prove attractive to woodland and wider countryside birds in the winter, until the fruit has been consumed. Dense scrub and trees may also host large numbers of roosting birds in winter, such as thrushes, finches and starlings.

Birds of conservation concern in Kent and Sussex woodlands

Gibbons *et al.* (1996) assigned all breeding and wintering British bird species to one of three groups based on their conservation status: red, amber and green. Green-listed species are of low conservation concern. These lists have recently been reviewed by Gregory *et al.* (2002), who

The red-listed song thrush breeds in many new woods in Kent and East Sussex.

Tim Loseby

Table 3.3 Breeding birds of woodland and scrub in Kent and Sussex, and their use of new woods

	Potentially nest in new woods/scrub	Feed in new woods/scrub	Conservation status	
	✓ with mature trees ✓✓ without mature trees		National list	Kent Red Data Book category
Grey heron				
Eurasian sparrowhawk	✓✓	✓		
Buzzard	✓	✓		
Kestrel	✓	✓	Amber	
Hobby	✓	✓		3
Pheasant	✓✓	✓		
Woodcock			Amber	3
Stock dove			Amber	
Woodpigeon	✓✓	✓		
Turtle dove	✓✓	✓	Red	2
Cuckoo	✓✓	✓	Amber	
Tawny owl	✓	✓		
Long-eared owl	✓✓	✓		
Green woodpecker	✓	✓	Amber	
Great spotted woodpecker	✓	✓		
Lesser spotted woodpecker			Red	3
Wren	✓✓	✓		
Dunnock	✓✓	✓	Amber	
Robin	✓✓	✓		
Common nightingale	✓✓	✓	Amber	3
Common redstart			Amber	1
Blackbird	✓✓	✓		
Song thrush	✓✓	✓	Red	2
Mistle thrush	✓	✓	Amber	
Garden warbler	✓✓	✓		
Blackcap	✓✓	✓		
Wood warbler			Amber	1
Common chiffchaff	✓✓	✓		
Willow warbler	✓✓	✓	Amber	
Goldcrest	✓✓	✓	Amber	3
Firecrest			Amber	1
Spotted flycatcher			Red	2
Long-tailed tit	✓✓	✓		
Marsh tit			Red	
Willow tit	✓	✓	Red	3
Coal tit	✓	✓		
Blue tit	✓✓	✓		
Great tit	✓✓	✓		
Nuthatch				
Treecreeper				
Eurasian jay	✓✓	✓		
Magpie	✓✓	✓		
Jackdaw				
Rook				
Carrion crow	✓✓	✓		
Starling	✓	✓	Red	
Tree sparrow			Red	2
Common chaffinch	✓✓	✓		
Greenfinch	✓✓	✓		
Siskin				1
Lesser redpoll			Amber	3
Common crossbill				
Bullfinch	✓✓	✓	Red	2
Hawfinch			Amber	3

Red Data Book 1: breeding species with fewer than 25 pairs in Kent

Red Data Book 2: more than 25 pairs, but red-listed nationally

Red Data Book 3: remaining species

forecast the population status in the UK for the period 2002–2007. The criteria remained essentially the same.

Red-listed species criteria:

- IUCN globally threatened species
- species showing an historic population decline during 1800–1995
- species showing a rapid decline in UK breeding population (> 50%) over the last 25 years
- species showing a rapid contraction in UK breeding range (> 50%) over the last 25 years.

Red-listed species require the most urgent conservation action.

Amber-listed species criteria:

- historic population decline during 1800–1995, but recovering; population has more than doubled over the last 25 years
- moderate decline in UK breeding population (25–49%) over the last 25 years
- moderate contraction in UK breeding range (25–49%) over the last 25 years
- moderate decline in UK non-breeding population (25–49%) over the last 25 years
- species with unfavourable conservation status in Europe.

Kent and Sussex woodland is home to 31 species of conservation concern as highlighted in the red and amber lists (Tables 3.3 and 3.4). The Government has identified 26 UK BAP species, of which eight occur in the woodlands of Kent and Sussex; all are included in the red list, and three – turtle dove, spotted flycatcher and bullfinch – have declined dramatically. Species of conservation concern have also been identified at a local level: for example, 24 woodland species have been added to the *Kent Red Data Book* by the Kent Ornithological Society, which aimed to highlight those species which are rare or localised in the county (Tables 3.3 and 3.4).

Fuller *et al.* (2005) recently reviewed the possible causes for the recent decline of woodland birds. Factors which emerged as having the potential to affect a wide range of woodland birds included: impacts of land use on woodland edge and habitats outside woodland; the impact of climate change on the breeding grounds; reduction of invertebrates; and reduced management of lowland woodland.

Table 3.4 Breeding birds open canopy woodland or young plantations in Kent and Sussex, and their use of new woods

	Potentially nest in new woods/scrub	Feed in new woods/scrub	Conservation status	
	✓ with mature trees ✓✓ without mature trees		National list	Kent Red Data Book category
Nightjar	✓✓	✓	Red	2
Tree pipit	✓✓	✓	Amber	3
Whinchat	✓✓	✓		
Stonechat		✓	Amber	1
Grasshopper warbler	✓✓	✓	Red	1
Lesser whitethroat	✓✓	✓		
Whitethroat	✓✓	✓		
Goldfinch	✓✓	✓		
Linnet	✓✓	✓	Red	2
Yellowhammer	✓✓	✓	Red	3
Reed bunting		✓	Red	2
Red Data Book 1: breeding species with fewer than 25 pairs in Kent				
Red Data Book 2: more than 25 pairs, but red-listed nationally				
Red Data Book 3: remaining species				

What birds are likely to occur in new woodland?

Based on Fuller's (1995) analysis of nesting and feeding requirements, woodland birds in Kent and East Sussex can be categorised as: birds which breed in woodland and scrub (Table 3.3); and birds of open canopy and young plantations prior to canopy closure (Table 3.4). Most of the breeding species associated with woodland in Kent and East Sussex breed in mature woodland and scrub (Table 3.3). Eleven species require a more open canopy, with small trees and shrubs (Table 3.4). A further eight species are occasional breeders (red-legged partridge, collared dove, barn owl, little owl, skylark and meadow pipit) or winter visitors (redwing and fieldfare).

Some woodland species are restricted to mature woodland, and are unlikely to be found in relatively young woodland, because of their sedentary nature (e.g. marsh tit and nuthatch), or habitat requirements (e.g. lesser spotted woodpecker). In contrast, willow warbler rapidly colonises distant new habitats. Other species nest in woodland, but feed mainly in surrounding habitats.

The stage of succession strongly influences bird colonisation and the development of bird communities in new woodland. The tree and shrub establishment phase, which lasts several years, attracts species of more open country such as skylark, meadow pipit and linnet. These may be joined by yellowhammer, tree pipit and whitethroat as the tree and shrub layer develops. In areas where young trees have closed canopy, species richness increases significantly, with the arrival of warblers, thrushes and chats. A new wood with a range of woodland habitat types, will obviously provide the best opportunity to maximise bird diversity: only early successional species such as skylark and meadow pipit may be lost as breeding species. Mature growth is of course problematic, as there will not be habitat available for hole nesters such as the woodpeckers and blue tit for many years. However, coppice, low growth shrubs and scrub can be used by the majority of woodland birds in Britain.

A Kentish woodland of just 10–15 years of age, with areas of closed canopy and some more open areas could support up to 44 breeding species. This includes scarce and strongly declining species such as bullfinch, chiffchaff, dunnock, song thrush, turtle dove, common nightingale and

Young woodland at Hucking in Kent supports breeding tree pipit and skylark.

René Pop

The amber-listed dunnock breeds in many new woods.

Tim Loseby

Parties of long-tailed tits are frequent visitors to new woodland throughout the year.

willow warbler. Thirty-seven species of birds were recorded in fourteen year old Comfort's Wood in Kent during breeding bird surveys in 2004/05 (Section 5.1).

3.5   Woodland bats

Bat diversity and status in Kent and Sussex woodlands

More than 30% of the mammalian fauna of the British Isles are bats (16 species). Thirteen species occur in Kent and Sussex, and use woodland for foraging and roosting (Table 3.5). Most of these have suffered significant declines in the last 100 years or so (Stebbings 1988; Hutson 1993; Harris *et al.*, 1995), probably due to agricultural intensification resulting in habitat loss, including roost sites (Hutson, 1993). Several bats are the subject of BAPs, including the pipistrelles and barbastelle, which occur locally in Kent and Sussex. Bechstein's bat and the barbestelle are both on the IUCN Red List of Threatened Species. Many bats have a close association with woodland and riparian woodland, and avoid arable land. Hedgerows and riparian woodland in particular provide for both foraging and commuting between roosting and feeding areas.

Hugh Clark

Hugh Clark

Species likely to benefit from new woodland include:

Brown long-eared bat (TOP LEFT)

Pipestrelles (TOP RIGHT).

Ancient woodland, with a wide age range of trees, a diverse canopy structure, good quality rides, open spaces and woodland edge provides good habitat for many bats. A landscape which includes such woodland, together with a mosaic of hedgerows, riparian woodland, scrub, unimproved grassland areas, ponds and rivers (both slow and fast flowing) will suit the feeding and commuting activities of all the British bats. All of these habitats provide insect food in abundance, which is one of the major factors which govern the suitability of a habitat for foraging bats. Such a landscape may once have been commonplace in Kent and Sussex, but this is not so today. Consequently, new woodland could provide important foraging habitat for bats and make a substantial contribution to bat conservation in the wider landscape, providing that it is designed for wildlife.

Recent studies have reported widespread and high usage of farm woodlands by bats, even in the early establishment phases (Central Science Laboratory, 2003). Nine species were found foraging and commuting, particularly pipistrelles and brown long-eared bats. More detailed studies are still required to understand precisely how new woodland can be most beneficial to bats. However, enough is already known about bat ecology to confirm the importance of new woodland location, and design; particularly of woodland edge, rides and open spaces.

Table 3.5 Bats occurring in Kent and Sussex

Species	Status	Commuting/foraging habitat	Food
Natterer's bat	Widespread, frequent	Forages in woodland, wet woodland, linear woods, woodland edge, open grassland, over water; commutes/forages along hedgerows	Flies, spiders
Daubenton's bat	Widespread, common	Forages along riparian woodland, over water, other woodland at certain times of year	Insects with aquatic larvae
Whiskered bat	Widespread, scarce	Forages in riparian habitats, woodland, woodland edge, open rides	Flies
Brandt's bat	Widespread, scarce	Forages in riparian habitats, woodland and areas close to water; commutes along hedgerows, linear woodland	Flies
Bechstein's bat	Very rare	Forages in mature woodland with good three-dimensional structure	Moths
Serotine	Frequent	Forages in pasture, lowland parkland, woodland edge, hedgerows	Beetles, flies, moths
Noctule	Widespread, frequent	Forages in wide range of habitats, including woodland edge/glades	Beetles, flies, moths
Leisler's bat	Widespread, rare	Forages in wide range of habitats, including woodland edge/glades, over woodland canopy	Flies, beetles
45 kHz pipistrelle	Widespread, common	Forages in wide range of habitats, including woodland edge, hedgerows, open ground	Flies
55 kHz pipistrelle	Widespread, common	Forages in wide range of habitats, including habitat edges, open ground, riverside/lakeside vegetation	Flies
Brown long-eared bat	Widespread, common	Gleans from foliage/other surfaces, favours woodland, woodland edge, parkland; commutes along linear features	Moths
Grey long-eared bat	Very rare	Gleans from foliage/other surfaces, favours woodland, woodland edge	Moths
Barbestelle	Widespread, very rare	Forages in woodland canopy, woodland edge, orchards	Moths

3.6 Woodland invertebrates

Invertebrate diversity in mature woodland

Woodland has the richest invertebrate fauna of any British habitat, which is due to its complex structure, diversity of niches and the relative stability of the mature state. Ancient semi-natural woodland also provides historical continuity, which is especially important to species which require very rare and specialised niches (Table 3.6), or which have only limited powers of dispersal. Most insect groups are represented in British woodland by a large number of species. Some plants, such as hawthorns, cherries, willows, birches and oaks, can support very high numbers of insects, exceeding 350 species in each case. In contrast, less than 25 species have been recorded on ivy, white poplar, honeysuckle and beech. This illustrates the value of different trees and shrubs to feeding invertebrates. Some invertebrates specialise in woodland of different states of succession, such as pioneer and climax. Woodland invertebrates also make extensive use of shrubs of the woodland edge and tall herb zones of rides for many purposes, including:

- pollen and nectar (for example social and solitary bees)
- plant sap (for example tree aphids)
- leaf-eating (for example leaf miners and leaf rollers)
- stem-nesting (for example solitary wasps)
- nest construction (for example leaf-cutter bees)
- structure (for example spiders)
- shelter (for example specialist woodland butterflies)
- foraging and hunting (for example ants).

Orange tip butterflies favour damper situations in woodland rides and glades, and often frequent new woods.

BELOW LEFT **Southern wood ant (*Formica rufa*) nests are threatened by overgrowth of rides and glades in ancient woodland.**

BELOW RIGHT **Bumblebee nectaring on a dandelion in a woodland ride.**

How important are new woodlands for invertebrates?

New woods do not have the diversity of structure or age necessary to provide the full range of habitat niches required by all invertebrates (Table 3.6). This may be alleviated to some extent through planting close to ancient woodland, hedgerows, or even through incorporating large remnant trees. The proximity of ancient woodland is far more important for invertebrate colonisation than for colonisation by birds. However, management practices in some ancient woods has resulted in a lack of structural diversity in the canopy, and little of the old and decaying wood necessary to support diverse invertebrate communities.

The artificial introduction of decaying wood into new woodland might attract some saproxylic species, especially if it was planted immediately adjacent to ancient woodland. Even then, many species would be unable to

Table 3.6 Invertebrate habitat in woodland. Features which occur in new woodland are emboldened. (Largely based on Elton 1966)

	Habitat	Microhabitat	Species and use
Trees and shrubs	**Living wood**		Wood borers
	Decaying wood	Rot holes	Saproxylic species and cover
		Heart rot	Saproxylic species
		Cavities	Saproxylic species and cover
	Bark	**Surface**	Predators and perches
	Damaged bark	Surface	Cover
		Loose	Saproxylic species and cover
		Sap runs	Specialists
	Foliage	**Canopy**	Food
		Understorey	Food
		Climbers	Food, cover, hibernation
	Flowers		Nectar
	Roots	**Living**	Gall causers
		Decaying	Saproxylic species
Woodland edge/rides	**Foliage**		Food and perches
	Flowers		Nectar
Herbs	**Foliage**		Food and perches etc
	Flowers		Nectar
	Roots		Food
Bryophytes			Cover
Fungi	**Soil**	**Mycelium and fruiting bodies**	Specialist mycophagous species
	Dead wood fungi	Mycelium and fruiting bodies	Specialist saproxylic species
Litter	**Leaves**		Saprophages and cover
	Dead wood	**Branches**	Saproxylic species
		Tree boles	Saproxylic species
Soil surface in rides	**Bare soil in sun**		Solitary bee nests
			Wasp nests
			Basking
Soil	**Soil particulate matter**		Specialist soil species
	Water	**Seepages**	Specialist species

colonise, and such action is unlikely to be sustainable, and therefore should be considered carefully. In new woods, there are usually at least a few trees which die after planting for a variety of reasons. If left, these will provide some habitat for a limited number of saproxylic species. New woodlands which are isolated from ancient woodland are most likely to develop an invertebrate fauna more characteristic of the wider countryside.

Rides, open spaces and traditionally managed coppice offer a diverse habitat which is very important for most woodland invertebrates. Coppice in particular can support a very rich fauna, although it may only be appropriate to consider coppice in new woodland where it is located within range of existing, invertebrate-rich coppice. Examples of this are discussed later in relation to specialist woodland butterflies. Shrubs provide a home to many invertebrates, including those associated with the lichens, algae and fungi found on their bark. Ward and Spalding (1993) report that over 2,000 invertebrates have been

Common bird's-foot-trefoil provides nectar throughout the summer in new woodland rides.

found on shrubs, of which about one third are genus specific. In general terms, rides and open space are important to most woodland invertebrates at some point in their life cycle. Whilst the larvae of many woodland invertebrates feed in shady or damp conditions, adults require warm sunshine and clear flight lines to an abundant supply of flowers for nectaring. With the disappearance of wild flower-rich meadows, woodland rides have become important refuges for both sun loving plants, and grassland invertebrate communities. **Without careful management, even these island sanctuaries are under threat. This is one of the areas where new woodlands can make a significant contribution to the wildlife landscape – whatever their size – providing suitable management is undertaken.**

TOP LEFT **Hoverfly (*Volucella inanis*) nectaring on hemp agrimony.**

TOP CENTRE **Six-spot burnet (*Zygaena filipendulae*) nectaring on scabious.**

TOP RIGHT **Large skipper nectaring on creeping thistle.**

Butterflies populations in mature woodland

During the latter part of the 19th century, permanent rides were constructed in heavily coppiced woodlands. Rides, glades and young coppice supported a diverse range of flora and fauna. Regular cutting and coppicing created a constant supply of open space and early successional growth, which is the perfect habitat for many woodland invertebrates. However, a reduction in the market for coppice products had a severe affect on woodland ecosystems. The subsequent decline in coppicing began towards the end of the 19th century, and continued through the 20th century, when the practice almost ceased throughout the broadleaved woodlands of southern England. It is perhaps the single most important element in the decline in the ranges of specialist woodland butterflies. The chequered skipper for example, which was still abundant in its East Midland stronghold as recently as the 1950s, had disappeared completely from England by the mid 1970s due to cessation of coppicing and the shading of rides. Other species which have also suffered major range losses include wood white, Duke of Burgundy, small pearl-bordered fritillary, pearl-bordered fritillary, high brown fritillary and heath fritillary. The Blean forest complex, north of Canterbury in Kent, is the last stronghold of the heath fritillary in eastern England. Extinction of the butterfly here was averted by careful conservation management, involving ride widening and renewed management of sweet chestnut coppice. The pearl-bordered fritillary was not so fortunate. It survived as a breeding species in Kent into the 21st century, but is now believed to be extinct, with no records for the past three years, despite careful searching. And the reason… changes in the management of rides and open space.

Can new woodlands help to conserve woodland specialist butterflies?

Twelve of the 16 British woodland specialist butterflies occur in Kent and/ or Sussex. Many of these have suffered dramatic declines, which can be partly or wholly attributed to changes in woodland management during the 20th century. With the exception of speckled wood and purple hairstreak, the others are local and uncommon in Kent and Sussex. It should be noted that together with white-letter hairstreak, these three butterflies are considered by Asher *et al.* (2001) to be wider countryside species because their habitats are more widespread in the landscape than just woodland. Five species may be recorded in new woodland, particularly where this is located close to existing colonies:

■ **The speckled wood** (*Pararge aegeria*) was once widespread, but had disappeared from most of its former range by the early part of the 20th century. However, in southern England it may now be found along tall hedgerows, and studies on long term changes in its distribution indicate that it has re-colonised much of its former areas over the last 60 years or so. This, coupled with its widespread grass food plants must make it a likely colonist of new woodlands.

■ **The purple hairstreak** (*Quercusia quercus*) on the other hand rarely strays far from its old home oak trees. It remains faithful to the extent that many colonies occur on remnant oak trees, which now stand isolated from woodland in hedgerows and byways. Nevertheless, Asher *et al.* (2001) report that it is generally expanding in Britain, and may well use new woodland, especially if it includes oaks and ash and is planted adjacent to an existing colony.

■ **The white-letter hairstreak** (*Satyrium w-album*) favours elms in sheltered hedgerows, scrub and woodland rides, where it can be found on both mature and younger non-flowering trees. It suffered during the Dutch Elm disease crisis in the 1970s, but has recovered since. Dispersal of this species is quite common and individuals have been recorded several kilometres from known colonies (Asher *et al.*, 2001). White-letter hairstreak could well colonise rides and the shrub edge of new native woodland planted with elms, particularly if they are associated with old woods or hedgerows where the butterfly already occurs. It also requires a diverse canopy structure of ash, oak and field maple where it feeds on honeydew and roosts.

■ **The brown hairstreak** (*Thecla betulae*) disappeared from Kent in the 1970s, and from East Sussex in the late 19th century. However, it still survives in nearby West Sussex in the Wealden woodlands. It has suffered from hedgerow removal and trimming. Ash is important for this species, for the populations of aphids which produce the honeydew upon which it feeds. A single colony breeds over a wide area, requiring sympathetic management of the landscape rather than protection of a single woodland. Butterfly Conservation and English Nature have produced information for landowners, detailing the requirement for non-trimmed, or layered hedgerows, with woodland edge, which act as focal points for the colony. Consequently, in areas where brown hairstreak occurs, blackthorn scrub associated with new woodland, and woodland edge could well benefit this species. This has been demonstrated recently by the successful colonisation of the M40 compensation area adjacent to Bernwood. Here, both brown and black hairstreak (*Strymonidia pruni*) butterflies expanded their existing colonies into new hedgerow and grassland habitat.

■ **White admiral** (*Limenitis camilla*) butterflies patrol shady woodland rides and edge, often in mature woodland. They are attracted to sunny glades to nectar on large patches of bramble. The white admiral is found in East Sussex and parts of Kent and is more widespread now than ever before, in contrast to most woodland specialists. It thrives when coppicing is discontinued, due to its preference for shady conditions where it can breed on honeysuckle. The White Admiral could benefit from new woodlands in areas where it is known to occur, particularly if honeysuckle is introduced when the canopy closes.

White admiral resting on St John's-wort.

Table 3.7 Colonisation potential of woodland specialist butterflies

		Colonisation potential
Silver-washed fritillary	*Argynnis paphia*	Significant recent range expansion (Asher *et al.*, 2001) suggests possible colonist of sympathetically managed new woodland
Purple emperor	*Apatura iris*	New woodlands planted in its strongholds would be beneficial if they included plentiful sallows along rides and woodland edge
Wood white	*Leptidea sinapsis*	Possible colonist in areas where butterfly is known to occur, if new woods managed sympathetically
Pearl-bordered fritillary	*Boloria euphrosyne*	Extinct in Kent: new woods in Sussex could serve as habitat linkages, facilitating movement between suitable existing habitat
Small pearl-bordered fritillary	*Boloria selene*	Extinct in Kent: new woods in Sussex might be beneficial if they created new rides around an existing old-woodland edge.
Heath fritillary	*Melitaea athalia*	Possible colonist in new woods in Blean (east Kent) if managed sympathetically
Duke of Burgundy	*Hamearis lucina*	Habitat could be restored in old woods, but unlikely to benefit from new woods

For many of the other woodland specialists, new native woodland in the short term is likely to 'enrich' the habitat mosaic, supporting existing colonies and providing corridors through which butterflies might move from one suitable ancient woodland to another, rather than providing breeding habitat *per se*. No new woodland has been planted in the British Isles for this purpose (Warren pers comm.), although with specialist advice, it should be feasible to do so for certain species (Table 3.7).

Heath fritillaries in the Blean complex, east Kent.

How important are new woodlands for butterfly conservation?

Twenty-four wider countryside species breed in the woodlands of Kent and Sussex. Their ability to colonise a new area is species dependent. Those species which do not breed in colonies: brimstone, large white, small white, green-veined white, orange tip, holly blue, red admiral, painted lady, small tortoiseshell, peacock and comma tend to range widely across the countryside, breeding in suitable habitat when they come across it. These species are the most likely early visitors to new woodland. Species which breed in discrete colonies tend to be more sedentary. Adults of some species will move between colonies within larger woodland blocks, and some will range several km from their home colony. Species which might colonise suitable habitat in new woodland include small skipper, large skipper, small copper, brown argus, common blue, marbled white, gatekeeper, and meadow brown. Attracting most species, whether they

Species found in new woodland rides in Kent and Sussex include:

RIGHT **Green-veined white nectaring on scabious.**

BELOW LEFT **Small skipper nectaring on thistle.**

BELOW RIGHT **Marbled white nectaring on knapweed.**

breed in colonies or not, requires the presence of larval foodplants and a plentiful supply of nectar-rich flowers for the adults (Section 4.3). With the possible exception of speckled wood and green-veined white, which prefer fairly shaded rides, this will inevitably depend on the presence and management of open glades and rides (Section 4.4).

New woods could make a significant contribution to the conservation of the wider countryside butterflies, many of which have declined significantly in abundance, despite range expansions (Table 3.8). Species which are causing concern are primarily those which rely on unimproved grassland in the wider countryside. Many now survive in small colonies in fragments of their former habitat, or equivalent types of habitat such as roadside verges. These include dingy skipper, brimstone, orange tip, green hairstreak, small copper, common blue, marbled white, gatekeeper, meadow brown, ringlet, and small heath. In the late 1990s conflicting advice was being given to guide the conservation of these butterflies. One approach focused on habitat quality in fewer sites, a second advocated the preservation of a larger number of sites within the dispersal range of a species, irrespective of quality. Bourn *et al.* (2002) considered these approaches in some detail. Their studies on three grassland species showed no correlation with the area of the habitat patch: strong correlations were found with habitat quality and isolation. They concluded that it is as important to maintain high quality habitat at least on part of a site, as it is to maintain as many contiguous sites as possible in the landscape. This emphasises the value of high quality open spaces in new woodland, and supports the view that with appropriate management, a new wood could host breeding populations of a large proportion of the wider countryside butterfly species.

Table 3.8 Butterflies which may occur in new woodland (data source Asher *et al.* (2001))

	Range and population
Wider countryside species	
Small skipper	Range expanding. Widespread and common. Distribution is probably limited by climate, rather than abundance of larval foodplants
Essex skipper	Range expanding. Colonies expanding within its range, possibly through increased use of roadside verges
Large skipper	Range expanding. Widespread and common. Distribution is probably limited by climate, rather than abundance of larval foodplants
Dingy skipper	Range declining, partially due to shading in woods. Only likely to colonise if wood adjacent to existing colony(s)
Brimstone	Range expanding. Strong correlation between distribution of butterfly and its foodplant. Less abundant due to habitat destruction, despite expanding range. Planting buckthorn or alder buckthorn would benefit this species
Large white	Range stable
Small white	Range stable
Green-veined white	Range stable
Orange tip	Range expanding, but less abundant due to decline in cuckooflower following drainage and grassland improvement. May do well in new woods in Kent/East Sussex if garlic mustard is present, and left undisturbed during flowering
Green hairstreak	Range stable, but less abundant, due to shading. Requires short turf, or scrub in sunshine, and suitable ant colonies to bury the pupae
Small copper	Range stable, but has suffered considerable decline in numbers. Particularly susceptible to climate, and may be lost from woodlands in cool, wet summers, to be recolonised in later warm, dry summers
Brown argus	Range expanding due to set aside, following earlier declines due to habitat loss. Long rotational ride management which encourages its annual foodplants to become established could benefit this species in new woodland
Common blue	Range stable. Has compensated to some extent for widespread habitat destruction by colonising new environments, though population has declined. New woods could benefit this species, providing areas of short swards are maintained in the rides and open spaces
Holly blue	Range expanding. More widespread within main distribution area. Open woodlands remain important for its populations
Red admiral	Regular migrant. No threat, but still needs nettles, which are less frequent than in the past
Painted lady	Regular migrant. Dependence on survival of suitable breeding areas outside Europe
Small tortoiseshell	Range stable. Remains ubiquitous
Peacock	Range expanding. Widespread and common
Comma	Range expanding. After a contraction possibly related to the decline in hop, currently undergoing dramatic expansion
Marbled white	Range expanding, though many colonies lost throughout 20th century. Seems to be making use of patches of habitat in areas where grassland has decreased; new woodlands can provide good habitat for this species
Gatekeeper	Range expanding, though colonies lost through agricultural intensification, and loss of hedgerows and unimproved grassland. Even small woodlands could be colonised
Meadow brown	Range stable. Common and widespread, but declining through agricultural intensification. Benefits from smaller habitat fragments, such as rides in woodlands
Ringlet	Range expanding. Many colonies lost through loss of native grasses, drainage and overgrazing. Uncut grassy rides in new woodland could be important for this species
Small heath	Range stable. Many colonies lost through loss of native grasses to arable or improved grassland. Now much less abundant locally, and causing considerable concern
Woodland specialists	
Brown hairstreak	Range declining. Loss of hedgerows major factor and widespread mechanical cutting
Purple hairstreak*	Range expanding. Widespread but numbers of colonies declining through loss of oakwoods
White-letter hairstreak*	Range slowly expanding. Recovering following Dutch Elm Disease in 1970s
White admiral	Range expanding. Benefiting from warmer climate and shadier woodland
Speckled wood*	Range expanding. Recolonised much of former area over last 60 years

*considered by Asher *et al.* to be wider countryside species

4 HOW TO CREATE A NEW WOODLAND FOR WILDLIFE

4.1 How to assess landscape character and survey wildlife habitats

This section describes how to evaluate potential woodland creation sites, including how to assess landscape character and how to survey wildlife habitats. The process is illustrated by the example of Victory Wood, which is being created at Lamberhurst Farm, a Woodland Trust property in east Kent (Section 4.1.6). This example is also used to illustrate selection of trees and shrubs (Section 4.2.2), grassland plants (Section 4.3.2) and woodland design (Section 4.4.3).

4.1.1 How to carry out a landscape character assessment

Landscape character is the study of landscape elements such as geology, land form, land cover, human influence, climate and history, which combine to provide an area with a unique local identity. Before adding woodland to a landscape, it is important to understand landscape character, so that proposed woodlands are appropriate, well designed and positioned to enhance it. Proposed new woodlands should fit well alongside other visual landscape elements in a locally characteristic way.

Understanding landscape character

There are four main stages to assessing landscape character:

1. Background reading

Consult the Countryside Agency's *Landscape Character Assessment Guidance for England and Scotland*, which is available on their website; and the regional guide *Countryside Character Volume 7 – South East and London* (Countryside Agency, 1999), which covers Kent and Sussex. This describes landscape character areas and briefly comments on trees and woodland.

To support new environmental stewardship schemes, Defra has outlined priority targets for the management of a variety of features in each character area. These targets can be viewed on the Defra website (www.defra.gov.uk).

All published larger-scale assessments of the area concerned should be reviewed. In the case of Kent and Sussex, many landscape assessments have been published over recent years. For example, the Kent Habitat Survey (KHS) (KHS Partnership, 2003) provides information on a wide range of habitats at various levels; district, character area and Area of Outstanding Natural Beauty (ANOB). It includes the ancient woodland inventory, and is particularly useful in showing statutory designations such as Sites of Special Scientific Interest (SSSI) etc, and the results of landscape level habitat surveys. The Landscape Assessment of Kent (Kent County Council, 2004) is intended for use in a variety of forward planning strategies: 114 local character area reports are included. This report is available on the Kent Landscape Information System (KLIS) website (http://extranet7.kent.gov.uk/klis/home.htm).

Next, proceed with finer detailed assessments which provide local guidance. At county level, both Kent and East Sussex County Councils have recently carried out county landscape assessments and produced tree and woodland strategies. These are available on their websites. Similarly, AONB management organisations have completed assessments for their areas, and the findings have often been incorporated into management plans and other guidance. In each case, the county or AONB is broken down into a number of character areas that describe the landscape of each, together with recommendations to conserve and enhance them.

Despite the written assessments available, there is no substitute for field observations. Drive around the area to determine directly how proposed planting sites fit into the landscape character area described in the publications.

2. Undertake a desk study of available maps and aerial photographs of the area

Look at aerial photographs to appreciate how landscape cover fits with topography, land use and settlement; to recognise the patterns made by trees, fields, hedges and woods; and how these patterns change across an area. The KLIS website offers a detailed description of habitats within Kent, derived from aerial photographs, backed up by ground surveys. Online maps are readily accessible at county level, down to field boundary level, which can be overlaid with various habitat data, including elevation, landscape character, soils, a limited number of habitat types, and maps describing statutory designations across Kent. The digital National Soils Map, which has a 1 km resolution, is produced by the National Soils Resources Institute of Cranfield University, but information for Kent can be freely viewed on the KLIS website.

Defra's Agricultural Land Classification (ALC), at a scale of 1:250,000 is also available from KLIS. Aerial photographs (available on the KLIS website and from www.old-maps.co.uk) are very helpful, particularly when integrating new woodland into an existing pattern of fields, hedgerows etc. Local authority websites also include information on local habitat action plans which involve woodlands. Information on the East Sussex County Council County (ESCC) Landscape Assessment will shortly be published on the ESCC website. A further source of geographic data, which includes soil maps and nature conservation designations, is the Government's web-based 'multi agency geographic information for the countryside' (www.magic.gov.uk).

3. Undertake field work to check and refine any conclusions drawn

In the field, record the character, condition, and aesthetics of the landscape in question. Where there may be archaeological interest, consult with archaeologists and local historians.

Design a field record sheet to ensure a repeatable and systematic approach. Walk over the area designated for planting and analyse the landscape, using a field survey sheet (see the *Countryside Agency's Landscape Character Assessment Guidance for England and Scotland* p31). A sketch map or photograph can also be an invaluable aid to identifying the key landscape characteristics of the area (Figure 4.1A–C).

An example of fieldwork: The landscape description for a 'Downland Valley', arising from a desk study, indicated the following features:

- wooded upper scarps
- large open scarp foot fields
- large, flat valley bottom fields with a weak landscape structure of small woods, overgrown hedges and trimmed remnant hedges with hedgerow trees.

Figure 4.1 Sketch maps drawn to identify key landscape characteristics for a 'Downland Valley'.

Figure 4.1A Analyse landscape and decide where local character boundaries might be

The lower valley has a larger, rectilinear, more open regular field pattern of a planned landscape, enclosed by the scarp

Wooded scarp with some open chalk grassland with scrub

The upper valley has a more enclosed, smaller scale pattern of woodland, hedges and pasture

Remnant hedges

Fragmented land cover

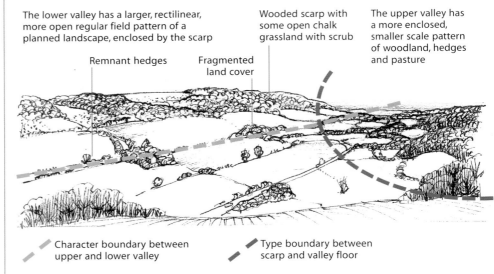

Character boundary between upper and lower valley

Type boundary between scarp and valley floor

Figure 4.1B Examine old maps to establish a picture of the history of landuse and the changes in land cover

The lower valley had a stronger, more complete landscape structure

The scarp ridge was less wooded with a greater area of species-rich grassland, and more intense open downland character

Large scarp fields are an historic feature

The upper valley was more wooded than the present day

Ancient woodland

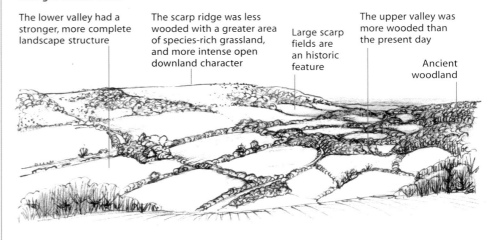

Figure 4.1C Plan for creating woodland to strengthen landscape character

Consider strengthening hedgerows to link with woodland

Do not plant on scarp, to retain the open downland character

Do not extend woodland up into scarpfoot fields

Leave some pastures within areas of woodland

Leave rectilinear fields open

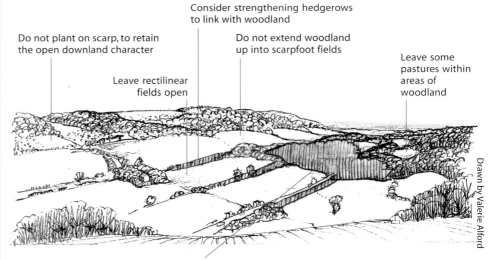

One option for introducing woodland to:
1. Increase the enclosure of the upper valley
2. Link fragmented areas of woodland and hedgerow
3. Include network of rides, glades and open spaces
4. Strengthen landscape structure

Drawn by Valerie Alford

The sketch produced in the field confirmed these features (Figure 4.1A) and allowed boundaries between local areas to be drawn. The landscape 'type' boundary separated the scarp and the valley floor. Local 'character boundaries' were also be drawn on the sketch. In this case, the upper valley appeared to differ in character from the lower valley, as it has a more enclosed, smaller scale pattern of woodland, hedges and pasture (Figure 4.1A).

Historic maps of the Downland Valley showed a stronger structure in the past, with many small woods in the valley floor, the same large scarp foot fields, but less woodland on the scarps than present day (Figure 4.1B). This history, taken with the context of the larger character area, may help to indicate where adding woodland may "weaken" character and where it will "strengthen" it. Recommendations were then drawn up for planting to enhance landscape character (Figure 4.1C).

4. Write up the landscape character assessment

In many cases, woodland creation is opportunistic, and the landscape character assessment, together with wildlife habitat surveys, merely confirm the suitability (or otherwise) of a chosen site(s) for woodland creation. In other cases, such as the example of Victory Wood (Section 4.1.6), the selection of woodland creation sites are dependent on the various assessments and surveys. In cases such as this, where sites are not fixed at the outset, other local landscape considerations are important, such as: planting adjacent to ancient woodland (see Section 4.4.1); creating linkages between existing patches of ancient woodland (see Section 4.1.6); or contributing to local or national habitat action plans, such as the creation of linear woodlands on the highways soft estate (see Sections 5.5 and 5.6).

4.1.2 What is involved in wildlife habitat surveys?

Wildlife habitat surveys should be cost effective, ecologically informative and easy to interpret. A rigorous ecological survey of the proposed site would encompass an extended Phase 1 habitat survey, soil survey and an assessment of conservation value. Taken together, these surveys can establish the suitability of the site for tree planting, and predict the effects of planting on the wildlife of both the planting site and the wider landscape.

Despite the information now available from various websites, ground surveys are still very important, because the online material does not provide sufficient detail to make the decisions described in this section. A good map of the area – preferably an Ordnance Survey (OS) 1:10,000 – is essential, both for surveying and planning. This shows the location and boundaries of the site, habitat which immediately borders it, and the location of the site within the broader landscape. Ordnance Survey 1:25,000 scale maps can be viewed on the OS website (www.ordnancesurvey.co.uk/oswbesite/).

Undertaking a Phase 1 habitat survey

A rapid Phase I assessment (Nature Conservancy Council, 2004) is a relatively simple, standardised technique which maps broad communities, and requires quite basic botanical skills. A surveyor should be able to cover 1–2 km squares within one day. Site topography and elevation are recorded, together with landscape features such as grassland and hedges, and vegetation structure such as high forest, coppice, linear woodland and grassland. In areas being considered for woodland creation, the effect of the present vegetation on woodland establishment will also start to become apparent: for example the presence of nettle, bramble and cow parsley indicate a fertile site, and competition for young trees, shrubs and grassland flora. The proximity of arable farmland may have been noted from online data, but the vulnerability of the site to spray drift will also become apparent from the field survey.

Commissioning a soil survey

Soil surveys are used to determine whether sites are suitable for planting trees, and if so, to help select appropriate species mixes (Sections 4.2 and 4.3) and to plan site preparation (Section 4.5.1). The digital National Soils Map indicates general soil types and hydrological properties, but laboratory-based analyses are required to determine pH, phosphorous index and other measures of nutrition. A survey may also provide evidence of drainage problems, water-logging or compaction which may impact upon tree planting (Section 4.5).

4.1.3 Wildlife habitat survey – classifying woodland and grassland communities in the wider landscape

Once the planting site has been selected, the next most important decision is to select the appropriate woodland type(s) for the site, and consequently the species to be planted. This can be controversial, with advocates for and against various approaches, ranging from recreation of the 'wildwood' by tree planting, to allowing woodland to regenerate naturally without intervention. Our ethos is to accelerate the return of a natural woodland and its wildlife, based on the most likely semi-natural woodland that would have grown on the site in the recent past and the type of woodland for which the site and its soils are now best suited, following agricultural improvement.

What ancient semi-natural woodland communities occur in the wider landscape?

The desk search of the geographic information systems described earlier, will have identified ancient woodland in the wider landscape, and any published information on these woods should be examined. Good records almost certainly exist for woodlands in English Nature's National Vegetation Classification (NVC) database and those with an SSSI designation. If not, a useful guide for undertaking an assessment is the *National Vegetation Classification: Field Guide to Woodland* (Hall *et al.*, 2004), but if there is any doubt, an ecologist should be employed to carry out an NVC survey. If neighbouring woodland is at an early stage of succession, it may not be possible to accurately assess its NVC type. Vegetation surveys on the planting site will also highlight features such as old hedgerows or remnant patches of trees, which may indicate which woodland type formerly grew on the site.

It is important that the woodland type selected is ecologically suited to each particular site *in its current condition*, as soils may have been significantly altered through decades of intensive arable farming. For example, an NVC survey recently carried out by the author at Lamberhurst Farm in east Kent (Section 4.1.6) showed that the arable land was bordered in part by lowland oakwood (W10a), containing areas of acid sessile oak-beech wood (W15): the pH range of these communities was 4.4–4.7. The pH range of the planting site was 5.9–7.5, with a phosphorous index of 0–3. In such circumstances... *should the new woodland design be based on the NVC survey of local oakwoods on base-poor soils, or should it reflect a community better suited to the base-rich soil of the planting site today, such as an ash-field maple wood?*

Different practitioners may have different opinions about this and the ultimate decision will be, at least partly, subjective. This issue is explored in more depth in the discussion on choice of species mixes for planting Victory Wood, at Lamberhurst Farm in Kent (Sections 4.2.2 and 4.3.2).

Using the National Vegetation Classification (NVC)

We recommend using the NVC because it is widely accepted as a robust classification of semi-natural vegetation in the British Isles, and it has been used extensively to describe the vegetation of protected sites. It has fewer categories than some classifications (such as Peterken's woodland stand type system (1981) and Rackham's ancient woodland classification (2003)) and has been criticised for this reason. However, the NVC does deal with trees, shrubs and ground flora together and is eminently suitable for sites where the prime interest is species diversity. Furthermore, new woodland design should be about planting a framework which accelerates natural colonisation and woodland development. The objective is not to exactly copy a precise woodland type. **Despite an NVC label, every wood is unique**.

How to undertake an NVC vegetation survey

In some cases, an expert may be able to provide a reasonably accurate assessment by observing the vegetation features. If additional information is needed, then a more systematic survey may be necessary.

The survey method used depends on the homogeneity of the stand (Kirby *et al.*, 1991). A series of quadrats are used to record vegetation data for comparison with NVC summary tables (Rodwell, 1991) and reference to the NVC field guide to woodland (Hall *et al.*, 2004). NVC makes recommendations of the quadrat sizes for each vegetation layer, and a number of different methods have been reported. However, for the purposes of this exercise, we recommend a minimalist approach to data collection, based on the method of Hall *et al.* (2004):

1. First identify an homogeneous area within the woodland for survey.

2. Set up the first of five 5 x 5 m quadrats and record the species present, and their percentage cover. If the data are unlikely to be used for comparative purposes, a 4 x 4 m or 10 x 10 m quadrat could be employed as in the NVC recording scheme.

3. Record the canopy and understorey cover of trees and shrubs over larger quadrats: the NVC recording scheme uses 50 x 50 m quadrats, but a 20 x 20 or 30 x 30 m quadrat should be sufficient.

   The abundance of each species can be recorded using percentage cover, or the Domin scale as follows:

Domin scale	% cover
10	91–100
9	76–90
8	51–75
7	34–50
6	26–33
5	11–25
4	2–10
3	frequent
2	sparse
1	rare

4. Repeat this process five times, with quadrats spread evenly around the stand.

5. If other vegetation types are suspected, repeat the process for a further sample area(s).

The contribution of different species to canopy cover is estimated as part of an NVC survey.

Use the data collected to determine the most appropriate NVC community classification, referring to the keys given in Rodwell (1991) or Hall *et al.* (2004). Computer programs are also available to calculate the 'goodness of fit' of data collected from quadrats to the expected species composition of semi-natural woodland communities and sub-communities recognised by the NVC. One such program, 'Tablefit' (Hill, 1996), can be downloaded from the Centre for Hydrology and Ecology website (www.ceh.ac.uk).

How to classify grassland communities in the wider landscape

The vegetation of new woodland rides and open spaces should not be left to chance, so it is necessary to identify any unimproved semi-natural grassland in the wider landscape. Good records may exist for such areas, particularly if they have a statutory designation such as SSSI or local nature reserve. If not, then a vegetation assessment should be carried out, to identify the community type. Grassland surveys are more straightforward and less costly than woodland surveys. As for woodland surveys, the current, modified soil environment will be a major factor in determining the species to be introduced.

Most arable soils are neutral or slightly basic and highly fertile, with high levels of phosphorous, nitrogen and potassium. Phosphorous is persistent in agricultural soils and can limit options for sowing natural grassland seed mixes. These factors strongly influence the species mix, and methods adopted for grassland creation. The presence of competitive weeds such as thistle, nettle, rosebay, cow parsley and dock, and coarse grasses such as false oat-grass and cock's-foot, are indicative of high nutrient levels. The soil pH should be measured and compared with that of the target NVC grassland type. The tolerance of the plant species to be planted to this pH should then be considered.

4.1.4 Assessing the conservation value of the planting site

Before undertaking field surveys of wildlife, local naturalists and conservation organisations (e.g. the Botanical Society of the British Isles, the Bat Conservation Trust, and Butterfly Conservation) should be consulted for records of rare species. Check whether the area is covered by any local Habitat Action Plans (HAP) or Biodiversity Action Plans (BAP) for species which may occupy the proposed woodland site. The National Biodiversity Network's (NBN) Gateway provides a vast amount of biological data from a wide range of sources. It can be easily accessed from the NBN's website (www.nbn.org.uk) and provides national and regional species distribution maps, and allows searches for all species recorded in SSSIs and 10-km squares; a useful starting point when considering the conservation value of an area.

Flora and fauna of the existing site

A simple baseline survey of flora and fauna can provide a wealth of information about the wildlife value of a site and its immediate surroundings. The costs of such surveys need not be high. Vegetation is important, and should be surveyed on any prospective woodland creation site. Birds are also important and can be used as indicators both at the local and landscape scale. The abundance of insectivorous birds such as warblers is directly related to the abundance of invertebrate prey and the vegetation structure. Butterflies are the easiest invertebrates to survey for the non-specialist: they are highly visible and relatively easy to identify. The requirement of adults for sunny rides, and abundant nectaring flowers can be indicative of both the structural quality of open areas, and potential feeding sources for a range of other invertebrates. The diversity of species and the presence of colonies will also give some indication about the quality of open space vegetation.

Bird surveys

Surveys of breeding birds may be based on the British Trust for Ornithology's Common Bird Census (CBC) mapping technique or the Breeding Bird Survey (BBS) transect method. The CBC is the most accurate method for determining the identity and numbers of breeding birds present, particularly on a small site, but the intensive observations required can be both time consuming (eight or more site visits are required) and expensive. Details of both techniques can be found on the BTO website (www.bto.org). An experienced bird surveyor should be able to recommend a simplified mapping technique which will establish the conservation value of the site. A winter bird survey can

Bird surveys should start early in the morning.

also be carried out, if the area might include important habitat for waterfowl or raptors etc. Additional information on rare and declining farmland birds, which may be present in the area, can be found on the RSPB 'Birds on your farm' web pages (www.rspb.org.uk).

Vegetation surveys

Use the standard methods for NVC surveys (see Section 4.1.3) and survey adjacent hedgerows as well as the proposed planting site. Neighbouring habitat of conservation value, such as ancient semi-natural woodland or unimproved grassland, should have been surveyed already. Discuss the methods adopted with the ecologist employed to undertake the survey. Make sure that rare or endangered plants or habitat are clearly identified by these surveys. Search arable land in summer for rare cornfield annuals. The effort required may be minimal, particularly on a site of less than 100 ha, and could involve no more than a few days survey work. Surveys of open ground vegetation along field margins and fence lines highlight beneficial species, which could be encouraged to colonise the rides and open spaces of the new woodland. This may reduce the number of species required in grassland mixes sown (see Section 4.3.2).

Butterfly surveys

These insects are a highly visible element of the wildlife of any site. Survey them using the 'Butterflies for the New Millennium' site transect method (Asher *et al.*, 2001), which involves a minimum of four visits to the site during the flight season. Provisionally schedule visits for early May, mid to late June, mid July, and mid to late August but if necessary, modify the schedule to encompass the flight periods of all possible butterflies and second broods. Transects across a 100 ha arable site can be completed on each occasion in less than one day.

Surveys of other fauna

Other surveys could be carried out to cover: invertebrates; bats; other small mammals; reptiles and amphibians; fungi; lichens; bryophytes; and soil microbes. Broad ranging invertebrate surveys are likely to be costly and time consuming. However, selected groups such as hoverflies may be chosen as 'indicators' of the diversity of other species in the community, and of habitat health; providing they are expertly surveyed using recognised transect methods. Employ specialists, who possess the necessary licences for these surveys.

European Protected Species

In England, a 'development' that adversely affects any European protected species will require a special Development Licence, issued by Defra. 'Development' is a broad term in this context, which includes projects which 'carry out operations on, over or under land', or involve the 'material change in use of land'. Consequently it is advisable to check as early as possible whether European protected species are present on areas destined for a change in land use, or in the vicinity of such areas; and if so, whether any disturbance is likely to be caused. This may require the services of an ecological consultant, who would be responsible for licence applications. Species which may be present include: bats; dormouse; great crested newt; and otter. More details and a complete list of European protected species can be obtained from the websites of Defra (www.defra.gov.uk) and English Nature (www.english-nature.org.uk).

Are there any valuable microhabitats on the site?

Bare ground along an existing track at Lamberhurst Farm, Kent provides valuable habitat for invertebrates.

Record any habitats of potential value to wildlife such as: remnant patches of unimproved species-rich grassland; nectar flowers for insects; veteran trees; fungi; bare ground; sunny banks; deadwood; habitat boundaries; ponds; streams; seepages; and similar microhabitats which may otherwise be overlooked. Ensure such habitats are protected, and provided with a sufficient buffer area to avoid damage.

These baseline surveys will establish whether the conservation value of the proposed site in its current state is high or low, and therefore whether it is suitable for establishing woodland. They will also identify whether any mitigation is necessary against disturbance of rare or protected species. If the site is rich in biodiversity, for example containing unimproved grassland, it should not be modified by tree planting.

4.1.5 Assess the future benefits for wildlife

When one of the aims of woodland creation and management is wildlife conservation, a good general knowledge of the flora and fauna of the wider landscape is essential, together with an understanding of how species disperse and colonise; particularly those which are able to colonise new woodland habitats. With this knowledge, one can design particular features for the benefit of priority species, such as hazel-rich woodland edge for dormouse, and predict the value of the site for wildlife in the longer term.

Are there sources of potential colonists nearby?

The precise location of a planting site is critical to successful colonisation. Locating new woodland next to existing woodland or species-rich hedgerows will confer a higher conservation value, especially if the woodland is ancient, and has robust populations of specialist woodland flora and fauna with the potential to colonise. Similarly, colonisation of the rides and open spaces will be enhanced by close proximity to any areas of relatively species-rich grassland.

Are there rare or endangered species in the wider landscape which might benefit?

Consult national conservation organisations to identify survey work already carried out in the local landscape, as part of national atlas projects. The Kent and Medway Biological Records Centre holds comprehensive sets of biodiversity data. Local wildlife organisations such as the Kent Wildlife Trust and the Kent Bat Group can identify local Biodiversity Action Plan species, which may benefit from woodland creation, for example bullfinch, song thrush and common nightingale. If no information is available, an ecologist could be employed to undertake similar surveys in the wider landscape to those described above, to include vegetation, birds, and possibly some invertebrates groups, bats or fungi. Commissioning such surveys is ultimately a decision for the site owner/manager, but a basic survey of vegetation and birds for example is relatively inexpensive.

Consider any negative impacts of the proposed new woodland

The impact of woodland creation on wildlife can be negative as well as positive. For example, planting too close to ancient woodland edge may damage or destroy a very valuable habitat (see example in Section 5.1). If pasture on the site is relatively species-rich, this should be protected and an alternative site found for tree planting (see example in Section 5.2). Woodland should not be planted where it would form a barrier between other habitats that could be linked, such as wetlands or grasslands.

Finally, decisions must be taken...

Directions have been given to assess the suitability of a site for woodland creation, which, taken together, may appear daunting, and potentially costly, but this need not be the case. Many of the assessments required can be undertaken by the landowner/manager, supported by an ecological consultant. Once all the information has been collated, it should be possible to determine how the woodland flora and fauna will develop as the trees and shrubs establish, the ride vegetation develops and the new woodland closes canopy. Table 4.1 summarises the assessment criteria, and gives some guidance towards prioritising the various factors.

The ancient woodland edge (right) will eventually be shaded by the new woodland edge (left), damaging valuable wildlife habitat.

Table 4.1 Summary of the main landscape character and site assessment criteria, including the potential for woodland creation for wildlife. Note: ASNW = ancient semi-natural woodland

Criterion	Potential for woodland creation for wildlife on agricultural land	
	High	Low
Habitat type and description		
Landscape character	■ Planting is a priority in local landscape assessment actions ■ Wooded landscape ■ ASNW adjoining the site, or close by ■ Opportunity to link areas of ASNW	■ Planting not a priority in local landscape assessment actions ■ Woodland not a feature of the local landscape, e.g. Romney Marshes ■ Adjoining designated area will not benefit from, or will be harmed by woodland creation ■ Area better suited to creation of another habitat type
Phase 1 habitat survey	■ Woodland and/or hedgerows within or bordering the site ■ Potential sources of colonists present ■ Site adjacent to woodland ■ Site has some protection from spray drift ■ Evidence of natural regeneration ■ Vegetation indicates low fertility	■ Few sources of woodland wildlife such as hedgerows ■ Site contains habitat of conservation value such as unimproved semi-natural grassland or wetland ■ Site vulnerable to spray drift ■ Site completely isolated from any woodland ■ Weeds present indicate high fertility
Soil survey	■ pH similar to ASNW in the wider landscape ■ pH has increased by < 2 units ■ P index 0–1	■ pH very high in comparison to ASNW or unimproved grassland in the wider landscape ■ Base-rich ■ P index > 2.0
Archaeological survey	■ No features present ■ Feature(s) would benefit from woodland creation	■ Feature(s) would be damaged by woodland creation
Planting location and design	■ Area for planting > 5 ha ■ Opportunity for extensive ride network	■ Area for planting < 1 ha ■ Area too small to include open spaces ■ Compaction, water logging or drainage problems
Woodland classification in the wider landscape		
Community type(s)	■ Adjoining ASNW/SSSI will benefit from protection of a new woodland buffer ■ New woodland provides habitat for expansion of wildlife from adjoining ASNW ■ New woodland provides corridor	■ No habitat likely to benefit from new woodland
Grassland classification in the wider landscape		
Community type(s)	■ Adjoining unimproved grassland benefits from protection of a new woodland buffer ■ New woodland open space provides habitat for expansion of wildlife in adjoining grassland	■ Adjoining semi-natural unimproved grassland would benefit from expansion onto the farmland site ■ Soil conditions on site suitable for recreation of a species-rich grassland
Wildlife on the existing site		
Birds	■ No farmland birds of conservation concern, such as corn bunting ■ Birds will benefit from new woodland edge	■ Established population of amber or red-listed arable farmland birds ■ Few woodland birds in the landscape
Vegetation	■ No rare species or vegetation communities which could be damaged by woodland creation	■ Rare arable weeds present ■ Species-rich grassland or other rare communities present
Butterflies	■ Populations of wider countryside butterflies in field margins which would thrive in managed woodland open space, such as skippers and blues	■ Meadow or pasture containing significant populations of rarer grassland species such as small heath or grizzled skipper
Other fauna	■ No species of conservation concern ■ Species present which will benefit from new woodland, such as dormouse	■ Rare or endangered species present which would suffer from woodland creation
European Protected Species Microhabitats	■ Any species present will benefit from woodland creation ■ None present which would be adversely affected by woodland creation	■ Disturbance would require licences and mitigation ■ Valuable microhabitats present
Future benefits for wildlife		
Wildlife in the landscape	■ Woodland, woodland edge and open spaces designed and managed for wildlife ■ Wildlife in the wider landscape will benefit from woodland creation	■ New woodland too small to include open spaces or a woodland edge shrub zone ■ Lack of source populations will mean that species diversity in the new woodland will remain low for the foreseeable future
Rare species in the wider landscape	■ Target species of local BAPs such as dormouse will benefit directly from woodland creation ■ Early stage growth will support species such as tree pipit and nightjar	■ No obvious BAP target species beneficiaries
Negative impacts on wildlife	■ No obvious negative impact on habitat or wildlife of conservation concern	■ Disturbance of protected species ■ Damage or destruction of habitats of conservation value such as ponds or unimproved grassland ■ Disturbance to adjacent habitats such as shading the edge of an ASNW ■ New woodland forms a barrier between habitats which benefit from being linked, such as wetlands ■ Species present could be extirpated, such as corn bunting and rare cornfield annual plants

4.1.6 Example of a landscape character assessment and wildlife habitat survey: Victory Wood

Lamberhurst Farm, the site for Victory Wood, is a Woodland Trust property which straddles the border of the Blean and the Eastern Fruit Belt local character areas. The site was acquired by the Woodland Trust in 2004, as 140 ha of arable land, including: a 1.4 ha meadow; 7.0 ha lowland oakwood; and a small 0.4 ha ash-field maple-dog's mercury wood. The site is underlain by London Clay; the soils are the Windsor Series, described as slowly permeable and moisture retentive clays. The area designated for tree planting (Figure 4.2), known as Clay Hill, is bordered to the southwest by Blean Wood, and to the northeast by Ellenden Wood SSSI: both are ancient woods within the Blean complex. The only link between these woods is a species-rich hedgerow and the southern boundary hedge. The new woodland will restore the skyline and reunite these two ancient woods (Figures 4.3 and 4.4).

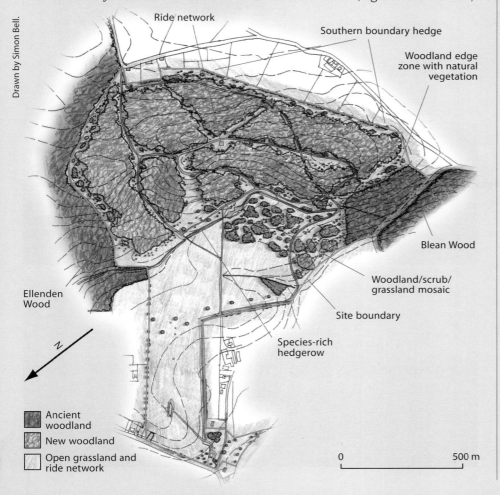

Drawn by Simon Bell.

Ride network

Southern boundary hedge

Woodland edge zone with natural vegetation

Blean Wood

Woodland/scrub/ grassland mosaic

Site boundary

Species-rich hedgerow

Ellenden Wood

Ancient woodland

New woodland

Open grassland and ride network

0   500 m

Figure 4.2 Map of Lamberhurst Farm, the site of Victory Wood; showing the location of new woodland on Clay Hill, scrub, rides and open areas.

Figure 4.3 An aerial perspective looking south across Lamberhurst Farm buildings, over a grazing area towards Clay Hill. The restoration of the landscape is evident from this scene and the design responds well to the landform. Woodland to the east (left) is Ellenden Wood; to the west (right) is Blean Wood.

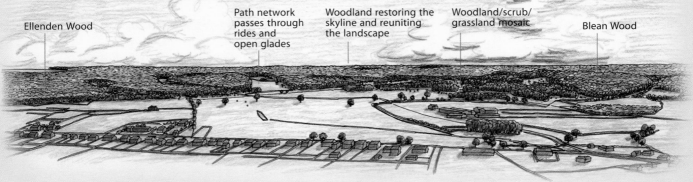

Drawn by Simon Bell.

Ellenden Wood

Path network passes through rides and open glades

Woodland restoring the skyline and reuniting the landscape

Woodland/scrub/ grassland mosaic

Blean Wood

Figure 4.4 Sketch showing the anticipated appearance of Victory Wood once established, looking south to Clay Hill from the bridge over the A229: compare with the photograph below which shows the same view today. The restored woodland on Clay Hill significantly improves the landscape and the mosaic of woodland, scrub and grassland responds to the landform and does not appear fragmented.

Woodland restoring the skyline

The woodland/scrub/grassland mosaic area on an important hill-spur

Blean Wood

Drawn by Simon Bell

bridge over the A229.

BELOW LEFT **Looking west across the ridges of Clay Hill – part of the area designated for tree planting.**

BELOW RIGHT **Looking north across Denstroude Lane to Clay Hill from a lane near Honey Hill.**

The *North East Kent Landscape Assessment* (Kent County Council, 1998) identifies the Blean as a local character unit. Key characteristics of the unit are densely wooded, rounded hilltops with sparse nucleic settlements and few roads within the woodland. Clay Hill, which is part of Lamberhurst Farm, is one of the smaller zones, specifically identified within this unit: one of the main management guidelines for the unit, which relates to Clay Hill, is to restore a native broadleaf woodland link with Ellenden Wood.

Landscape character, soil, archaeological and ecological surveys carried out at this site in 2005 are summarised in Table 4.2, using the criteria listed in Table 4.1. They confirm the suitability of the site for woodland creation. Planting commenced in late 2005, and parts of the site include demonstration plots for woodland creation, using the information presented in this book.

Table 4.2 Summary of the key landscape character and site assessment criteria for Lamberhurst Farm, which support the creation of Victory Wood

| Criterion | Potential for woodland creation at Lamberhurst Farm | |
	High	**Low**
Habitat type and description		
Landscape character	■ Woodland creation identified as one of main aims of local landscape assessment actions ■ Heavily wooded landscape ■ ASNW adjoining the site ■ Opportunity to link areas of ASNW	
Phase 1 habitat survey	■ ASNW and species-rich hedgerows within and bordering the site ■ Sources of colonists present ■ Site protected from spray drift ■ Evidence of some natural regeneration	■ Weeds present indicate high fertility in some parts of the site
Soil survey	■ P index 1–2 over much of site ■ pH has increased by < 2 units in some parts of the site ■ Soils ideal for tree growth	■ pH high in comparison to neighbouring ASNW ■ Base-rich from many years of liming ■ P index 1–3 over parts of site
Archaeological survey	■ Most features have disappeared ■ Opportunity to restore landscape to its historical pattern	
Planting location and design	■ Extensive area for planting high forest, woodland edge and a network of rides and glades	
Woodland classification in the wider landscape		
Community type(s)	■ Adjoining ASNW/SSSI will benefit from protection of a new woodland buffer, and restored link between Blean and Ellenden Woods ■ New woodland provides habitat for expansion of wildlife from adjoining ASNW	
Grassland classification in the wider landscape		
Community type(s)	■ Soil conditions on site suitable for recreation of species-rich grassland	■ No unimproved grassland in the local landscape to act as source for wild flowers
Wildlife on the existing site		
Birds	■ Many species present will benefit from new woodland, woodland edge and open spaces	■ Large population of red-listed Skylark ■ Territorial corn bunting on site in spring, possibly breeding
Vegetation	■ No rare arable weeds present ■ No rare species or vegetation communities which could be damaged by woodland creation	
Butterflies	■ Healthy populations of wider countryside butterflies in field margins which would thrive in managed woodland open space, such as skippers and blues	
Other fauna	■ Not surveyed	
European Protected Species	■ Dormouse and great crested newt likely to benefit from habitat creation	
Microhabitats		■ Trackway with areas of bare ground will be lost
Future benefits for wildlife		
Wildlife in the landscape	■ Woodland, woodland edge and rides created and managed for wildlife ■ Wildlife in the wider landscape will benefit from woodland creation, such as woodland birds, foraging bats, woodland and grassland invertebrates, shade plants, fungi and lichens	
Rare species in the wider landscape	■ Target species of local BAPs such as dormouse will benefit directly from woodland creation ■ Early stage growth will support species such as tree pipit and nightjar	
Negative impacts on wildlife		■ Skylark population will decline, though some birds should breed on extensive open areas of site ■ Corn bunting likely to be disturbed

4.2 How to select trees and shrubs

Our ethos for woodland creation for wildlife is to create conditions, very early in the life of the new woodland, which accelerate wildlife colonisation. This can be achieved through a carefully designed planting scheme, with particular emphasis placed on landscape character, the choice of planting material – trees, shrubs, tall herbs and grassland plants – and woodland structure. Equal consideration must be given to the design and subsequent management of each component of the woodland habitat: high forest, woodland edge, rides and glades.

The National Vegetation Classification (NVC) is recommended as a guide to species selection, but it should not be relied upon solely to formulate the species mix for a wood of a given type. Every wood is unique, and may contain subtle variations in its tree community, even within small areas. This section considers the steps necessary to devise planting mixes for a new wood, and illustrates the process with a description of mixes recommended for planting at Victory Wood in east Kent.

4.2.1 Five steps to selecting appropriate planting mixes

1. Identify the most appropriate woodland/scrub communities for the site

Ecological assessments, carried out for the landscape character assessment, should indicate the various woodland communities in the local landscape (see Section 4.1) and the trees and shrubs that are characteristic of them. Soil and site characteristics should also be considered (see Section 4.1.3). If there is little or no reference ancient woodland in the local landscape, soil and site characteristics become the primary selection criteria.

2. Select the core species for the high forest planting mix

Consult Rodwell (1991) for complete lists of species occurring in the relevant communities (known as 'floristic' tables). These tables present species lists for woodland communities, which are further divided into sub-communities: consult the latter if this level of detail is known. Species lists for most communities contain too many tree and shrub species to contemplate planting them all – a realistic number is six to 12. In the case of the primrose-ground ivy sub-community of ash-maple woodland (W8a) for example, 36 woody perennials are listed, more than half of which occur at low frequencies.

Select the 'core' species for the high forest mix, i.e. those most characteristic of the woodland type. Choose them from the most common or frequently occurring trees and shrubs (frequency values of III to V). Local survey data should help to identify those species which are most characteristic of local woodland communities. These form the basis of the planting mix.

3. Expand the high forest planting mix to include other trees and shrubs, and produce a woodland edge mix – which together provide a diverse range of wildlife services

This is the most important stage of the process. Still referring to the complete list of plants for the community, select trees and shrubs – characteristic of local woodland – from the list of species with lower frequencies (I and II). One of the key criteria which should be applied at this stage is the resources which they provide for wildlife. This is especially important for shrubs and trees of the woodland edge, which in the early years after planting will become home to many birds, insects and plants. The information provided in Tables 4.3 and 4.4, and Figure 4.5, will help you to devise mixes which add to the structural diversity of the canopy and the woodland edge; and **facilitate and accelerate the natural colonisation of wildlife, and hence the establishment of a diverse woodland ecosystem**.

When selecting trees and shrubs, particular consideration should be given to the following:

■ **How valuable is the species to invertebrates?** Foliar, sap, nectar, pollen and fruit feeding insects are very important constituents of woodland biodiversity. They provide an essential source of food for bats, and the majority of woodland birds during the breeding season, including the critical post-fledging period (Table 4.3).

■ **What time of the year is fruit available?** Select a mix of trees and shrubs which will provide an almost year round supply of fruit for animals and insects. Fruit is a vital food for many mammals, insects and woodland birds – particularly in the post-fledging period, and throughout the autumn and winter months (Table 4.4). Check the fruiting season of each species being considered for planting. Whilst many species bear fruit in the autumn, far fewer have fruit in late winter, spring and summer (Figure 4.5). With the onset of climate change, some trees and shrubs, such as hawthorn and blackberry already flower and fruit several weeks earlier than normal in some places. If these fruits are consumed early, then this may have serious implications for birds and animals which rely on them later in the winter. Therefore, make sure that species which naturally fruit in late winter, such as guelder-rose, holly, crab apple and ivy are well represented.

■ **How will the planted species contribute to a diverse vegetation structure?** Canopy cover and density affect colonisation by ground layer plants; diversity of cover along the woodland edge is critical for both feeding and nesting birds, and insect populations. With a good range of trees and shrubs, and an appropriate design (see Section 4.4), structural diversity should be assured.

■ **Identify rare species in the planting mix and those likely to colonise naturally.** Do not plant species if they are likely to colonise naturally, for example birches, bramble and ivy. Rare species, or those with a limited distribution are not generally considered appropriate for planting because their native distribution patterns are of intrinsic importance. Information may be found in local and national floras.

4. **If possible, look at variations in tree communities in nearby woodland, and introduce some variety into the planting mixes**

Woodlands are rarely homogeneous, so it is important to consider variations in tree communities within a wood, as well as among woods (see example of Victory Wood in Section 4.2.2) to properly integrate new woodland into the landscape.

5. **Determine the planting percentages**

Next, determine the numbers of trees and shrubs of each species to be planted. Determine the planting percentages by referring to actual frequency values recorded in local woodland (see example for Victory Wood, Section 4.4.3), in consultation with the frequency tables in Rodwell (1991) (e.g. Table 4.5), to achieve similar combinations of species and patterns. When several woods are being planted, try to avoid homogeneity between them.

TOP LEFT **Willows such as almond willow support a very high diversity of insects.**

TOP RIGHT **Oaks support a very high diversity of insects; here a purple hairstreak rests on the foliage of a young sessile oak.**

RIGHT **In early spring, the nectar and pollen of blackthorn attracts insects, which in turn attract predators such as great tit.**

Tim Loseby

LEFT **Hoverfly (*Scaevi pyrasti*) nectaring on bramble.**

RIGHT **Male bumblebee (*Bombus vestalis*) nectaring on bramble.**

Siskin and other finches feed on alder cones throughout the winter.

Tim Loseby

Dense beech and oak foliage causes heavy shading, and a poor ground flora.

Structurally diverse woodland edge is very good for wildlife.

BELOW LEFT **Elder fruits in summer when few other shrubs are in fruit.**

BELOW RIGHT **Hawthorn fruits are consumed in autumn/winter.**

Thrushes such as redwing rely heavily on fruits in winter.

www.markhamblin.com

Yew fruits are consumed by a variety of birds in autumn/winter.

LEFT **Guelder-rose fruits are an important mid-winter food resource.**

RIGHT **Ivy fruits are an important mid/late winter food resource.**

Table 4.3 Invertebrates associated with trees and shrubs

	Number of invertebrates		
	Total*	Specialists*	Butterfly and macromoth larvae**
Willows	752	217	>100
Birches	521	112	152
Native oaks	423	–	26
Blackthorn	384	43	97
Prunus spp.	384	43	22
Hawthorns	356	29	115
Alders	283	40	50
Hazel	253	22	72
Bramble agg.	237	32	64
Rosa spp.	215	44	41
Field maple	193	60	19
Rowan	160	14	20
Broom	124	26	33
Gorse	71	16	13
Ash	68	–	25
Wild privet	66	4	23
Common juniper	63	26	11
Aspen	60	26	44
Dogwood	55	7	11
Buckthorn	46	10	11
Guelder-rose	44	7	3
Wayfaring-tree	44	7	5
Elder	36	4	6
Holly	36	2	4
Traveller's-joy	35	10	14
Spindle	33	6	7
Elms	31	8	62
Alder buckthorn	28	2	9
Yew	26	2	4
Ribes spp.	25	19	19
Beech	23	–	39
Honeysuckle	19	10	32
White poplar	12	–	6
Ivy	5	2	17

* data cited in Day *et al.*, 2003: sourced from the Centre for Ecology and Hydrology's Phytophagous Insect Data Bank and York University's Ecological Database of the British Isles

** source Crafer, 2005

Table 4.4 Fruit types and frugivores of trees and shrubs in Kent and East Sussex (adapted from Snow and Snow (1988) and personal observations by the author)

Species	Fruit type	Species attracted	
		Dispersal agents	Seed and pulp predators
Dogwood	Drupe	Thrushes, robin, blackcap, starling, magpie, crow, green woodpecker	
Hawthorns	Drupe	Thrushes, robin, starling, wood pigeon	Blue tit
Spindle	Arillate	Thrushes, robin, blackcap	Great tit, marsh tit, long-tailed tit
Alder buckthorn	Berry	Thrushes, starling	
Ivy	Berry	Thrushes, robin, blackcap, starling	Wood pigeon
Holly	Drupe	Thrushes, robin, blackcap, wood pigeon	
Wild privet	Berry	Thrushes, robin, blackcap, magpie	Bullfinch, wood pigeon, blue tit, marsh tit
Honeysuckle	Berry	Thrushes, robin, starling	Bullfinch, blue tit, marsh tit
Crab apple	Pome	Thrushes, robin, starling, crow	Chaffinch, great tit, blue tit
Wild cherry	Drupe	Thrushes, blackcap, garden warbler, starling, magpie, jay, crow, wood pigeon	
Blackthorn	Drupe	Thrushes, robin, starling, crow, magpie	
Buckthorn	Berry	Thrushes, robin, blackcap, starling	Bullfinch
Field-rose	Fleshy receptacle with achenes	Occasional thrushes	Greenfinch
Dog-rose	Fleshy receptacle with achenes	Thrushes, robin, blackcap, wood pigeon	Greenfinch, blue tit
Elder	Drupe	Thrushes, robin, blackcap, garden warbler, whitethroat, lesser whitethroat, starling, spotted flycatcher, crow, jay, magpie, moorhen	Wood pigeon, collared dove, bullfinch, great tit, blue tit, marsh tit
Common whitebeam	Pome	Thrushes, starling, crow, jay, magpie	Wood pigeon, bullfinch, greenfinch, chaffinch, brambling, great tit
Rowan	Pome	Thrushes, blackcap, garden warbler, lesser whitethroat, starling, magpie, jay	Bullfinch, blue tit
Yew	Arillate	Thrushes, robin, blackcap, starling	Greenfinch, great tit
Wayfaring-tree	Drupe	Thrushes, robin, blackcap, garden warbler, lesser whitethroat	
Guelder-rose	Drupe	Thrushes, robin, blackcap	Bullfinch

Note: Green woodpeckers also consume berries in the autumn/winter; waxwings which occur in variable numbers each year will eat almost any fruit, but tend to congregate in more sub-urban and urban locations

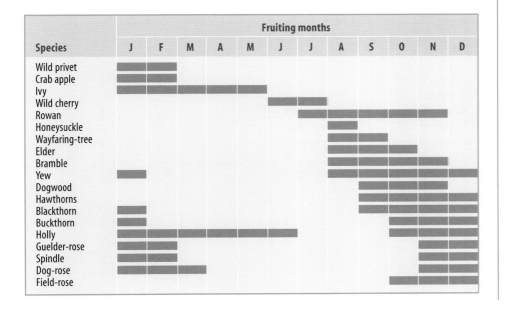

Figure 4.5 Fruiting phenology of shrubs referred to in planting schemes for Victory Wood.

Table 4.5 Woody perennials and their frequency values in ash-maple woods (W8a), oakwoods (W10a), and their seral counterparts (W21 and W24) (after Rodwell, 1991)

Species		Frequency			
		W8a	W10a	W21	W24
Ash	*Fraxinus excelsior*	IV	I		
Field maple	*Acer campestre*	II	I	I	
Hazel	*Corylus avellana*	V	III	II	I
Hornbeam	*Carpinus betulus*	II	I		
Pedunculate oak	*Quercus robur*	IV	III		
Sessile oak	*Quercus petraea*	I	III		
Silver birch	*Betula pendula*	II	III		
Downy birch	*Betula pubescens*	II	I		
Small-leaved lime	*Tilia cordata*	II	I		
Small-leaved elm	*Ulmus minor*	II			
Goat willow	*Salix caprea*	I			
Yew	*Taxus baccata*	I	I		
Holly	*Ilex aquifolium*	I	II	I	
Grey willow	*Salix cinerea*	I		I	
Crab apple	*Malus sylvestris*	I	I	I	
Wild cherry	*Prunus avuim*	I	I		
Rowan	*Sorbus aucuparia*	I	I		
Wild service-tree	*Sorbus torminalis*	I			
Aspen	*Populus tremula*	I	I		
English elm	*Ulmus procera*	I		I	
Sweet chestnut	*Castanea sativa*	I	I		
Sycamore	*Acer pseudoplatanus*	I	II		
Midland hawthorn	*Crataegus laevigata*	I	I	I	
Hawthorn	*Crataegus monogyna*	III	I	V	II
Spindle	*Euonymus europaeus*	I		I	
Ivy	*Hedera helix*	II	II	IV	II
Wild privet	*Ligustrum vulgare*	I	I	II	
Honeysuckle	*Lonicera periclymenum*	II	III	I	
Blackthorn	*Prunus spinosa*	I	I	III	I
Dog-rose	*Rosa canina* agg.	II	I	III	I
Raspberry	*Rubus idaeus*	I	I		
Bramble	*Rubus fruticosus* agg.	IV	V	IV	V
Elder	*Sambucus nigra*	I	I	II	I
Dogwood	*Cornus sanguinea*	II		I	
Wayfaring-tree	*Viburnum lantana*	I	I	II	
Guelder-rose	*Viburnum opulus*	I	I	II	
Gorse	*Ulex europaeus*		I		
Broom	*Cytisus scoparius*		I		
Beech	*Fagus sylvatica*		I		
Alder	*Alnus glutinosa*		I		
Lime	*Tilia x europea*		I		
Field-rose	*Rosa arvensis*			I	
Buckthorn	*Rhamnus cathartica*			I	
Black bryony	*Tamus communis*			II	
Traveller's-joy	*Clematis vitalba*			I	
Common juniper	*Juniperus communis*			I	

Frequency values (how often a plant is found on moving from one sample of vegetation to the next):

IV and V – community constants (61–80% = IV, 81–100% = V)

III – common or frequent species (41–60%)

II – occasional (21–40%)

I – rare (1–20%)

4.2.2 Examples of species selection: Victory Wood

The selection of species for planting is illustrated using different parts of Lamberhurst Farm, the site of Victory Wood in east Kent (Section 4.1.5), following the guidelines described in Section 4.2.1. The landscape and ecological character assessment (Section 4.1.5) confirmed its suitability for planting trees, and identified the most appropriate woodland types for planting.

Agricultural land at Lamberhurst Farm; the distant ridge will form part of Victory Wood.

View west from Lamberhurst Farm across Blean Wood, an ancient lowland oakwood.

1. Identify the most appropriate woodland/scrub communities for the site

The area designated for planting Victory Wood is 73 ha of arable land at Lamberhurst Farm. Woodland was cleared from this area within the last 60 years or so. The ancient semi-natural woodland bordering the site to the north-east and south-west is primarily lowland sessile oakwood, with small patches of ash-field maple-dog's mercury woodland along a stream gully, and small patches of rare acid sessile oak-beech woodland within the core oakwood. The northern and southern boundaries of the planting area are protected by species-rich hedgerows, and should be maintained as such, or partially incorporated into the new woodland edge.

Brown clay and occasional heavy clay loam topsoils, which cover much of the site, are base-rich. Consequently the pH has risen since the original woodland was cleared, from <5.0 to a mean of 6.4. Some areas have naturally calcareous topsoils and subsoils with a pH >7.0. The site is low in N and has a P Index in the range 0–3. Current soil conditions would support species-rich neutral grassland in the woodland open spaces, particularly where the topsoils and subsoils are calcareous. Other areas are only just outside the pH range of acid grassland, so re-establishing a more calcifugous community could be considered. The sward along the arable field margins is species-poor, and is dominated by soft-brome and black-grass. It is classified as a common field speedwell-black grass community (OV8).

Lowland oakwood is the most appropriate woodland community for the majority of the planting site (Box 1, page 74).

In the north-east corner of the planting area, the soil conditions (pH >7; P index of 1) and topography support the planting of a smaller area of ash-field maple-dog's mercury woodland (Box 2, page 74), in an area adjacent to the same woodland type in Ellenden Wood. This will add considerable variety to Victory Wood, through the inclusion of ash and field maple in the high forest (W8a), and species such as wild cherry, grey willow, goat willow, dog-rose, dogwood, spindle and crab apple in the woodland edge.

2. Select the core species for the high forest planting mix

The full list of trees and shrubs associated with lowland oakwoods (W10a); ash-field maple-dog's mercury woodland (W8a); and their associated scrub communities (W21 and W24) is reproduced in Table 4.5. The frequencies detailed in this table give a useful indication of how often a species occurs in a given vegetation type.

Oakwood

The most common or frequent (III–V) trees and shrubs of oakwood high forest are:

- pedunculate oak
- sessile oak
- silver birch
- hazel

Sessile oak is the dominant oak in adjacent ancient woodland, so this must be reflected in the composition of the final mixes (Table 4.6). Various climate change scenarios suggest that sessile oak will be steadily disadvantaged in the South East, compared with pedunculate oak – hence it is important to include both oaks in the final mixes. Silver birch may arrive naturally, but it is included in the planting mix to ensure its presence early on, as it is particularly valuable to wildlife (Section 4.2.3).

Ash-maple wood

The most common or frequent trees and shrubs of ash-maple high forest are:

- ash
- pedunculate oak
- hazel
- hawthorn

Ash and oak are the two characteristic canopy trees of ash-maple woodland: the dominance of sessile oak in local woodland must again be reflected in the composition of the final mix (Table 4.6). Similarly, the dominance of Midland hawthorn in the local landscape must also be reflected in the final mix.

3. Expand the high forest planting mix to include other trees and shrubs, and produce a woodland edge mix – which together provide a diverse range of wildlife services

High forest planting mixes

Seven other trees characteristic of local woodlands and the W10a community type were selected for the oakwood mix (Mix 1):

- beech
- downy birch
- hornbeam
- wild service-tree
- hawthorn
- Midland hawthorn
- holly

Beech, downy birch and hornbeam all contribute to the high canopy, but were primarily included to reflect their presence in local woodland communities. Wild service-tree is a rarer tree in local woodland, which is included for its value to wildlife, as well as its intrinsic conservation value. In addition to hazel, three other understorey species are included: all are characteristic of the high forest understorey in local woodland, and all are important for wildlife (Section 4.2.3).

Three other species were added to the ash-maple high forest mix:

- hornbeam
- small-leaved elm
- field maple

Hornbeam is characteristic of local woodland, and is consequently included as a key high forest species. A small number of small-leaved elms are included for their value to wildlife, as well as the conservation value of the species itself. Elms are in recovery following the mass losses due to Dutch elm disease, and a planted tree may well reach maturity before succumbing to the disease. Planting a small number should at least enable a continued turnover of trees in the understorey. If there were any difficulties in sourcing elms, the percentage of one of the other species would be adjusted to compensate. Field maple completes the mix as the third component of the understorey – and is included primarily as a characteristic species of local ash-maple woodland.

Woodland edge planting mixes

All woodland edge species of lowland oakwoods and ash-maple woodland in Kent were considered as potential components of the respective edge mixes, with the final selection being made on the basis of their value to wildlife, using the criteria outlined in Section 4.2.1. The rationale for selection of each of the fifteen species is presented in detail in Section 4.2.3. We have used a single mix for each woodland type (Table 4.7), but it is important to vary the density of planting and spacing along the edges to create structural diversity and to provide opportunities for natural regeneration (Section 4.4).

Some natural regeneration is likely, but this will probably be very slow. The main candidates for removal from the planting list are the birches, but these

Table 4.6 High forest planting mixes for the oakwood and ash-maple areas

	Planting percentage	
	Oakwood type	Ash-maple type
Canopy trees		
Sessile oak	40	25
Pedunculate oak	5	2.5
Beech	15	–
Downy birch	2.5	–
Silver birch	2.5	–
Hornbeam	10	20
Wild service-tree	5	–
Ash	–	25
Small-leaved elm	–	2.5
Understorey		
Midland hawthorn	7.5	5
Hawthorn	2.5	–
Holly	2.5	–
Hazel	7.5	5
Field maple	–	15

Table 4.7 Woodland edge planting mixes for the oakwood and ash-maple areas

	Planting percentage	
	Oakwood edge	Ash-maple edge
Wild cherry	–	5
Grey willow	–	5
Goat willow	–	5
Midland hawthorn	20	12.5
Hawthorn	2.5	2.5
Holly	10	5
Hazel	30	10
Field maple	–	5
Blackthorn	10	15
Field-rose	2.5	–
Dog-rose	–	10
Elder	10	10
Dogwood	–	5
Honeysuckle	2.5	2.5
Wayfaring-tree	5	–
Guelder-rose	2.5	–
Gorse	2.5	–
Broom	2.5	–
Spindle	–	2.5
Crab apple	–	5

Table 4.8 High forest planting mixes representing localised oakwood communities

	Planting percentage	
	Mix 2	Mix 3
Canopy trees		
Sessile oak	50	60
Pedunculate oak	5	5
Downy birch	2.5	2.5
Silver birch	2.5	2.5
Hornbeam	20	–
Aspen	–	5
Rowan	–	5
Understorey		
Midland hawthorn	7.5	7.5
Hawthorn	2.5	2.5
Holly	2.5	2.5
Hazel	7.5	7.5

Oak with beech sub-canopy and understorey in Ellenden Wood.

are included to ensure the presence of the species in the rapidly developing woodland.

Although several of the species are rare, or associated with ancient woodland – notably wild service-tree and Midland hawthorn – they are so characteristic of local woodland, that their inclusion in the planting mix is justified.

4. Look at variations in tree communities in nearby woodland, and introduce some variety into the planting mixes

Nearby Ellenden Wood includes several distinct woodland communities, which may be natural, or influenced by man. To reflect some of this variation, two other mixes have been designed (Table 4.8) for planting at a lower frequency. Mix 2 represents areas where beech is absent, and hornbeam is a more prominent member of the community. Mix 3 represents areas dominated by oak, with small numbers of aspen and rowan added specifically for their value to wildlife (Section 4.2.1). In addition, there are small patches of rare acid sessile oak-beech woodland within Ellenden Wood. Because of its rarity, and concerns over the long term performance of beech as the climate changes, a mix based on this community was not included.

5. Determine the planting percentages

The high forest mixes are predominately trees, with 20–25% shrubs included for the development of the understorey. The planting percentages (Tables 4.6 and 4.8) were based on canopy cover values recorded in neighbouring Blean and Ellenden Woods, with reference to Rodwell's frequency values for the appropriate woodland type (Table 4.5). Similarly, the planting percentages for the woodland edge mixes were also guided by reference to the cover percentages recorded in local woodland. For example, the oakwood edge mix is dominated by blackthorn, elder, hawthorns, hazel and holly; smaller numbers of the additional shrubs make up the difference.

4.2.3 Summary of the selection criteria for Victory Wood planting mixes

- **Ash**: characteristic of W8a high forest; adds to structural diversity of the canopy; supports a diverse range of lichens from an early age.

- **Aspen**: although infrequent in W10a, included in one of the minor oakwood mixes as characteristic locally and seed production sporadic; slow to reach site naturally; contributes to canopy structure; important for its high diversity of lichens; rich invertebrate fauna; important for insectivorous birds.

- **Beech**: although infrequent in W10a, included in high forest as characteristic locally: contributes to canopy structure; supports far fewer invertebrates than oaks, but provides nuts for birds such as tits, Eurasian jay, common chaffinch and wintering brambling; supports a diverse range of lichens.

- **Birches**: characteristic of high forest in W8a and W10a communities; contributes to canopy structure; supports high insect diversity; particularly valuable foodplants for moth larvae; although wind dispersed, sources may be too distant to colonise naturally.

- **Blackthorn**: characteristic of woodland edge in both types; supports a high diversity of insects; provides very important early spring nectar source for insects; key autumn/winter fruit resource for birds.

- **Bramble**: characteristic of W8a and W10a communities, but predicted natural colonist so excluded from mixes; forms important component of the field layer; particularly attractive to insectivorous birds such as chiffchaff and wren; attracts a wide range of frugivorous birds, including several warblers; flowers important for nectaring butterflies in mid/late summer; dead stems provide nest sites for some woodland solitary bees and wasps.

- **Broom**: although infrequent in W10a, included in woodland edge; supports a good diversity of insects.

- **Crab apple**: although infrequent in W8a, included in woodland edge mix; important late-winter fruit resource when other fruit becomes scarce; supports good diversity of insects.

TOP LEFT **Lichens colonising a ten year old ash tree in new woodland.**

TOP RIGHT **Blackthorn sloes provide an important fruit resource in autumn/winter.**

Bramble flowers attract a great variety of insects.

Blackberries provide fruit in late summer/ autumn for a wide variety of birds, including insectivores.

TOP LEFT **Dog-rose hips provide an important fruit resource in winter.**

TOP CENTRE **Dogwood drupes are consumed by a wide variety of birds in early winter.**

TOP RIGHT **Hawthorn foliage supports a high insect diversity and its flowers provide an important source of pollen and nectar in spring.**

Hazel supports a high diversity of insects.
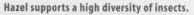

- **Dog-rose**: although infrequent in W8a, included in woodland edge; late summer flowers of *Rosa* spp. provide valuable nectar sources.

- **Dogwood**: although infrequent in W8a, included in woodland edge; early winter fruits.

- **Elder**: although infrequent in both types, included in woodland edge; fruits for a short period late summer when few other shrubs are in fruit; consumed quickly by diverse range of birds; foliage and flowers attract relatively few insects.

- **Field maple**: characteristic of W8a high forest and woodland edge; may be rapidly colonised by lichens.

- **Field-rose**: although infrequent in W8a, included in woodland edge.

- **Guelder-rose**: although infrequent in W10a, included in woodland edge; an important mid- to late-winter fruit resource, particularly attractive to bullfinches.

- **Hawthorns**: characteristic of high forest and woodland edge in W8a and W10a communities; supports a high diversity of insects; very important source of nectar for insects in early summer; important foodplant for moth larvae; key autumn/winter fruit resource for birds.

- **Hazel**: characteristic understorey species of high forest and woodland edge in W8a and W10a communities; high diversity of insects; important foodplant for moth larvae; fruit is an important autumn food source for dormouse.

- **Holly**: characteristic of woodland edge in W8a and W10a communities; fruits for much of the year, from October well into the spring, therefore important in late-winter when other fruit becomes scarce; winter fruits favoured by bullfinch; very poor for insects, though foodplant of holly blue butterfly; potential natural colonist.

- **Honeysuckle**: characteristic of high forest and woodland edge of W10a; although infrequent in W8a, included in woodland edge; fruits briefly late summer, attracting a range of frugivorous birds, including bullfinch

Tim Loseby

LEFT **Bullfinch feeding on honeysuckle.**

RIGHT **Spindle berries provide a minor mid-winter fruit resource.**

LEFT **Wayfaring-tree fruits in the late summer providing a resource for both insectivorous and frugivorous birds.**

RIGHT **Willow flowers support a wide range of insects, and are particularly favoured by bumblebees in the early spring.**

and marsh tit; used by dormice for nesting material; potential natural colonist of high forest.

- **Hornbeam**: infrequent in W8a and W10a communities, but included in high forest as characteristic locally; contributes to canopy structure; supports relatively few insects, but important for hornbeam-specific insects.

- **Ivy**: characteristic of W8a and W10a communities, but predicted natural colonist so excluded from mixes; late autumn flowers important source of nectar for insects overwintering as adults; fruits late winter/ early spring, so increasingly important resource as other fruits are exhausted.

- **Oaks**: characteristic of high forest in both types; exceptionally valuable for insects; supports a diverse range of lichens.

- **Rowan**: although infrequent in W10a, included in high forest; not present in neighbouring woodland, but included for contribution to canopy structure; slow to reach site naturally; summer/autumn fruits important for warblers and favoured by red-listed bullfinch.

- **Small-leaved elm**: rare due to Dutch elm disease; planted to support local populations.

- **Spindle**: although infrequent in W8a, included in woodland edge; mid-winter fruit for birds; planted to support local populations.

- **Wayfaring-tree**: although infrequent in W10a, included in woodland edge; late summer fruits important for warblers prior to migration; predicted natural colonist.

- **Wild cherry**: although infrequent in W8a, included in woodland edge; contributes to edge structure; fruits for a short period mid summer – when few other shrubs are in fruit – consumed quickly by larger frugivorous birds.

- **Willows**: infrequent in W8a, but included for planting on moister woodland edge; very high diversity of insects; important foodplants for moth larvae; flowers provide valuable early source of nectar.

Mature oak woodland.

Box 1 The character of oak-bracken-bramble woodland (W10a)

W10a woods form part of the core dry oakwoods in southern Britain, also occurring on surface-water gleys. Pedunculate oak is the most frequent tree; but locally, and in more free draining soils, sessile oak may be found. Oaks occur with silver birch, sometimes occasional beech, Scots pine and sycamore. Hornbeam is a low frequency canopy tree, and limes are especially rare in Kent and Sussex. Coppiced versions often lack oak, or are reduced to a few standards, and can be dominated by hornbeam. More common forms of oak-bracken-bramble woodland are those dominated by hazel, with or without oak. Hazel occurs with hawthorn and Midland hawthorn in older stands in the South East. Blackthorn and holly may be found in the margins of these woods, and occasionally rowan. Crab apple, elder and guelder-rose are also associated with this woodland. The field layer is dominated in the summer by bracken in more open canopy woodland, but where the canopy is denser, bramble and honeysuckle occur, and occasional broom, gorse and raspberry are likely. Where the woodland edge is adjacent to arable fields, a compressed edge of hawthorn or blackthorn scrub, with bramble-Yorkshire- fog underscrub occurs. On free-draining soils, the edge may be dominated by a narrow strip of birch and bracken.

Few studies describe the seral stages leading to W10 woodland. Natural precursors are probably varied, but limited by soil moisture and pH. Rodwell (1991) considers that over brown earth with free, but not excessive drainage, the less calcicolous types of *Arrhenatherum* grassland are likely to invade, with *Holco-Juncetum* and *Holcus-Deschampsia* grasslands establishing on more water-logged, mesotrophic soils (neither very acid or very alkaline). In the absence of grazing pressure, the grassland may be quite rapidly invaded by characteristic trees and shrubs. On moister soils, these might include hawthorn, blackthorn, bramble, and rose spp, which are typical of hawthorn-ivy communities (W21) (Table 4.5). On drier soils, silver birch may dominate. Oak may also be an early colonist.

Mature ash-field maple-dog's mercury woodland.

Box 2 The character of ash-field maple-dog's mercury woodland

W8 woods have a rich flora, which depends to some extent on coppicing. Unlike oakwoods and hornbeam-woods, which are outliers of continental woodlands, ash-woods are characteristic of the British Isles, particularly those which are carpeted with bluebells. Each stand type has a seral scrub counterpart, although Rodwell (1991) points out that, on ex-agricultural land, it is difficult to predict the natural course of succession: quite diverse communities can lead to ash-field maple-dog's mercury woodland. This gives some degree of latitude in designing planting mixes. However, the most common scrub types in lowland Britain are W21 hawthorn-ivy scrub and W24 bramble-Yorkshire-fog underscrub. Bramble-Yorkshire-fog, which frequently occurs on abandoned farmland often develops into W21 in neutral or base-rich soils. On deeper, moist and richer neutral soils a more species-poor blackthorn scrub may dominate (W22). A mosaic may develop with patches of hawthorn and blackthorn scrub interspersed with bramble and Yorkshire-fog (Rodwell 1991). There are four sub-communities of hawthorn-ivy scrub, and three sub-communities of bramble-Yorkshire-fog underscrub. Trees may invade at the same time, or follow initial scrub development, depending on edaphic factors. Lightweight seeds of pioneer willows and birches are wind-dispersed, and will arrive first. The heavier wind-dispersed seeds of ash and sycamore may arrive if parent trees occur within 100 m or so of the site. Oak and beech may also be dispersed into the site by birds.

In Kent and Sussex, a recognisable stand of ash-field maple-dog's mercury woodland, containing ash, oak, hazel, field maple and hawthorn could arrive naturally within 50 years or so, depending on the proximity of seed sources. Rarer trees and shrubs will usually take much longer than this, although chance colonisation events can occur at any time. A representative shade ground flora may take 100–200 years to develop. Studies of similar woodland of differing ages in Cambridgeshire found that even after 100 years, hazel, field maple and oak were still absent (Peterken 1981).

Sub-community W8a: primrose-ground ivy

In this community, ash and hazel are constant, occurring in variable proportions, together with pedunculate oak (Rodwell, 1991). Emergent ash trees are very common, and can shade out oak and hazel if the stand is dense. Field maple is a constant, but not so common as an emergent. It can tolerate ash shade, and casts dense shade itself. There is a lower frequency of birches, hornbeam and English elm. Scattered small-leaved lime, crab apple, wild cherry, sessile oak, spindle, rowan, and aspen may be found. Grey and goat willow colonise in wetter conditions. In addition to hazel, which is most abundant (particularly in coppice, less so in high forest), the underwood includes hawthorn, honeysuckle, bramble and ivy. Scattered Midland hawthorn (older parts of stands), elder, blackthorn, dogwood, wayfaring-tree, guelder-rose, holly, wild privet, dog-rose, bramble and raspberry occur. Other species recorded at low frequency include beech, yew, sweet chestnut, and sycamore.

4.3   How to select herbs and grasses for rides and open spaces

Our ethos for the creation of rides, glades and open spaces in woodland for wildlife is essentially the same as that for areas of high forest and woodland edge i.e. to create conditions which will facilitate and accelerate natural colonisation, and the establishment of a diverse ecosystem as rapidly as possible.

4.3.1 Five steps to selecting an appropriate planting mix

Five steps should be followed, which are similar to those applied to the choice of trees and shrubs:

1. **Identify the most appropriate grassland and tall herb communities for each site**

   Semi-natural unimproved grassland is a very rare habitat in Kent and East Sussex. Consequently, landscape character assessments (see Section 4.1) would have to extend over large areas to encompass this habitat, and it may be necessary to rely heavily on the literature, if no such habitat is present in the vicinity of the planting site.

2. **Select the core species for the planting mix**

   Consult Rodwell (1992) for lists of species occurring in the relevant communities. These tables include main grassland communities and their sub-communities: the latter should be consulted if this level of detail is known. For most communities, only a small proportion of the plants can realistically be sown. If possible, also find out what species grow locally in similar grassland types.

   Select the 'core' species for the grassland mix, i.e. those most characteristic of the grassland type. Choose them from the plants most characteristic of grassland communities (known as 'community constants', with frequency values of IV and V (see Table 4.5 for explanation of frequency values)): these species are presented as the first block of species in Rodwell's floristic tables. Consult local survey data to ensure that species chosen are also characteristic of local grassland communities. These form the basis of the planting mix.

3. **Expand the planting mix to include other plants of these communities – found in local grassland – which provide a diverse range of wildlife services**

   Still referring to the complete list of plants for the community, select plants from the list of species with lower frequencies (I–III). Plants chosen must be typical of natural grassland vegetation found locally; particularly species tolerant of a wider range of soil pH; and species which can compete on soils of higher nutrient status. The information provided in Tables 4.9–4.12, and Figure 4.6, will help you to devise mixes **which add to the structural diversity of the sward and attract wildlife into woodland rides and glades; especially insects, which in turn encourage insectivorous birds and mammals**.

   When selecting herbs and grasses, particular attention should be given to the following:

   - **How valuable are the species to invertebrates?** Grassland plants provide valuable pollen, nectar and foliage resources for invertebrates, which in turn provide an important food resource for foraging woodland birds, bats and other fauna (Tables 4.9–4.12). The grassland in rides and open spaces offers important nectaring opportunities for saproxylic species from the high forest. Members of the daisy family (Asteraceae) and carrot family (Apiaceae) are particularly attractive to insects. Composites, such as: yarrow, which occurs in neutral grassland; goldenrod; thistles (*Cirsium* spp.); and ragworts (*Senecio* spp.) attract insects with long tongues, such as butterflies and moths. Umbellifers, such as hogweed and wild angelica, are more suited to insects with smaller mouthparts, such as beetles and flies. Bumblebees forage for nectar and pollen in a wide range of flowers, although there are believed to be individual preferences amongst species. Nectar-feeding butterflies and other wider countryside insects also visit a variety of flowering plants. Some of these plants will almost certainly arrive naturally, for example wind-dispersed seeds of sow-thistles, dandelions and thistles.

■ **What time of the year do the species flower?** Flowering time is an important consideration. For example, butterflies, moths and bumblebees require an abundant supply of flowering plants throughout the flight season – which extends from March through to late October – particularly in the peak summer season (Figure 4.6). Try to select a mix of flowering plants which, together with predicted colonisers such as thistles, provide a resource of pollen and nectar throughout the season.

LEFT **Spotted longhorn beetle (*Strangalia maculata*) feeding on teasel pollen.**

RIGHT **Bumblebee worker (*Bombus pratorum*) collecting pollen from cuckooflowers.**

Brown argus nectaring on scentless mayweed.

LEFT **Meadow brown nectaring on marjoram.**

RIGHT **Male bumblebee (*Bombus lapidarius*) nectaring on knapweed.**

■ **How will the species contribute to a diverse vegetation structure?** Woodland rides are very important for insects, especially if they provide high quality open space, with a transition from high forest, through scrub and taller herbs to short grassland (Section 4.4). In some cases, grassland structure may be critical for colonisation of an insect to take place, or for a colony to remain viable; insect larvae may develop in soil, herb vegetation, leaf litter or dead wood, but adults require open structured flowers for nectar, such as umbellifers and composites (Table 4.9). Factors of importance to all insects are:

— flowering phenology for the supply of nectar and pollen
— plant structure
— plant abundance
— location of the plants with respect to temperature, light and shade
— sward height
— competition from other herbs.

It is not possible to take all these factors into account when selecting a grassland mix. However, the general principles are important, and will influence the species choice. The grassland must provide an abundant supply of flowering plants throughout the flight season, for nectar-feeding adults (Figure 4.6). These should be close to the various larval

Table 4.9 Soil requirements, regeneration strategies and colonisation potential of plants providing nectar and pollen for insects

Species		Favourable soil conditions			*Regen. strategy	Colonisation potential
		Acid	Neutral	Basic		
Wild angelica	Angelica sylvestris	X	X	X	S	Poor
Betony	Stachys officionalis	X	X	X	V,S	Poor
Bird's-foot-trefoils	Lotus spp.	X	X	X	Bs	Poor
Bluebell	Hyacinthoides non-scripta	X	X	X	V,S	Poor
Bramble	Rubus fruticosus	X	X	X	V,Bs	Good
Clovers	Trifolium spp.	X	X	X	V,S,Bs	Moderate
Colt's-foot	Tussilago farfara	X	X	X	W	Good
Common fleabane	Pulicaria dysenterica	X	X	X	W	Good
Cow parsley	Anthriscus sylvestris	X	X	X	S	Good
Cuckooflower	Cardamine pratensis	X	X	X	V,Bs	Poor
Dandelions	Taraxacum spp.	X	X	X	W	Good
Ivy	Hedera helix	X	X	X	V	Moderate
Hogweed	Heracleum sphondylium	X	X	X	S	Good
Knapweeds	Centaurea spp.	X	X	X	V,S	Moderate
Ragged-robin	Lychnis flos-cuculi	X	X	X	W	Moderate
Ragworts	Senecio spp.	X	X	X	W,Bs	Good
Red campion	Silene dioica	X	X	X	Bs	Moderate
Sow-thistles	Sonchus spp.	X	X	X	W,Bs	Good
Thistles	Cirsium spp.	X	X	X	W,Bs	Good
Watermint	Mentha aquatica	X	X	X	V,Bs	Poor
Wild teasel	Dipsacus fullonum	X	X	X	S	Moderate
Meadowsweet	Filipendula ulmaria		X	X	V,Bs	Poor
Oxeye daisy	Leucanthemum vulgare		X	X	S,V,Bs	Good
Primrose	Primula vulgaris		X	X	V,Bs	Poor
Hemp-agrimony	Eupatorium cannabinum			X	W	Good
Red valerian	Centranthus ruber			X	W	Good
Small scabious	Scabiosa columbaria			X	S	Poor
Violets	Viola spp.			X	S,V	Poor
Wild marjoram	Origanum vulgare			X	V,Bs	Moderate (local)
Wild privet	Ligustrum vulgare			X	S,V	Moderate
Wild thyme	Thymus polytrichus			X	V,Bs	Poor
Bugle	Ajuga reptans	X	X		V,Bs	Poor
Broom	Cytisus scoparius	X			Bs	Poor
Devil's-bit scabious	Succisa pratensis	X			S	Poor
Tormentil	Potentilla erecta	X			V,Bs	Poor

*Natural regeneration strategies (Grime *et al.*, 1990):
V—Vegetative expansion: new shoots remain attached to parent until well established
S—Seasonal regeneration: seeds or vegetative propagules produced in single cohort
Bs—Persistent seed bank: viable, but dormant seeds present throughout the year
W—Numerous, widely dispersed seeds: wind-dispersed widely, but may be of limited persistence

food plants. The size and visibility of a plant, or whether it is growing in isolation or as part of a small colony may determine its suitability for egg-laying. There is considerable variation in the use of species by insects. Some species, such as the speedwells (*Veronica* spp.) are little used, whilst others such as thistles and knapweeds have a high insect diversity associated with them. Whatever species are selected, it is important to introduce a broad mix of plants to create a diverse sward of grasses and herbs. This will support the varied food and niche requirements of a diverse range of insects.

■ **Can we ensure that a wide variety of foodplants are available for butterfly and moth larvae?** Larvae of most of the non-specialist woodland butterflies – even those with very restricted diets such as small skipper and marbled white – can find their food plants growing on a wide soil pH range (Table 4.12). Whilst most plants host some macromoth species, some support very large numbers, for example heathers (82), docks (96), annual meadow-grass (36), dandelions (66), plantains (66), chickweeds (56), common bird's-foot-trefoil (30) and groundsels (33) (Crafer, 2005). In many circumstances, for example the neutral soils of Victory Wood (Section 4.3.2), a simple mix can be devised, which in theory will provide food plants for larvae of all non-specialist woodland butterflies and a diverse range of macromoths. Other habitats, such as acid grassland have relatively poor plant diversity, and may support only a small number of breeding butterflies

Figure 4.6 Flowering phenology of plants providing nectar for insects.

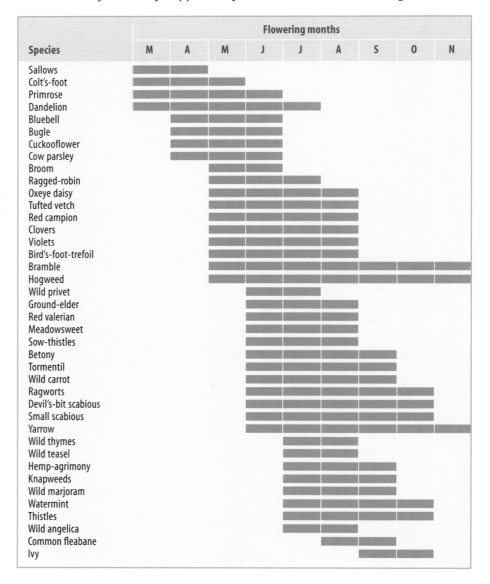

and moths. Efforts to plant a wider range of larval foodplants on such sites to attract a greater diversity of butterflies, which are inconsistent with the natural vegetation, are discouraged. Whatever plants are introduced, establishment of larval foodplants does not guarantee colonisation by butterflies, moths or any other insects. Management is essential to provide the necessary variety of sward heights and densities to suit different species (see Section 4.4). Grazing is the best method, but within the confines of woodland rides, mowing may be the only option (Section 4.5), although rabbits may well contribute to this process.

Tall herb zone along the north side of an east-west woodland ride.

■ **Identify any species in the planting mix likely to colonise naturally and any species which are rare.** Species may not require planting if they are likely to colonise naturally, for example dandelions and thistles; slow colonising species might be included in more isolated woodland open spaces. Species which are rare, or have a limited distribution are not considered appropriate for planting because their native distribution patterns are of intrinsic importance and they may require specialised habitat management. Information may be found in local and national floras.

4. **Determine the planting percentages**

Once the make-up of the final planting mixes have been decided, determine the percentages of grasses and wildflowers of each species to

Table 4.10 Butterfly larval foodplants

	Main foodplants in grassland and open areas in woodland
Wider countryside species	
Small skipper	Yorkshire-fog; rarely other grasses such as timothy, false brome
Essex skipper	Cock's-foot, but may use other grasses such as creeping soft-grass, timothy, false brome, meadow foxtail, tor-grass, common couch
Large skipper	Cock's-foot; occasionally purple moor-grass and false brome
Dingy skipper	Common bird's-foot-trefoil; occasionally horseshoe vetch, greater bird's-foot-trefoil
Brimstone	Buckthorn , alder buckthorn
Large white	Wild or cultivated crucifers, particularly *Brassica oleracea* vars.
Small white	Cultivated crucifers; sometimes wild crucifers, including wild cabbage, hedge mustard, charlock, mignonette
Green-veined white	Wild crucifers, including wild cabbage, hedge mustard, large bitter-cress, cuckooflower, charlock
Orange tip	Cuckooflower and garlic mustard; occasionally large bitter-cress, charlock, winter-cress, hedge mustard, turnip, hairy rock-cress
Green hairstreak	Gorse, broom, Dyer's greenweed, buckthorn, dogwood; common rock-rose, common bird's-foot-trefoil on chalk grassland, possibly in woodland
Small copper	Common sorrel, sheep's sorrel; occasionally broad-leaved dock
Brown argus	Cranesbills
Common blue	Common bird's-foot-trefoil; others include greater bird's-foot-trefoil, black medick, lesser trefoil, white clover, restharrow
Holly blue	Holly, ivy; others include a wide variety of shrubs such as dogwood, bramble, spindle
Red admiral	Nettle; sometimes small nettle
Painted lady	Thistles (*Carduus* spp. and *Cirsium* spp.); wide range of other plants including mallows, common nettle, viper's bugloss
Small tortoiseshell	Nettle, small nettle
Peacock	Nettle
Comma	Nettle; others include hop, willows, currants
Marbled white	Red fescue; possibly supplemented with sheep's-fescue, Yorkshire-fog, tor-grass
Grayling	Sheep's-fescue, red fescue, bristle bent, early hair-grass
Gatekeeper	Fine grasses including bents, fescues, meadow-grasses
Meadow brown	Fine grasses including bents, fescues, meadow-grasses, coarse grasses including cock's-foot, false brome
Ringlet	Meadow-grasses, coarse grasses including cock's-foot, false brome, common couch, tufted hair-grass
Small heath	Fine grasses including bents, fescues, meadow-grasses
Woodland specialists	
Brown hairstreak	Blackthorn, occasionally other *Prunus* spp
Purple hairstreak*	Oaks
White-letter hairstreak*	Wych elm, English elm, small-leaved elm
White admiral	Honeysuckle
Speckled wood*	Cock's-foot, false brome, Yorkshire-fog, common couch and other grasses

*considered by Asher *et al.* 2001 to be wider countryside species be sown in consultation with the frequency tables in Rodwell (1992). Refer to actual frequency values recorded in local grassland (see example for Victory Wood, Section 4.3.2).

When this has been achieved, one further step is necessary, which may result in some modification of the final species mix:

5. Establishing a sward

Select the most appropriate method of establishing a sward, as described in Section 4.4.4; and find out where to obtain a species-rich seed mix or supply of green hay which is close to the specification. Try to ensure that the material has local provenance, as described in Section 4.5.6. The Flora Locale website (www.floralocale.org) is a useful source of information on suppliers. Complex seed mixes can be expensive, so it may be necessary to compromise, for example by: reducing the areas sown; reducing the number of species included in the mix; or using a harvested meadow mix which is likely to contain a similar, but not identical compliment of species.

Table 4.11 Use of butterfly foodplants by macromoth larvae (after Crafter, 2005)

Species		Number of species
Docks	Rumex spp.	95
Plantains	Plantago spp.	66
Dandelions	Taraxacum spp.	66
Bramble	Rubus fructicosus	64
Chickweeds	Stellaria spp.	56
Annual meadow-grass	Poa annua	36
Groundsels	Senecio spp.	33
Nettle	Urtica dioica	30
Broom	Cytisus scoparius	30
Common bird's-foot-trefoil	Lotus corniculatus	20
Couches	Elytrigia spp.	17
Ivy	Hedera helix	16
Common sorrel	Rumex acetosa	13
Dogwood	Cornus sanguinea	11
Gorse	Ulex europaeus	10
Buckthorn	Rhamnus cathartica	9
Sheep's sorrel	Rumex acetosella	8
Dyer's greenweed	Genista tinctoria	8
Alder buckthorn	Frangula alnus	7
Sheep's-fescue	Festuca ovina	7
Rock-roses	Helianthemum spp.	7
Red fescue	Festuca rubra	4
Wood meadow-grass	Poa nemoralis	4
Tall fescue	Festuca arundinacea	4
Yorkshire-fog	Holcus lanatus	3
Rough meadow-grass	Poa trivialis	3
Holly	Ilex aquifolium	3
Cock's-foot	Dactylis glomerata	3
Crane's-bills	Geranium spp.	3
Bents	Agrostis spp.	2
Smooth meadow-grass	Poa pratensis	2
Garlic mustard	Alliaria petiolata	1
Cuckooflower	Cardamine pratensis	1
Common stork's-bill	Erodium cicutarium	1
False brome	Brachypodium sylvaticum	1

Table 4.12 Soil requirements, regenerative strategy and colonisation potential of larval foodplants of open countryside butterflies and some macromoths

Species		Favourable soil conditions			*Regen. strategy	Colonisation potential
		Acid	Neutral	Basic		
Broad-leaved dock	Rumex obtusifolius	X	X	X	Bs	Good
Nettle	Urtica dioica	X	X	X	V,Bs	Good
Garlic mustard	Alliaria petiolata	X	X	X	S,Bs	Good
Cuckooflower	Cardamine pratensis	X	X	X	V,Bs	Poor
Common stork's-bill	Erodium cicutarium	X	X	X	S,Bs	Moderate
Common bird's-foot-trefoil	Lotus corniculatus	X	X	X	Bs	Poor
Ivy	Hedera helix	X	X	X	V	Moderate
Alder buckthorn	Frangula alnus	X	X	X	S	Moderate
Red fescue	Festuca rubra	X	X	X	S,V	Good
Yorkshire-fog	Holcus lanatus	X	X	X	S,V,Bs	Good
Common couch	Elytrigia repens	X	X	X	V,Bs	Poor
Sheep's-fescue	Festuca ovina	X	X	X	S,V	Poor
Annual meadow-grass	Poa annua	X	X	X	S,Bs	Good
Rough meadow-grass	Poa trivialis	X	X	X	V,Bs	Good
Creeping bent	Agrostis stolonifera	X	X	X	V,Bs	Good
Sheep's sorrel	Rumex acetosella	X			V,Bs	Moderate
Broom	Cytisus scoparius	X			Bs	Poor
Holly	Ilex aquifolium	X			S	Poor
Velvet bent	Agrostis canina	X			V,Bs	Good
Gorse	Ulex europaeus	X			Bs	Poor
Common sorrel	Rumex acetosa	X	X		S,V	Poor
Spreading meadow-grass	Poa humilis		X	X	V,Bs	Good
Wood meadow-grass	Poa nemoralis		X	X	V	Poor
Giant fescue	Festuca gigantea		X	X	S	Moderate
Tall fescue	Festuca arundinacea		X	X	S,V	Moderate
False brome	Brachypodium sylvaticum		X	X	S,V	Moderate
Cock's-foot	Dactylis glomerata		X	X	S	Good
Dove's-foot crane's-bill	Geranium molle		X	X	S,Bs	Moderate
Dyer's greenweed	Genista tinctoria		X	X	S	Poor
Buckthorn	Rhamnus cathartica			X	S	Moderate
Common rock-rose	Helianthemum nummularium			X	Bs	Poor
Dogwood	Cornus sanguinea			X	S	Moderate
Narrow-leaved meadow-grass	Poa angustifolia			X	V,Bs	Good
Smooth meadow-grass	Poa pratensis		X		Bs	Moderate

*natural regeneration strategies (Grime et al., 1990):
V–Vegetative expansion: new shoots remain attached to parent until well established
S–Seasonal regeneration: seeds or vegetative propagules produced in single cohort
Bs–Persistent seed bank: viable but dormant seeds present throughout the year

4.3.2 Examples of species selection: Victory Wood

The selection of herbs and grasses for the woodland rides and glades is illustrated for Victory Wood, following the guidelines described in Section 4.3.1.

1. Identify the most appropriate grassland and tall herb communities for the site

Farming practices have increased the pH of the soils in the area designated for tree planting. Consequently, rides and open spaces over much of the area could support species-rich neutral grassland, particularly where the topsoil and subsoil are naturally calcareous. However, there are some areas where the soil pH is still just below 6.0, which is only just outside the pH range of acid grassland: re-establishing a more acid grassland community could be a longer term aim for these areas. Due to the high clay content and fertility of the soil, topsoil removal in the woodland open spaces could be considered at this site also.

Swards along the arable field margins are relatively species-poor, and are dominated by soft-brome and black-grass. Other species include occasional false oat-grass, Italian ryegrass, thistles, willowherbs, cut-leaved crane's-bill, common bird's-foot-trefoil, meadow grasses, bristly oxtongue, common fleabane, creeping buttercup, bramble, ragwort and sow-thistles. The fields themselves were not cropped in the previous year, and no weed control was undertaken. These areas are dominated by black-grass, soft-brome and broad bean. The weed burden on this site must be reduced to a minimum before the introduction of wild flowers, which will require the application of herbicides prior to the preparation of the seedbed, following prescribed methods for arable revision to species-rich grassland (section 4.5.1).

Black grass is one of the characteristic plants of field margins at the site of Victory Wood.

Species-rich neutral grassland

2. Select the core species for the planting mix

The main grassland type appropriate for the open areas is a species-rich neutral grassland community (MG5). It is important to select all of the MG5 community constants to provide the foundation of the new grassland community (Table 4.13).

Table 4.13 Species-rich neutral grassland seed mix suitable for the open spaces in Victory Wood

Sowing mix		% by weight
Grasses		
Common bent [a]	Agrostis capillaris	20
Sweet vernal grass	Anthoxanthum odoratum	5
Crested dog's-tail	Cynosurus cristatus	25
Cock's-foot [a]	Dactylis glomerata	2.5
Meadow fescue [a]	Festuca pratensis	2.5
Red fescue [a]	Festuca rubra	20
Smooth meadow-grass [a]	Poa pratensis	5
Total		80
Wild flowers		
Yarrow	Achillea millefolium	1
Garlic mustard [a]	Alliaria petiolata	1
Cuckooflower* [a]	Cardamine pratensis	1
Common knapweed*	Centaurea nigra	3
Meadow vetchling	Lathyrus pratensis	2
Autumn hawkbit	Leontodon autumnalis	1
Oxeye daisy	Leucanthemum vulgare	1
Common bird's-foot-trefoil* [a]	Lotus corniculatus	3
Ribwort plantain	Plantago lanceolata	1
Meadow buttercup*	Ranunculus acris	1
Bulbous buttercup*	Ranunculus bulbosus	1
Yellow-rattle	Rhinanthus minor	1
Common sorrel [a]	Rumex acetosa	1
Red clover	Trifolium pratense	1
White clover*	Trifolium repens	1
Total		20

* nectar plants
[a] butterfly larval foodplants

Table 4.14 Seed mix for more acidic open spaces of Victory Wood

Sowing mix		% by weight
Grasses		
Common bent*	Agrostis capillaris	30
Sweet vernal grass	Anthoxanthum odoratum	2.5
Cock's-foot [a]	Dactylis glomerata	2.5
Wavy hair-grass	Deschampsia flexuosa	5
Sheep's-fescue	Festuca ovina	30
Yorkshire-fog [a]	Holcus lanatus	2.5
Annual meadow-grass [a]	Poa annua	5
Timothy	Phleum pratense	2.5
Total		80
Wild flowers		
Common stork's bill	Erodium cicutarium	2
Common bird's-foot-trefoil*[a]	Lotus corniculatus.	2
Sheep's sorrel*	Rumex acetosella	10
Lesser trefoil*	Trifolium dubium	2
Dove's-foot crane's-bill*[a]	Geranium molle	2
Tormentil	Potentilla erecta	2
Total		20

* nectar plants
[a] butterfly larval foodplants

3. Expand the planting mix to include other plants of these communities – found in local grassland – which provide a diverse range of wildlife services

Other plants characteristic of unimproved neutral grassland locally were then selected using Tables 4.9–4.12; and Figure 4.6 as a guide. These were chosen to provide nectar plants for woodland insects throughout the flight season, particularly the critical summer months. Larval foodplants for non-specialist woodland butterflies (Tables 4.10 and 4.12) and species which support a diverse range of macromoth larvae were also considered (Table 4.11). The 22 plants selected (Table 4.13) provide resources for the larvae of at least 11 non-specialist woodland butterflies. In addition, green hairstreak and holly blue feed on shrubs, and would be likely to colonise scrub or woodland areas. The vanessids (red admiral, small tortoiseshell, peacock, comma and painted lady) feed on nettle and thistles, which are almost certain to colonise parts of the site naturally. In view of an existing brown argus colony on site, cut-leaved crane's-bill could also be included.

Yorkshire-fog was initially selected as one of the core grasses of species-rich neutral grassland, but it is likely to colonise rapidly, or arise from the seedbank: it is also highly competitive, so for this reason it was not included in the mix. Site disturbance at planting will almost certainly result in a greater range of thistles, sow-thistles, hogweed and bramble in some abundance, which will provide important additional nectar sources for insects. No species were included in the mix which would be classified as rare in Kent.

4. Determine the planting percentage

Eighty percent (by weight) of fine grasses is generally believed to produce a meadow with a more natural appearance, and to reduce the impact of weeds. The mix is dominated by grasses identified as community constants (20–25% of the mix); other grasses were included at much lower percentages (2.5–5.0%). The wild flower component of the mix was divided fairly evenly between the species, with slightly higher percentages of species identified as community constants.

Acid grassland

2. Select the core species for the planting mix

On a small part of the site, the development of a more acid grassland community is a longer term aim. The NVC classification for unimproved acid grassland occurring in Kent and Sussex is sheep's fescue-common bent-sheep's sorrel (U1). In the absence of any natural habitat in the vicinity, the typical sub-community (U1b) was chosen as a guide for species selection. Three community constants were included, which vary little between sub-communities: sheep's fescue, common bent and sheep's sorrel (Table 4.14).

3. Expand the planting mix to include other plants of these communities – found in local grassland – which provide a diverse range of wildlife services

Other plants were selected from the list of species occurring in U1b communities, using Table 4.9 and Figure 4.6 as a guide, to provide some nectar plants for woodland insects. These are poorly represented in the mix: reflecting the character of acid grassland floral communities. The adjacent area of species-rich grassland also being created will be much more substantial, so it will not be necessary to increase species richness in the acid grassland areas. Nevertheless, the acid mix does include the larval foodplants of several non-specialist woodland butterflies typical of acid grassland (Table 4.14), particularly Yorkshire-fog and cock's-foot for small skipper and Essex skipper respectively; sheep's sorrel for small copper;

bents and fescues for gatekeeper, meadow brown and small heath; and dove's-foot crane's-bill for brown argus.

Site disturbance at planting will almost certainly result in a greater range of thistles, sow-thistles, hogweed and bramble in some abundance, which will provide important additional nectar sources for insects. No species were included in the mix which would be classified as rare in Kent.

4. Determine the planting percentage

The mix is dominated by the two grasses identified as community constants (30% of the mix respectively); other grasses were included at much lower percentages (2.5–5.0%). The wild flower component of the mix was divided fairly evenly between the species, with the exception of sheep's sorrel, which is a constant in the acid grassland community.

ABOVE LEFT **Small skipper is a likely colonist of the rides and glades of Victory Wood.**

ABOVE CENTRE **Gatekeeper is a potential colonist of Victory Wood.**

The planting mix for neutral grassland at Victiory Wood includes:

LEFT **Yellow rattle**
RIGHT **Common sorrel**
ABOVE RIGHT **Yarrow**
BOTTOM **Oxeye daisy.**

4.4 How to design a new wood

4.4.1 How to design the high forest planting

What structure should you aim for?

The most valuable mature woods for wildlife are those which provide a diverse range of habitats and structure (Figure 4.7), including:

- closed-canopy woodland with a well developed ground flora; a shrub layer up to about 5 m tall; an understorey of low stature trees and immature canopy species; and a canopy layer of mature trees
- areas of open canopy and small trees/shrubs
- a well-structured shrub layer along internal and external woodland edge
- rides and glades, including a field layer of grasses, ferns and wild flowers
- mature stems with holes; standing and fallen dead and decaying wood.

Figure 4.7 Structural variation in mature woodland.

Drawn by Tharada Blakesley

High quality ancient semi-natural woodland is not dominated by any single habitat type or structural feature; a balance between them encourages a rich woodland flora and fauna. **The key to success in designing woodland for wildlife is to understand these structural requirements, and to ensure that in new woodland, they are diverse and provide a high quality habitat.**

Is the size of the new wood important?

To some extent, biodiversity is dependent on the size of a new wood; an aspect of planning, which is often determined by non-biological constraints. Bird communities, in particular, tend to be more diverse in larger woods (Ford, 1987; Fuller, 1995; Woolhouse, 1983). Including areas of open canopy or small trees/shrubs in the design creates habitat for early successional bird species such as tree pipit, whitethroat, linnet and yellowhammer. Scrub and young trees may be retained to support birds such as common nightingale, turtle dove, whitethroat and bullfinch. These areas also contribute to the overall amount of woodland edge habitat, which is critical to the biodiversity of new woodland. Woodland of 5 ha or more will comfortably accommodate the range of structures listed above, with a reasonable balance among them, although even woods of 2–5 ha can support a valuable degree of structural diversity.

Woods smaller than 2 ha – a common sight in Kent and East Sussex – are often dismissed in the literature as too small to be of value to biodiversity conservation. Even these woods can make a positive contribution, albeit

Tim Loseby

www.markhamblin.com

TOP LEFT **Blue tits will nest in new woods if boxes are provided, otherwise, they will use the habitat for feeding, particularly post-fledging family parties.**

TOP RIGHT **The Eurasian jay is a frequent visitor to new woods.**

LEFT **Common nightingale habitat in new woodland at Comfort's Wood.**

with a reduced range of vegetation structures. In small woods, populations of birds may be limited to just one or two pairs of a species, which will inevitably be vulnerable to events such as predation. Consequently, small woods rely on immigration of birds from one year to the next, without ever developing stable populations. The value of small woods depends on their position in the landscape; planting next to mature woodland, particularly where management has been abandoned, may add to the structural diversity of the whole, and provide areas of scrub and open space to compliment the closed canopy of the mature woodland. So, even opportunities to plant small plots of land should be given serious consideration.

What are the key factors to consider when designing the high forest?

It is impossible to design a new woodland that resembles the structure of an ancient woodland in a single step, but it is possible to enhance the processes of succession that will eventually lead to it.

For the design of high forest, five factors should be considered:

1. **Size and use** – the range of habitats and structure will be constrained for small woods < 2 ha.

2. **Areas of open space** – these are essential for light-requiring ground flora and they allow natural regeneration (or later planting) to diversify age structure.

3. **How should canopy trees be grouped?** Single species groups avoid competition and blocks of 36 trees, planted 2 m apart should ensure that at least one tree will reach the canopy or sub-canopy; variation could be introduced for example by varying group size and spacing.

4. **How should understorey trees and shrubs be grouped?** Both single species and intimate mixes should be considered; group size is less critical than for canopy trees, and may be much smaller.

5. **Planting pattern** – trees and shrubs could be planted in straight lines, sinuous rows or more randomly, whilst maintaining specified spacing; groups of trees and shrubs should be located randomly, whilst trying to avoid shrub dominance over slower growing canopy trees.

In practice, each factor may be varied, producing almost infinite possibilities within a design: examples of how this can be achieved are given for Victory Wood in Section 4.4.3. **For successful woodland creation for wildlife, adopt a simple design, which is easy to plant and manage and which provides a framework, within which natural regeneration and wildlife colonisation are enhanced.**

4.4.2 How to design a woodland edge

What structure should you be aiming for?

The woodland edge marks the boundary between high forest and 'other vegetation', (e.g. arable land, grassland, tall herb vegetation or scrub) or the internal boundary between high forest and rides or larger glades. A distinct zone of shrubs or coppiced trees included along such boundaries will be very attractive to wildlife. Plant species to include in a woodland edge mix are described in Section 4.2, where the emphasis is placed on creating:

- a structurally diverse habitat for many species of insects, foraging birds and bats
- areas of dense foliage, at different levels, for nesting birds, mammals and basking insects
- shrubs and trees that fruit for much of the year
- nectar sources for insects, to complement sources in the open ground flora.

Birds, which favour the woodland edge, include dunnock, wren, long-tailed tit, and summer visitors such as common nightingale, blackcap, garden warbler and chiffchaff. The woodland edge also provides valuable hunting areas for raptors and owls, such as sparrowhawk, barn owl and tawny owl. Many of the birds, which inhabit the edges of mature lowland woods are those which also favour the young growth of new woodlands, such as most of the woodland warblers.

LEFT **A woodland edge lacking a shrub zone is very poor for insects, birds and foraging bats.**

RIGHT **This woodland edge looks attractive because the trees have not been pruned, but it lacks structural diversity and is poor for wildlife; note the ride is frequently mown, also creating very poor habitat for wildlife.**

What are the key factors to consider when designing the woodland edge?

Before attempting this design, it is helpful to study a natural woodland edge or mature area of scrub, to visualise what the planting is being designed to achieve. For the design of the woodland edge, four factors should be considered:

1. **Area of woodland edge** – decide how much of the new wood can be designated as woodland edge, considering the extent of the woodland perimeter; the desired internal ride network; and the number of glades envisaged. The width of the edge may be constant or variable (a minimum of three rows is essential). To encourage structural diversity and natural regeneration, open spaces should be incorporated into the woodland edge design.

2. **Orientation of rides** – position rides east-west if the wood is large enough to accommodate this.

3. **How will the shrubs and trees be grouped?** Planting these as intimate mixes rather than single species groups, 2 m apart, should produce structural diversity and enhance biodiversity recovery; variable rather than uniform spacing could also be considered.

Observing the structural diversity of a natural woodland edge, such as this one at Yocklett's Bank in Kent, can help the design process.

4. **Planting pattern** – straight lines, sinuous rows or more random planting should be considered, reflecting the planting pattern of the high forest areas; consider the growth rates and sizes of different species, planting taller species along the inner rows.

The woodland edge is confined to a much smaller area than the high forest, but it will support a disproportionately high level of wildlife. Consequently, its design is very important, and opportunities should be taken to introduce as much structural diversity as possible.

4.4.3 Examples of woodland design: Victory Wood

A 5 hectare compartment based on the Victory Wood planting scheme has been chosen to illustrate the process of woodland design, including areas of high forest, woodland glades, woodland edge and rides.

Design of the high forest

Key design features:

1. **Size and use** – 5 ha compartment; an ash-field maple-dog's mercury woodland created for wildlife conservation

   High forest planting area occupies 3.41 ha, of which:
   3.25 ha are occupied by trees and 0.16 ha by permanent glades

   Woodland edge planting area occupies 0.5 ha

   Rides (central and peripheral) occupy 1.09 ha.

Figure 4.8 Example of a 5 ha compartment, based on the planting sceme at Victory Wood.

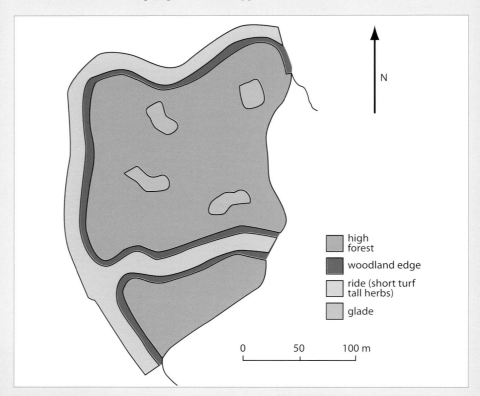

N

high forest

woodland edge

ride (short turf tall herbs)

glade

0   50   100 m

2. **Areas of open space** – four small glades, each of 400 m² (0.04 ha) randomly sited between groups of trees and shrubs (Figure 4.8): these will support light requiring ground flora, and will provide some structural diversity, but they will require continued management.

3. **How will canopy trees be grouped?** Single species; blocks of 36 trees to avoid competition and to ensure that at least one tree will reach the canopy or sub-canopy; birches scattered randomly; uniform 2 m spacing to encourage canopy closure.

4. **How will understorey trees and shrubs be grouped?** Mixed species groups to encourage structural diversity; blocks of 20 shrubs.

5. **Planting pattern** – to achieve a more naturalistic appearance, planting in sinuous lines, 2 m apart; planting along these lines in a staggered pattern (2 m apart); groups located randomly.

How to calculate the number of trees required

To calculate the number of trees, and the number of groups required, the following simple calculation can be performed:

Area of high forest planting = 3.25 ha

At 2 m spacing, 2,500 trees/shrubs planted per ha
Therefore, for 3.25 ha; number trees/shrubs required = 2,500 x 3.25 = 8,125

To calculate requirement for each species, multiply total number of trees/shrubs by proportion of each species;
for example, number of hornbeam trees required = 0.2 x 8,125 = 1,625

To calculate the number of groups of each species, divide the number of trees/shrubs by the group size (36 for trees, 20 for shrubs);

for example;
number of hornbeam groups = 1,625/36 = 45
number of shrub groups = 2,031/20 = 102 groups.

Canopy trees	Planting percentage	Number plants required	Approximate number of groups
Sessile oak	25	2031	56
Pedunculate oak	2.5	203	6
Hornbeam	20	1625	45
Ash	25	2031	102
Elm	2.5	203	6
Understorey shrubs – intimate mix	25	2031	102

Design of the woodland edge

This design adopts a uniform edge width, with three rows of shrubs and trees, planted 2 m apart. Three planting patterns have been devised, varying in planting density, each based on unit lengths of 50 m. The scheme described meets the criteria for new 'native' woodland by the English Woodland Grant Scheme, which allows a shrub element of up to 25% of the grant-aided area.

High density areas

Three rows of shrubs and trees planted 2 m apart; random planting with no grouping. To achieve some gradation of height; growth rates and size should be considered to determine whether species should be planted towards the inner or outer edge of the shrub zone. Consequently, plant willows, holly, crab apple, hazel, field maple and wild cherry along the inner edge.

Medium density areas

This design reduces the planting density by simply leaving 25% of planting spaces unoccupied, to provide greater structural diversity.

Low density areas

This design reduces the high density planting by leaving 50% of planting spaces unoccupied, to encourage some natural regeneration and provide greater structural diversity.

Key design features

1. **Area of woodland edge** – 10% of total area (0.5 ha); width of edge 6 m (three rows of shrubs and trees); ride width 15 m.

The unoccupied spaces in the shrub edge of this new woodland add to its structural diversity.

2. **Orientation of rides** – peripheral ride and an east-west central ride.

3. **How will the shrubs and trees be grouped?** Intimate planting mix; uniform 2 m spacing.

4. **Planting pattern** – sinuous lines, 2 m apart; planting along these lines in a staggered pattern (2 m apart); faster growing or taller species predominately along the inner edge.

Optional design features for this compartment

Here, four modifications are proposed to the design of the compartment described above. The planting scheme which results from them would be more complicated to layout, but would increase structural diversity of the high forest area, and allow a greater opportunity for natural colonisation.

- **Location of open areas** – the area and number of permanent, randomly sited glades could be increased in the high forest area from 0.16 to 0.5 ha, accounting for 10% of the total compartment area. Glades would vary in area from a minimum of 1,000 m², providing increased opportunities for natural regeneration, development of the light requiring ground flora; and along the internal edges, more shade tolerant ground flora.

- **Spacing of trees and shrubs within groups** – this could be varied to encourage more structural diversity: standard 2 m spacing, with occasional groups spaced at 3 m or 5 m to promote a more open and natural appearance and create opportunities for natural regeneration.

- **Species composition and size of canopy tree groups** – single species groups retained, but size varied: in addition to groups of 36 trees, occasional groups of 16 and nine trees could be included, particularly close to the woodland edge; this would increase structural diversity.

- **Area of woodland edge** – this could include deep scallops of predominately shrubs rather than tall herbs or grassland, which effectively varies the width of the woodland edge from 6 m (three rows) to 15 m (eight rows). This would provide considerable structural diversity, attractive to a wide range of woodland edge species.

4.4.4 How to design and establish the vegetation of rides and glades

What structure should you aim for?

The open spaces of rides and glades support a great diversity of wildlife, and can help to conserve the flora and fauna of another threatened and diminishing habitat, unimproved semi-natural grassland. Rides on wetter soils may support a marshy flora, whilst those on drier soils can develop a heathland flora. Rides also serve as corridors for dispersal by many species and for hunting by others. Like the woodland edge, ride vegetation needs to have some structural, as well as floral diversity. This creates a range of habitats capable of supporting a high density and variety of insects, from bare ground and short turf, through tall herbs to the woodland edge. Plants which should be included in a ride/glade mix are described in Section 4.3. For nature conservation purposes, an area of open space equivalent to 25% or more of a new wood would be valuable.

LEFT **Abundant nectar sources in the tall herb zone of a 'new woodland' ride, 15 years after planting.**

TOP RIGHT **Species-rich tall herb zone at Bentley Meadow.**

BOTTOM RIGHT **Although quite narrow, this east-west ride in Straits Enclosure, Alice Holt, is good for woodland butterflies such as silver-washed fritillary and purple emperor.**

Silver washed fritillary nectaring on thistle in Straits Enclosure, Alice Holt.

However, the biodiversity potential of rides and open spaces in woodlands planted on agricultural land in Kent and Sussex over the last 25 years or so often remains unfulfilled. In addition to poor or non-existent zones of shrubs along the woodland edge, rides may be mown repeatedly resulting in a low diversity of plants, or they may be narrow and shaded. Such rides are quite unsuitable for many woodland insects and their predators because they lack nectar sources and food plants. Even where foodplants have colonised, such as Yorkshire-fog and timothy grasses favoured by the small skipper, in the absence of abundant sources of nectar, dispersing adults are unlikely to colonise such areas. Occasional bramble patches may attract insects, but they will not sustain breeding populations through the spring and summer months.

TOP LEFT **This woodland ride is frequently mown throughout the summer, and is consequently very poor for wildlife.**

RIGHT **Common spotted-orchid has been recorded in the rides of several farm woodlands in Kent.**

Common fleabane provides an excellent source of nectar for insects in late summer.

In special circumstances, one of the management objectives of a new wood could be to provide habitat to attract rare species such as pearl-bordered fritillary or heath fritillary butterflies, although the author is unaware of any woodland creation schemes designed specifically to encourage colonisation by rare woodland specialist butterflies. However, this could be attempted in the future, providing specialist habitat design and management guidelines were devised by experts.

Heath fritillary occurs in Ellenden Wood, less than 100 m from the new woodland creation site at Victory Wood.

Butterflies illustrate very well some of the key ecological issues which underpin ride design and management. Most woodland butterflies rely on sunlit rides and glades, which must support a plentiful supply of larval foodplants, and an abundant supply of flowers for nectaring. These open spaces usually offer protection from wind, and a warmer microclimate for species which like to bask, such as comma, the fritillaries and white admiral. Wood white and ringlet are exceptions, as they prefer light shade, whilst green-veined white and speckled wood will tolerate deep shade. The adults of most species will use a range of flowers for nectaring, whilst their larvae are likely to feed on just a few species. This is particularly so for the woodland specialists such as white admiral, which feeds only on honeysuckle. Wider countryside species may also have a narrow range of foodplants, for example small tortoiseshell requires either nettle or small nettle. However, the presence of the right foodplant and an abundant supply of nectar is not always sufficient to allow a species to colonise a particular wood. The habitat and micro-climate in which the foodplant is growing is also critical for breeding to take place. Some species such as the marbled white prefer tall grassy areas, whereas others such as the small heath require short vegetation. Oates (2004) has shown that the pearl-bordered fritillary requires "plentiful leaf litter plus adequate violets without (too much) grass, plus tree/scrub seedling and re-growth development and over good spring weather". If the grass is too long, the habitat becomes unsuitable, even with plentiful violets. This is the reason why this species is now believed to be extinct in Kent. Rides in which it bred in the last two remaining woods were allowed to become overgrown.

TOP **A shady north east-south west ride in Ham Street Woods, Kent supports several woodland butterflies.**

BOTTOM **White admirals favour shady woodland rides, often in mature woodland, but visit sunny glades to nectar.**

How to design rides

Light penetration is affected primarily by the orientation of the ride, its width and the height of the trees along the high forest edge. Within an east-west ride, the north side is sunny and warm, the south side cooler and moister. East-west rides are sunnier for longer than north-south rides during the summer months. For a detailed account of aspect and the duration of direct sunlight, refer to Ferris and Carter (2000). It is important that light reaches the central zone of short turf or bare ground, as well as the areas of taller herbs and shrubs. Rides must be sunny and warm to support nectaring insects, whilst also providing cool, shady conditions for larvae of the same species. Increasing the width of east-west rides creates more sunny areas, although there is a risk that they become wind tunnels, particularly with prevailing westerly winds. This can be alleviated by angling rides to the north or south near the edge of the wood, by scalloping and by closing off some ride sections with standard trees.

Tree height usually cannot be manipulated, unless a broad zone of shrubs is planted to grade into the high forest on the southern side. In many woodlands, both old and new, rides are often too narrow, but this can be avoided in new woodland, providing the site is large enough. **The width of rides should be approximately one, to one and a half times the height of the high forest edge. For new woodland, assume that trees will grow 20–30 m tall, so rides should not be narrower than 20 m and preferably wider than 30 m.** The width of north-south rides is not as critical, so if space is limited, they can be narrower. They are likely to support a different flora to their east-west counterparts, which is more typical of light-woodland shade; consequently they provide important habitats in their own right. Woods larger than 5 ha should easily accommodate a simple ride network, whereas those of 2–5 ha should have at least a single ride.

Ride management

The ideal ride management system for an east-west ride is a three-zone system (Warren and Fuller, 1993), modified for new woodland (Figure 4.9). Zones or strips of differing habitat are created, from a central track of short dry turf with bare areas, through tall herb swards rich in wild flowers (on neutral or calcareous soils), grasses, sedges and rushes, to the graduated scrub and coppice zone of the woodland edge. Such designs must be maintained by appropriate mowing and cutting regimes to enhance and retain biodiversity. Cuttings should be removed to avoid damage to the habitat through soil enrichment.

Figure 4.9 Profile of a three-zone ride management system.

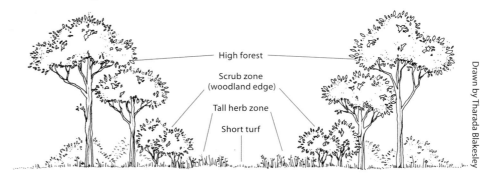

High forest

Scrub zone (woodland edge)

Tall herb zone

Short turf

Drawn by Tharada Blakesley

The short turf or central zone should be approximately 2 m wide, and mown once or twice a year to create areas of short turf and to maintain access. Occasional areas of bare ground should be encouraged – particularly along south-facing woodland edges – so such areas should not be re-vegetated. Bare ground is often exposed accidentally during mowing, mimicking the results of grazing by large herbivores. In sunny positions, bare ground will warm up rapidly, and may be as much as 10°C higher than the surrounding vegetation. It supports a rich and characteristic insect fauna (Key, 2000) and is used by insects for basking, egg laying and by solitary bees and wasps for burrowing. Predatory beetles, ants, flying insects and some spiders scavenge, hunt or ambush their prey on bare ground, whilst snakes bask on it in early morning sunshine. Log piles and brash will provide similar opportunities.

Tall herbs should be mown every 4 years with a side-mounted flail, on a rotational basis, to create a mosaic of tall grasses and herbs of four different ages in the ride network, preferably in equal amounts, but certainly sufficient to maintain viable populations of insects. Some insects, such as wood white butterflies cannot tolerate this level of disturbance, but this would only be an issue in specialised circumstances. The woodland edge or scrub zone should be cut or coppiced on a rotation of 8–20 years to create a mosaic of structural diversity and different aged shrubs. If shrubs have been planted fairly close together, they should be cut more frequently. Woodland edges which have regenerated naturally may have a low density of trees and shrubs and require less frequent cutting.

The basic three-zone system can be improved by incorporating a scalloped woodland edge – particularly along south facing edges. Scallops should be up to 20 m long and 20–50 m deep, to provide bays that offer more shelter from the wind (Warren and Fuller 1993). Scalloping replaces straight woodland edges with more natural, diffuse ones. It increases the total amount of woodland edge and diversify wildlife habitats. Some scalloped areas may be coppiced, with others maintained as tall herbs or grassland. Gently curving rides also provide an alternative to long straight rides.

Although a three-zone ride network requires continuous management, it provides increased habitat diversity and attracts a rich variety of woodland flora and fauna. Therefore, where woodland is created primarily for biodiversity conservation, it should be seriously considered. Indeed, rides in any new woodland would be best designed like this, if funds and space allow.

How to establish the vegetation of rides and glades

The planting design for ground vegetation in rides is relatively straightforward compared with high forest and the woodland edge. All plant species can be introduced in a single seed mix, uniformly across the ride area.

There are five options for introducing grassland plants to agricultural land, some of which will require sward killing and cultivation in preparation:

- sowing a sward (basic mix of grasses, or a species-rich seed mix)
- spreading green hay
- oversowing and slot seeding
- planting container grown plants or plugs
- natural regeneration.

Due to the relatively small areas likely to be involved in a woodland creation scheme, each may be applicable in certain circumstances. Table 4.15 presents the main advantages and disadvantages of each method for such areas, and gives examples of where each might be employed.

Can areas be left to regenerate a sward naturally?

If semi-natural grassland, high in biodiversity occurs nearby and if soil nutrient levels are relatively low, then natural colonisation of the site is possible, given a sympathetic management regime. Such an approach might also be considered, even in the absence of adjacent areas of semi-natural grassland, provided soil fertility is low. In such cases, a diverse flora should colonise open areas within 10 years or so; the time taken for the planted trees to close canopy. An appropriate 'natural' grass seed mix could be sown to exclude unwanted weeds (Section 4.3.2), allowing other species to colonise. Such land may also be considered for conservation grassland as well as woodland.

In an otherwise arable landscape with no semi-natural grassland nearby, natural swards will be composed of plant species typically found in NVC grassland communities of lower botanical nature conservation value, such as rank grassland (MG1a,b), improved permanent grassland (MG6) and reseeded grassland (MG7). They may also take on the character of an open vegetation community, characteristic of field margins and fence lines. Such grassland is likely to contain a poor diversity of flora and insects, and will take a very long time to attain any significant biodiversity value. In these circumstances, consider sowing a native grass and wild flower mix.

Table 4.15 Sward establishment options for woodland open spaces, and larger grassland areas

Options	Advantages	Considerations	Suitable sites
Sowing a 'natural' grass seed mix	■ Mix of grasses can establish sward on more fertile site, followed by species-rich hay spreading or oversowing after 3 years or so ■ Control over species planted, though not over establishment ■ More cost effective for relatively small areas of woodland open space ■ Simple mix increases the chances of success ■ Seed mixes can be related to local conditions and known vegetation types (NVC)	■ Seed mix should be determined for each site, considering: objectives, management, and site characteristics ■ Provenance can be difficult to ascertain ■ Risk to genetic structure in the wider landscape if non-local seed sown adjacent to existing unmanaged natural grassland ■ Any natural colonisation of herbs from adjacent species-rich habitat slow in comparison to sowing ■ High soil fertility and/or pernicious weed problems may require repeated cultivation and spraying for 12 months or so prior to sowing	■ Land with a P Index 0–1 ideal; 2 is marginal ■ Sites which match a local seed source ■ Suitable for woodland rides where relatively small areas are sown
Sowing species-rich grassland mixes	■ More rapid establishment of a diverse sward ■ Early introduction of wild flowers to enhance value for insects and other wildlife ■ Control over species planted, though not over establishment ■ Seed mixes can be related to local conditions and known vegetation types (NVC) ■ More cost effective for relatively small areas of woodland open space	■ Mix should be formulated for each site, or an appropriate wild-harvested seed mixture used ■ Site must not be dominated by coarse grasses or pernicious weeds – if stress tolerant species are likely to be present, may need two stage process ■ If stress-tolerant species do not survive, may require repeat sowing or hay spreading after 3 years or so ■ Provenance can be difficult to ascertain ■ Risk to genetic structure in the wider landscape if non-local seed sown adjacent to existing unmanaged natural grassland ■ Some ground preparation required to open-up sward ■ May be expensive ■ Hay may need to be removed on sites with a high P-index	■ Long term pasture with higher N and low P (note these may also be considered for grassland restoration) ■ Land with a P Index 0–1 ideal; 2 is marginal ■ Particularly suitable for woodland rides where special mix is required ■ Oversowing can be done in zones along rides in existing swards
Species-rich green hay spreading	■ Richer sward likely ■ Fresh seed – high viability ■ Lower cost than seed ■ Local provenance may be easier to source ■ Local species mix	■ Sourcing hay may be difficult ■ Hay must be very fresh ■ Species introduced determined by diversity and abundance of source flora ■ No guarantee of which species will be viable in the mix ■ Site must not be dominated by coarse grasses or pernicious weeds ■ Most suitable for existing sward with little weed burden ■ Ground preparation required, and grazing or light rolling after strewing	■ Land with a P Index <2 ■ Donor site must match the restoration site closely ■ Sites previously sown with a species-poor mix, and harvested annually ■ Particularly suitable for woodland rides where small areas can be prepared
Potted seedlings or plugs	■ Plant in bare ground or sward ■ Self seed ■ Introduce targeted species to an existing botanically interesting sward e.g. butterfly foodplant or insect nectar plant ■ Introduce species difficult to propagate through seed	■ Expensive – mortality can be high ■ Requires careful planting and aftercare until established ■ Plants can be swamped by existing vegetation ■ Unsuitable for highly fertile sites ■ Provenance can be difficult to ascertain ■ Unsuitable for archaeological sites	■ Small areas ■ Long term pasture with high N and low P (note these may be considered for grassland restoration) ■ Grassland with P Index 0–2 ■ Suitable for woodland rides where a small number of target species are required ■ Planting can be done in zones along rides or in specific areas
Natural regeneration	■ Seed/hay not required ■ Species-rich swards may develop in the longer term, particularly on sites adjacent to existing unmanaged natural grassland ■ Colonisation can be accelerated through livestock movement if unmanaged natural grassland close by ■ Local provenance assured ■ Low cost option	■ Lack of seed bank in most sites ■ Requirement for low P levels eliminates a lot of agricultural land ■ Requires nearby unmanaged natural grassland ■ May take a decade or more to establish ■ Perennial weeds in existing seed bank or invading can cause problems	■ Smaller sites in close proximity to unimproved natural grasslands or reseeded areas ■ Long term pasture with higher N and low P (note these may be considered for grassland restoration) ■ Low risk from perennial weeds ■ Rapid response is not required ■ Seed bank already contains some target species ■ Evidence of colonisation by desirable species in set aside ■ Cost is an important issue ■ Archaeological interest

4.5   How to plant and manage new woodland

Tree planting methods have been described in detail elsewhere, and many techniques are standard practice (e.g. Williamson, 1992; Agate, 2000 and 2002). In this section, methods are highlighted which are particularly suitable for woodland creation for wildlife in South East England, with the reasons for their choice explained.

4.5.1 How to prepare the site

The form and extent of site preparation depends upon the nature of the planting site in terms of soil structure and type, topography, drainage, previous land use and current vegetation cover. This information should have been gathered at the site assessment stage (Section 4.1.2).

What are the key factors to consider when planning site preparation ?

1. **Soil texture** is a measure of soil particle sizes. Light soils contain a high proportion of sand (large particles); they drain easily and have a low water-holding capacity. Loams contain a mix of clay (very small particles), sand and silt (medium sized particles). They are easy to cultivate and provide an ideal medium for plant growth. Heavy soils have a high clay content which is often associated with poor drainage; susceptibility to waterlogging in winter and drying and cracking in summer. Even if suitable tree species for the site have been chosen, planting can still be difficult on heavy soils. If the site is large enough, such soils can be improved by deep cultivation. Otherwise, notch or pit planting techniques should be used (Section 4.5.2).

2. **Soil structure** – use of heavy machinery may cause compaction to depths greater than normally cultivated. Repeated ploughing to the same depth may create a thin zone of compacted soil at the base of the cultivated layer – known as a plough pan. If nothing is done about this, water will not penetrate the soil and it becomes waterlogged in winter and hard and dry in summer. Consequently, trees suffer from poor aeration and drainage, and roots fail to penetrate into the soil, causing poor growth and instability. Soils can be loosened, and plough pans broken up by ripping or subsoiling prior to planting.

3. **Ground vegetation** – herbicide or mulch treatments should be applied to reduce competition between the planted trees and grasses or herbs (Section 4.5.4). An area of 1 m² around individual trees, or a 1 m strip if the trees are planted in rows, is recommended. Vegetation between rows will be less competitive; it may be mown, or allowed to grow rank to encourage wildlife onto the site (which may include unwanted voles), although ultimately it will be shaded out by the closing tree canopy.

    The sward at the site of Victory Wood for example, is dominated by black-grass, soft-brome and Italian rye-grass (Section 4.3.2). Such sites require clearance of the vegetation in the ride areas prior to sowing with the selected grassland mix.

4. **Sowing ground vegetation prior to planting** – an alternative approach for arable, set-aside or transport corridors is to sow a grass sward over the whole site – rather than just over areas designated as rides or glades. This might be more appropriate where appearance is important, such as roadsides, where an even grass sward is more desirable than a weed community dominated by plants such as thistles, ragworts and bristly oxtongue. However, grasses are likely to be more competitive than ruderals, and hence the growth of trees may be reduced if grasses are not controlled around tree bases.

4.5.2 How to plant trees and shrubs

What type of stock should be planted?

Planting stock should be chosen to achieve high survival rates, good establishment, rapid growth to canopy closure (which will shade out arable weeds) and affordability. Trees are available in various forms: bare-root (i.e. with no soil attached to the roots at purchase); cell-grown (similar sizes to bare-root, grown in cells of 150 – 500 ml); container-grown; and root-balled (peripheral roots cut in the field, but inner roots bound in soil). For woodland creation for wildlife, small young trees achieve good establishment and growth. Larger trees are sometimes planted for their 'instant visual impact', but they are more susceptible to damage during lifting, transportation and planting, and they establish more slowly following planting.

Therefore, select bare-rooted trees or cell-grown ones, 30–100 cm tall and 1–3 years old. For woodlands planted for wildlife, bare-rooted transplants (1 + 1: grown from seed, transplanted after one year, lifted one year later) are a good choice, based on price and good establishment. Transplanting on the nursery encourages a healthy, fibrous root system, which aids establishment: consequently transplants (1 + 1), or undercuts (1 u 1: not moved but roots trimmed *in situ* after one year) are likely to establish better than seedlings (1 + 0 or 2 + 0), which have not been lifted prior to dispatch.

Trees grown in cells, such as rootrainers, have the advantage that roots – which have been trained downwards – are protected by the ball of compost surrounding them. This means that there is a wider opportunity for planting, because these trees can be planted whist still in active growth in late summer/autumn. In contrast, bare-rooted trees must be planted in the dormant season (late November to early March). Cell-grown trees are likely to establish better because of the protection afforded to the roots during transportation and planting, but they are more expensive. This is why most woodland planting is carried out with bare-rooted stock. However, some evergreen species such as yew, box and holly are usually supplied container-grown.

TOP **Bags of bare-root trees awaiting planting.**

BOTTOM **Heeled in trees at a planting site.**

Clive Steward

How should plants be handled?

Handle all plants carefully, and protect their roots from drying at all times. Bare-root trees, in particular, need careful packaging and transport to the planting site. They should be transported in plastic sacks, which are white on the outside to reflect heat and black inside to reduce frost damage. Handle the sacks with care, and, if necessary, store them in a cool, dark building. Roots will dry out very rapidly once the sacks are opened, so plant the trees as quickly as possible. Bare-root trees may be 'heeled in' once on site to minimise exposure of their root systems to drying.

Planting techniques

Once planting commences and trees are being handled, their roots must be kept as moist as possible, by being covered at all times. Any damage to delicate fine roots results in poor establishment and reduces chances of survival. Notch planting is the easiest and quickest way to plant bare-rooted and cell-grown trees up to 100 cm tall. Push a spade into the ground and rock it backwards and forwards to create a 'notch'. Then ease the transplant into the hole from the side to avoid damaging, or bending the roots upwards. Close the notch by treading carefully around the stem. Make 'T'-shaped notches for plants with larger roots systems. Notch planting can also be used to plant trees directly into a sward. A particularly resilient sward may require the removal of a turf prior to making the notch: this can be discarded or replaced around the base of the tree, inverted to a depth of about 30 cm.

Where larger trees are used, pit planting may be required: a pit is dug large enough to accommodate the root spread and deep enough so that the root collar is just at soil level. The advantage of this method is that it breaks up the soil, which aids root penetration. When digging pits on clay or compacted soils, break up the pit sides to aid root penetration. Planting trees in pits is much more time consuming and therefore more expensive than notch planting. Consequently it is not usually used for young transplants (e.g. 1 + 1), which survive well if notches are prepared correctly.

On larger, flat sites, machine-planting may also be an option. Planting machines create a furrow into which the trees are planted. The furrow is then closed behind. This method is much faster than manual planting and survival rates can be better as tree roots spend less time in contact with the air. However, difficulties can be encountered on clay soils where the sides of the furrow may be 'smeared', thus restricting root penetration and not allowing the furrow to be closed correctly. This latter scenario can also create ideal vole runs.

Notch planting at Victory Wood, Kent.

4.5.3 How to protect trees and shrubs

The main causes of damage and loss, which trees can be protected from, are wild animals, domestic stock, people and wind. The type of protection required depends on the anticipated problems and the scale of the planting. Most sites require some protective measures so these must be considered when planning and budgeting. The following discussion highlights some of the main problems that occur in woodlands planted for wildlife, and some of the more commonly used approaches to protect against them.

Potential problem species will have been identified in the survey of fauna (Section 4.1.4). It should therefore be possible to predict potential threats to young trees from the animal species recorded. Culprits might include field voles, deer, rabbits and hares.

Voles are ubiquitous, and cause damage on most sites by attacking the basal 20 cm of planted trees. They prefer taller ground vegetation, such as that found in the inter-rows of woodland created for wildlife and along ride edges. If the areas around the trees are kept free of weeds by herbicides, voles are less likely to attack the trees. However, mulch encourages animals to approach the base of the trees. In this case, tree shelters or guards are essential. Birds of prey hunt voles, so they should be encouraged into planted sites by providing artificial perches. At Victory Wood for example, sparrowhawk, peregrine, hobby, kestrel, marsh harrier and barn owl have all been observed hunting. They will take some voles, in addition to adding to the conservation value of the new woodland.

Rabbits and brown hares can also cause damage to the bark of young trees up to 75 cm above ground level. Rabbits in particular can occur in high numbers on some sites. The best option is to erect rabbit fencing, but tree shelters and guards can provide some protection, and may be more economical on small sites. Hares are unlikely to be a serious problem in woodland planted for wildlife, because their population densities are very low. The brown hare is a red-data species in Kent, so the presence of hares in young woodland should be viewed as a positive contribution to wildlife conservation.

Deer are the most serious threat to new woodland, browsing new shoots up to 2 m above ground. In Kent, two or three species of deer are present. Roe deer are widespread, though more common towards the High Weald, whilst fallow deer favour old parkland. It is also possible that sika deer are present. Although roe and fallow deer have gradually been moving eastwards across north Kent, they have yet to reach the Blean. In other parts of the region, such as the High Weald, some form of protection may be required. The minimum fence height for roe deer is 1.2 m for areas < 2 ha, and 1.5 m for areas > 2 ha. For muntjac and fallow deer, 1.5 m is recommended. For more details on fence construction, consult the Forestry Commission's Practice Note on deer fencing (Pepper, 1999). Deer find certain species such as ash and willows more palatable, and hence taller tree guards may be required for these species; 1.2 m guards should be sufficient for roe deer and muntjac, but 1.8 m would be required for red deer, sika and fallow deer.

Squirrels rarely attack young trees, but can do serious damage by stripping bark as the trees begin to close canopy. They favour smooth-barked species such as beech, but will attack other species as well. If beech is a significant component of new woodland, and there is a healthy population of squirrels in the area, this creates an obvious dilemma for the woodland designer. Such a problem arises at Victory Wood (Section 4.2.2) where beech is a major component of the local ancient oakwoods. In this case, the landowner must decide whether the woodland design should be modified in anticipation of future squirrel problems, e.g. by reducing the beech component. This particular decision is further complicated by concerns over climate change and the long-term future for beech in the South East. In this instance, the landowner decided to significantly reduce the numbers of beech planted.

What are the options for tree protection?

There are two main forms of tree protection: individual protection (spiral guards, tubes etc.) and fencing off groups or areas of trees. The method chosen will depend upon the following factors:

- **The scale, density and shape of the planting area**: for larger, more regularly shaped blocks – areas > 1 ha – fencing will be a cheaper option than individual protection, but will not be effective against voles.

- **Location within the wider landscape**: some individual tree protection can be visually intrusive.

- **Need for access**: individual tree protection allows greater freedom of movement into new woodland, but access provision, especially for future management, must be allowed for when fencing.

- **Level of risk**: if protection around an individual tree is damaged, only that tree is at risk; if a fence is damaged, the whole area is at risk.

- **Maintenance**: regular maintenance, especially of fencing, is vital.

- **Effect on wildlife**: the effect of fencing on blocking movement of other wildlife such as badgers must be addressed, e.g. through the use of badger gates.

Individual tree protection comes in a wide range of shapes and sizes, but two main types are usually used for woodland planted for wildlife: spiral guards and plastic tree shelters.

Spiral guards are wrapped around trees to reduce bark stripping by rabbits, hares and voles. They are only really suitable for sturdy trees, whose height is greater than the standard 45–60 cm guards. The disadvantage of these is that they cannot be used on trees which are shorter than 75 cm without inhibiting growth. Ideally, they should be used with a cane to keep trees upright. Vole guards however are normally just 20 cm tall, so they do not affect tree growth.

Plastic tree shelters come in a range of brands and heights, depending upon the nature of protection required. Tree shelters supported by stakes are effective against all wild animals; although they must be buried at least 1–2.5 cm into the ground to ensure protection against voles. They improve tree survival and enhance growth by providing a sheltered, humid micro-environment. They also protect trees from foliar acting herbicides making weed control easier and less expensive. However, they do have some disadvantages. For example, in areas of high public access, they can attract unwanted attention. After accelerated early growth, trees may not be able to support themselves when tubes are removed and they may require staking. Some species, particularly beech, do not respond well to tree shelters.

1.2 m stock-proof deer fence at Victory Wood.

4.5.4 How to take care of trees and shrubs after planting

Aftercare of newly planted woodland is vital if the objectives behind its creation are to be achieved. All the care and attention invested to plant the trees may amount to nothing if sites are not subsequently managed properly. Until the root systems of young trees become well-established, they obtain moisture and nutrients from the surface soil layer, in direct competition with weeds. Weed control is therefore an essential element of aftercare. It may be needed for 3–5 years, depending on the site, the tree species mix, the vegetation into which trees were planted and whether mulches were used. Grass swards require weeding for longer than arable weed communities, because grasses are more competitive.

This site was sown with a commercial fescue mix prior to planting sessile oaks; no weed control was undertaken; it is dominated by fescues and soft-brome, with few broadleaves; and has little value for wildlife. In the third season after planting, the majority of trees were still alive (90%), but hidden from view: tree growth is being severely retarded by the competition.

Weed control

Currently, the most popular weed control method is herbicide application, for which timing is critical. Areas around tree bases should be clear of weeds and grass all year, but especially in the spring, when weeds and grasses are at their most competitive. In practice, foliar acting herbicides may offer sufficient control, without recourse to residual herbicides. Some local authorities do not allow the use of residual herbicides because their persistence in the soil may affect subsequent attempts to establish ground flora. Residual herbicides were used more in the past, because they tend to be simpler and cheaper to apply. However, many of them only control weeds pre-emergence and must be applied to bare earth. Consequently, they have been used in the pre-planting phase, with foliar acting herbicides being used subsequently.

Alternatives to herbicides, such as mulches are being developed. Mulches suppress weed growth around planted trees, increase soil water retention and in some cases increase soil temperature. Ideally, mulches should last at least three growing seasons, and make repeat applications of herbicide unnecessary. To achieve this with sheet mulches, good quality proprietary brands are essential and to be effective, they must be 1 m wide. Some plastic mulches are thin and can rip easily, which can make planting more difficult and greatly restrict inter-row access if mowing is required. Ripping can be caused naturally by animals (including voles) and wind, but also deliberately by people in areas with good public access.

Areas not protected by mulch will be rapidly infested with weeds on an ex-arable site. If weed control is not carried out, weeds will grow densely, but they will not affect tree growth unless they collapse across the planted trees in late summer. Inter-rows could be mown, but in the examples illustrated (page 103), this was not undertaken as a mower could not get between the sheets of mulch without damaging the edges. The weed community which develops can be beneficial for wildlife (Section 4.3), particularly invertebrates, ground nesting birds and winter seed-eating birds. An alternative strategy on arable land is to sow a grass mix to exclude pernicious weeds such as ragworts and thistles. A simple mix based on that devised for ride areas can be sown, and mown regularly. This benefits grassland biodiversity and the appearance of the site, provided that the area around the trees is kept weed free.

Mulching materials can also include cardboard, straw, and loose materials such as composted bark and wood chips. Cardboard has not been widely used. Although cheap, it must be replaced annually to be effective. Loose materials such as composted bark are widely used in urban landscaping, and if sufficient depth is applied (approximately 10 cm) they should be effective against weed growth for one year, before a repeat application is necessary. Composted wood chips or other chipped tree waste may have the added advantage of introducing a substrate for fungi and habitat for some invertebrates.

Mulch mats come in varying sizes.

One other current development of interest is soil inversion, which is achieved with a deep plough which inverts up to 1 m of soil. In theory, this buries the weed seed bank in the upper layers and permits trees to be planted in a weed free, but initially less fertile substrate. However, if the soil inversion is not deep enough, this can lead to vigorous ruderal communities which may be difficult to control. The reduced competition should allow the tree to get away more quickly and with less need for herbicide application. Another possibility for weed control, practiced locally by East Sussex County Council, is topsoil stripping. The advantage of this method is that it reduces fertility, and creates revenue which can be used to offset planting costs through the sale of the topsoil.

Vigorous weed growth in a plot where soil inversion was not deep enough.

LEFT **Mulch of woven permeable fabric in its third season: note vigorous weed growth in the inter-rows, which were too narrow to be mown.**

RIGHT **Despite vigorous weed growth, and some invasion of the mulched area, the planted oak is benefiting from the weed-free zone maintained around it by the woven fabric.**

LEFT **Although largely clear of weeds, grasses have emerged through the planting hole in this black plastic sheet mulch.**

RIGHT **Straw mulch can still inhibit weed growth in the third growing season.**

Beating up

This is the process of replacing trees in plantations that die soon after planting or during establishment. In woodland created for wildlife, some losses are inevitable, and the response to these will be dependent on the numbers of trees involved, and the pattern of the losses. If fewer than 10% of trees are lost, and these are scattered throughout the new wood, there may be little cause for concern. Larger-scale losses inevitably affect the structure of the high forest areas, and may delay canopy closure. This could be due to low quality planting stock or poor planting technique.

Losses may also be incurred if there is a poor match between the species planted and the site conditions; for example wild cherry and sweet chestnut planted on wet sites (see case studies in Sections 5.1 and 5.3). Under such circumstances, both the choice of trees and the soil environment should be considered before replacement planting is undertaken.

Contractors and procurement

Planting and managing new woodlands may be carried out by contractors, a landowner's own workforce, or volunteers. There are advantages and disadvantages to each approach relating to the costs and the quality of the work undertaken.

Contract labour is common for tree planting, especially on larger scale plantings. If a contractor is used, it is important to select one with the experience, skills and organisation to carry out the work efficiently and correctly. Selection of contractors may be guided by membership of a relevant industry body e.g. the British Association of Landscape Industries (BALI), but of more importance perhaps is seeing examples of the contractor's work. Local authorities and organisations who plant regularly usually maintain approved lists. Contracts should state that the contractor is responsible for buying the stock, planting and maintenance, normally over 3–5 years. The contract should specify where responsibility lies for replacement of dead trees and the required condition of the site at the end of the contract period e.g. 95% stocked, trees establishing well. This places the onus on the contractor to use good stock and carry out the planting and maintenance correctly. The required maintenance works should be identified at the outset and should include weeding (including noxious weeds), tube/guard/fence maintenance, replacement of dead trees, straightening of leaning trees and replacement of mulches if required.

Competitive quotations should be sought on the basis of detailed plans and drawings, a detailed specification and instructions for how the work should be carried out. The most cost effective quote should be accepted, not necessarily the lowest price. A formal contract should be entered into, possibly based upon the Joint Council for Landscape Industries (JCLI) form of contract. In such documentation, it is agreed how and when work will be carried out, when it will be completed, how much it will cost, and the duties and liabilities of both parties to the contract. Importantly, the contractor should be made liable for defective work and provision made for retaining part of the contract sum by the employer to ensure that the contractor honours his guarantee for the work. Damages for non or late completion of the contract can be included.

An 'in house' workforce enables more direct control, but a specification, plans and drawings will still be required.

Volunteer labour

The use of volunteers to carry out planting can work very well as long as the planting is relatively small scale. It is important not to overwhelm a small group of volunteers with a large planting project, because the work may not be completed within the planting season. Productivity tends to be lower with volunteers than with contractors or a specialist labour force, but obviously labour costs are lower. Materials must still be purchased, stored and transported to the site, and normally all organisation must be carried out by the body commissioning the planting. One big advantage of using local people or organisations such as schools or colleges is that of 'local ownership' of a project. It also encourages the view that the new wood contributes in some way to the local community and should be valued and cared for accordingly.

Fire

The risk of fire is high in recently planted woods because there will be a period when dense ground vegetation has not been shaded out. The risk will be particularly high after prolonged dry periods in early spring or late summer. Mowing of the inter-row vegetation and rides may help, particularly in vulnerable areas e.g. near housing. Risks should be identified at the design stage and the most vulnerable areas left open to be regularly mown. A fire plan should be drawn up, to include contacting the local fire brigade and providing them with a plan of the site and access keys.

Fence/guard/tube removal

Individual tree protection will have served its purpose within 5–7 years. If tubes or spirals are left on after this they can restrict tree growth and should therefore be removed. Spiral guards are easier to remove than tubes. Removing tubes may also result in an initial 'flopping' of trees which had previously been supported by the tube and whose height growth against diameter growth had been exaggerated due to the presence of the tube. To ease this problem and encourage a more robust stem, tubes can be slit halfway down to allow some movement; this will encourage stem thickening prior to complete removal the following year. Where possible, redundant tubes should be collected for recycling. Deer fencing will be required for 10–15 years as trees will be vulnerable to fraying and bark stripping during this time. Stock fencing may be permanently required.

Pruning

Pruning is described in detail in many other publications; only the essential details are presented here as they relate to wildlife. If wildlife is the sole objective, the woodland may be allowed to develop naturally, with minimal interference to the structure of the trees. If the objectives are broader than just wildlife, and include timber production, pruning will be necessary during the establishment phase to assist the development of the trees, but this can still benefit wildlife.

Foresters prune to improve the form of a tree and produce a straight stem with knot free wood and a higher timber quality; a strong central leader is encouraged with minimal side branching, which aids establishment and accelerates canopy closure. Lateral branches are cut back close to the stem every two years or so until the tree is about 10 years old; multiple leaders are cut back to a single leader. If a wood has been designed both for timber and wildlife, with appropriate areas of understorey trees and edge planting, then the wood as a whole is likely to benefit from some pruning in the early years; the accelerated height growth of the pruned trees themselves provides greater structural diversity, whilst the lower level foliage is retained along the woodland edge, together with those trees which are not pruned.

Timing can be important, depending on the species. Most pruning should be carried out between late June and December, avoiding the period of early spring growth. Oaks, ash and wild cherry should be pruned in July or early August, to minimise the risks of infection through cut surfaces. Pruning should not be carried out on all trees, just the selected 'final' crop trees which may be 10–15% of the initial number planted.

LEFT **Regular pruning of every tree has created a very open understorey in this new wood, with little structural diversity – photographed in May.**

RIGHT **Woodland on the same site, which has never been pruned – photographed in May.**

Thinning

Thinning for forestry purposes has been well documented, but for woods planted primarily for wildlife, guidance is more subjective, and a visual assessment of a new wood is critical. Where trees have been planted 2 m apart, consider thinning the woodland after 10–15 years – when the trees are taller than 6 m – if it is likely to increase structural diversity.

Heavy thinning is usually beneficial to wildlife, allowing good light penetration through the canopy, encouraging the development of both ground vegetation and the shrub layer, as well facilitating natural regeneration of trees. A close visual inspection should be carried out to identify those trees whose removal would be beneficial to the structural diversity of the woodland as a whole, and the development of the high forest area in particular. These might include individuals whose canopies are overlapping, where removal of one tree would benefit the development of the other, and the canopy in general. Small trees which are becoming suppressed by shading should be removed, provided the balance and variety of tree species are not seriously affected. In some cases it may be necessary to actually thin a good quality 'timber' tree, in order to reduce its domination and to allow others to come through. Whatever thinning is undertaken, leave the felled trees on site, since deadwood is a scarce and valuable habitat resource in new woodlands.

4.5.5 Direct seeding

Woodland can be created by sowing tree seeds directly into their final position on site, rather than by planting young trees raised in a nursery. It is an ancient practice, much less used nowadays than the conventional direct planting of trees. In this section, an overview of the methods, and their suitability for woodland creation for wildlife in South East England are considered (Table 4.16). More detailed accounts of the techniques have been presented by La Dell (1983) and most recently in a comprehensive Forestry Commission Practice Guide (Willoughby *et al.*, 2004) which updates all their previous guidance.

Direct seeding is a technique which is not yet fully developed; a lot is known about some species, but others need further research and development (Willoughby *et al.*, 2004). Success for any species or mix of species in terms of germination and establishment is not guaranteed, and the outcome can be unpredictable. It may differ considerably from the woodland community, which the practitioner had in mind. Consequently, it cannot be recommended as a method of creating new woodland for wildlife at this time. However, there are good opportunities to carry out direct seeding trials and contribute to the development of the knowledge base. Where woodland is being created for wildlife, experimental plantings could combine a mixed approach of conventional planting and direct seeding. Conventional planting could be employed to establish the framework of the wood; including the species characteristic of the woodland type chosen for the site, planted in the appropriate proportions. Direct seeding could then be employed to introduce some of the understorey trees and woodland edge species.

How to prepare the site

As with sowing any grass or arable crop, preparation of a good seed bed is essential. Subsoiling and ploughing break up any plough pan or compaction and rotavating and harrowing provide the required tilth. Willoughby *et al.* (2004) recommend that existing vegetation is completely killed in the summer before sowing by using a broad spectrum contact herbicide. If a grassland community is present, suitable for sward enhancement to create

Table 4.16 The advantages and disadvantages of using direct seeding to create woodland for wildlife

Issues	Woodland creation for wildlife by direct seeding	
	Advantages	**Disadvantages**
Selection of site	Appropriate for good quality agricultural soils	Not suitable for heavy clay soils which are wet during the winter months
Applicability to a wide range of trees and shrubs	Some success with a small range of trees and shrubs	Limited to a few species: oak, sycamore and ash extensively tested by the Forestry Commission; far less is known about other trees and shrubs, but there has been some success with wild cherry, hawthorn, field maple, dogwood and birch. The Forestry Commission currently recommends that ash, oak and/or sycamore form a minimum of 75% of design
Cost	May be a slightly cheaper option if initial seeding is successful, depending on the mix; conventional agricultural machinery could be used for preparation and sowing; weed control required for fewer years than conventional planting; no need for guards	Failure to germinate or establish would require repeat seeding, which would prove expensive; oak seed, which is a major component of many woodlands is very expensive, and is likely to restrict the woodland design
Seed predation and germination	Predation may be a minor issue on agricultural land distant from established woodland	Woodland for wildlife is often established close to existing woodland, which may increase predation by small mammals; germination rates can be highly variable and unpredictable
Time to canopy closure	Likely to close canopy much quicker than conventional planting, and hence shade out arable weeds and create a suitable environment for woodland plants	Assuming germination is successful, stem density is unpredictable: dense stands may actually be poorer for wildlife without thinning, which adds further expense, and in some circumstances, such as tightly budgeted roadside plantings, may not be feasible
Appearance during the establishment phase	Unkempt appearance may benefit some wildlife after the first year when weeds controlled; could reduce vandalism on certain sites	Unkempt appearance may not meet requirements for sites such as roadsides, where 'neatness' is important; high small mammal populations in such sites might attract predators such as barn owls, with the risk of road casualties
Species present, and appearance of the closed canopy woodland	The structure of the wood may have a much more 'natural' appearance, in terms of the variety of tree heights, density and open spaces, especially if thinning has taken place	Although 'naturalistic', the tree community may differ from that envisaged by the designer in species diversity and frequency; consequently it may not closely resemble the woodland community upon which the design was based – even with thinning – and not fit the local landscape character
Applicability to the woodland designs for Victory Wood (Section 4.1.6)	Could be trialled in small compartments	Planting schemes for Victory Wood do not fit the Forestry Commission's current recommendation for a minimum of 75% ash, oak and/or sycamore; soils may be too heavy

rides and open spaces, it should be protected. Otherwise the site will require sowing with a grass mix, or species-rich grassland mix.

How to sow seeds of trees and shrubs

The two main methods of sowing tree seeds are broadcast sowing, where seeds are distributed randomly, and drilling where seeds are sown in lines. Larger-sized seeds such as oak tend to be drilled as they need to go in deeper, to about 10 cm depth. They are then covered by rolling, or if other species are to be sown after, by harrowing. Smaller seeds are broadcast-sown after any larger seeds, normally to a depth of around 2 cm and then lightly rolled. On lighter soils, seed should be sown deeper than on heavier soils, because moisture retention in the former will be much less.

Tree seeding can take place either in the autumn, using untreated seed, or in the spring, using treated seed. Untreated autumn-sown seed will receive a natural pre-treatment from winter weather. Spring-sown seed will not have that natural treatment and dormancy will need to be broken artificially. Willoughby *et al.* (2004) report that autumn sowings are likely to be more successful as the seed germinates earlier and is less likely to suffer from heat damage and spring drought, although they may suffer more from predation. If wet sites are to be sown, autumn sowing should be avoided as the seed may rot over winter.

Using nurse crops

Watson (1996) describes a method known as "Temperate Taungya" where tree seeds are sown within an arable crop. The theory is that the arable crop greatly reduces seed predation by birds, provides protection to the emerging tree seedlings, and can be harvested with minimal damage to the tree seedlings. Annual weeds on ex-arable sites tend to be light-demanding at the seedling stage. Nurse crops such as short-growing wheat or barley shade out weeds early in the year and will be dying, with reduced water uptake, by June, when tree and shrub seedlings are germinating and growing. La Dell (1983) supports this view but Willoughby *et al.* (2004) conclude that nurse crops are detrimental to woodland establishment and do not recommend them. In biodiversity terms, nurse crops should certainly not be dismissed as they can reduce the need for herbicide applications during the establishment phase.

Sowing rates

The proportion of viable tree seed that will become established varies greatly. Willoughby *et al.* (2004) report that even under favourable conditions, the percentage of seed surviving to form seedlings at the end of the first year can range from 0% to 50%. They recommend that 200,000 viable seeds per hectare (of all species combined) should be sown with the intention of establishing 10,000 per hectare of reasonably evenly spaced and vigorous trees by year 10. Watson (2002) supports this target, but where biodiversity objectives may be of more importance, lower stocking levels may offer more diversity within the newly stocked area.

Woodland Trust

Four year old woodland created by direct seeding in Hampshire: oak, ash, hazel, dogwood, hawthorn, blackthorn, sweet chestnut and wild cherry have all successfully established.

What species are suitable for sowing?

A major limitation of direct seeding is that our knowledge is restricted to a fairly narrow range of species. Most is known about oak, sycamore and ash – which have been extensively tested by the Forestry Commission. Far less is known about other trees and shrubs, but there has been some success with wild cherry, hawthorn, field maple, dogwood and birch. The Forestry Commission currently recommend that ash, oak and/or sycamore form a minimum of 75% of the sown propagules, which would not be appropriate for any NVC woodland types. It is also important to note that seed cost varies tremendously with species, and with such high density sowing rates required, the tendency in some planting has been to use cheap, readily available seed such as sycamore and ash.

How can the site be protected and maintained?

Some exponents of direct seeding argue that the higher number of seedlings present make protection against deer and rabbits unnecessary as they are able to absorb damage because of the higher numbers present. However, this has not been proven and in most situations some form of protection, most commonly fencing, will be required (see Section 4.5.3). It has been argued by some that initial maintenance is also unnecessary, particularly where the tree seed is sown with a nurse crop. There is no real evidence to support this and it is recommended that suitable weed control operations are carried out, although it is much more complicated under this system due to sometimes dense, and irregularly spaced trees. Willoughby *et al.* (2004) give detailed prescriptions for use of overall sprays, whereas La Dell (1983) highlights the use of mulches, including straw, which may offer a more wildlife friendly option. Pruning and thinning requirements are similar to those described in Section 4.5.3.

4.5.6 Where can plants be obtained?

Trees and shrubs

Even amongst professionals, the definition of provenance and origin can vary: here, provenance is defined as the location from which plant material was collected, i.e. where the parent plants were growing; origin refers to the location from which the parental material originated. In some cases, the provenance and origin will be identical, but in others, the plants may have originated far away, and hence the origin – if known – may be quite different to the provenance.

Large numbers of trees and shrubs being planted in Britain still originate from seed collected in central and eastern Europe, as imported seed is cheaper than UK sources. The problem with this material is the potential for eroding the genetic diversity of our native plants through hybridisation. Imported plants will have evolved under different environmental and climatic conditions, so their response to UK conditions is unpredictable. For example, frost tolerance and flowering and fruiting phenologies may be quite different. If plants of European origin flower and fruit at slightly different times, this could have profound implications for invertebrates, whose lifecycle may not be in synchrony with these 'exotic' trees and shrubs.

Our knowledge of the adaptive genetic diversity of most of our native trees and shrubs, and the implications of planting imported stock is still very limited. It seems sensible to adopt the precautionary principle supported by organisations such as the Forestry Commission and Flora Locale, which urges practitioners to use local origin or local provenance plant material where possible. The Flora Locale website (www.floralocale.org) publishes detailed information on sourcing native plants.

The UK Forestry Standard (Forestry Commission, 1998b) includes the following national aims which apply to the creation of native woodlands: to maintain and restore natural ecological diversity; and to maintain genetic integrity of populations of native species, so far as is practicable. Plants for the creation of native woodland for wildlife should be of local provenance, and preferably local origin, although this is not always possible. The Forestry Commission identifies four broad regions of provenance in the UK, which are further divided into seed zones; within each seed zone are two elevation zones, above and below 300 m. Kent and Sussex are located in zone 405, which covers the whole of South East England. As a minimum requirement, designers and contractors should try to ensure that new woodland designs specify plants of local provenance, whose seed is sourced from the appropriate seed zone. If this is impossible to obtain, it should be sourced from an adjacent seed zone.

It is better to collect seed locally – either from adjacent woodland, or woodland within the local designated character area, or alternatively the larger character area. In theory, this should be best adapted for the conditions of the prospective planting site. The best source of local origin material is ancient semi-natural woodland. In addition to the age of the woodland, extensive coppicing and a 'natural' appearance provides further evidence to support the possibility that the trees are really of local origin. Although many trees are outbreeding, it is still important to collect seed from a large number of individuals to maximise the adaptive genetic diversity of the species. This is particularly important with the onset of climate change, and the unpredictable climate which the trees may have to endure as they mature. There is no hard and fast rule governing the number of parent trees, but between 25 and 50 individuals within the local population should be selected if possible. Each parent tree should be at least 50–100 m from the next. Approximately equal amounts of seed collected from each tree should be bulked before planting to ensure maximum genetic variability within the batch.

Ground flora

Issues relating to herbaceous plants and grasses are very similar to those relating to trees and shrubs. For example, according to Flora Locale, practically all grass seed used in the UK is imported: most originating in North America or Australia. Consequently the guidelines for sourcing trees and shrubs also apply to herbaceous plants, seed mixes and green hay used for sowing and planting in woodland. Sources of plants and seeds of native origin are available from the Flora Locale website. Companies offering herbaceous plants often have seed sourced from one or a few locations. The chances that seed of a particular species was collected anywhere near the prospective planting site is therefore small. Special seed collections can be commissioned, but these are likely to prove expensive.

A more attractive option may be to use meadow mixes harvested locally. The mixes offered by the High Weald Meadows Initiative (www.highweald.org) are a good example, although these are in high demand, and it may not be possible to obtain exactly what is required. This organisation offers a Weald Native Origin Wildflower and Grass species mix which is harvested mostly from local MG5a grassland, but it includes a few MG5b and MG5c sites. Their meadows contain all of the grasses, and many of the herbs identified in the selections for Victory Wood (Section 4.3.2), although there is no guarantee with any mix that all species present in the sward will be represented in the harvested seed. However, as with many commercial mixes, there are many more species included than those likely to be specified, if the methods described earlier (Section 4.3.1) are followed. This can be advantageous, but sometimes mixes contain less desirable species, such as agricultural varieties of grasses and clovers.

In the case of grasses, it may be too expensive to commission seed collections, certainly for large areas of rides and open spaces. It is important therefore to ensure that any mix purchased is made up of native species and varieties, **avoiding agriculturally improved varieties** which are often included in so called 'native' mixes.

In some cases, landowners may have access to a useful seed resource without realising it. The roadside along the Hastings Spine and Spur road (Section 5.5) is a good example of this: the estate includes areas of rank grassland classified as false oat-grass (MG1). Also within the roadside estate is a 1.3 ha meadow which contains 47 herbs and grasses, resembling a crested dogstail-common knapweed grassland (MG5): a natural grassland community found in Kent and Sussex. If this meadow was cut in late summer, the hay could be used to enrich the grassland in other areas of the roadside estate, rather than discarding it, as is the current practice. Furthermore, the roadside estate is immediately adjacent to an SSSI, managed by the Sussex Wildlife Trust, which contains a large area of species-rich neutral grassland. A small proportion of this meadow could be harvested for green hay, specifically for enriching rank grassland on the roadside estate.

5 CASE STUDIES – NEW WOODS IN KENT AND EAST SUSSEX

Many new woods have been planted in Kent and East Sussex over the last 20 years or so. Some already have considerable wildlife value, but most are poor for wildlife, and are likely to remain so for years to come, without some form of intervention. The case studies described here illustrate many of the issues raised in Chapter 4 on woodland design and management practices. These woods were not created specifically for wildlife, so no criticism of their original design or current management is intended. The factors considered in the case study woods include:

- landscape character
- the site and its location
- the structure and design of the wood
- high forest and woodland edge planting mixes
- ground flora
- woodland fauna, including birds and butterflies
- contribution to local BAPs.

For each case study, a landscape character assessment was carried out following the guidelines in Section 4.1.1. Vegetation surveys were carried out in spring (high forest) and summer (rides and open spaces) using the NVC vegetation survey method (Section 4.1.3). Birds were surveyed using a simplified mapping technique based on the BTO Common Birds Census; each site was searched systematically on two occasions in the breeding season. Butterfly transects followed the method described in Section 4.1.4. Of all the insect groups, butterflies were surveyed because they are uniquely placed to act as indicators of the state of health of an ecosystem (Liley *et al.*, 2004). Thomas *et al.* (2004) have recently shown that butterflies are declining more rapidly than either plants or birds, which emphasises their important role as indicator species.

Collectively, the case study woods reveal a remarkable diversity of wildlife for their age, although there is considerable variation between them. The following descriptions show that whilst some are currently very good for wildlife, others are poor. All could provide good wildlife habitat if managed appropriately.

Lichens colonise new woods from a very early age.

5.1 Comfort's Wood

Map of Comfort's Wood showing numbered compartments

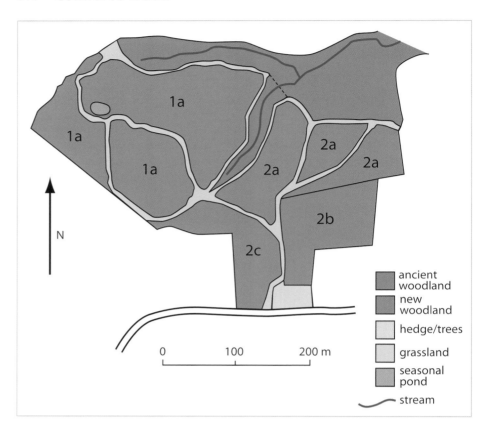

N

	ancient woodland
	new woodland
	hedge/trees
	grassland
	seasonal pond
	stream

0   100   200 m

LEFT **Planting within a few metres of ancient woodland will facilitate colonisation by woodland plants.**

TOP RIGHT **A seasonal pond in Comfort's Wood acts as a source of ancient woodland plants, and adds to the biodiversity value of the site.**

BOTTOM RIGHT **Pendulous sedge is one of seven ancient woodland vascular plants which can already be found in the new planting.**

LEFT **Song thrush is one of five red-listed species breeding in Comfort's Wood.**

RIGHT **Garden warbler has been regularly recorded in Comfort's Wood.**

Tim Loseby

René Pop

5.1.1 Landscape character and site description

Comfort's Wood is in the Cranbrook: Kentish High Weald local character area, which is part of the High Weald character area and the High Weald Area of Outstanding Natural Beauty. The western part of the Cranbrook: Kentish High Weald is characterised by small fields, rough grazing meadows, orchards, belts of coppice and overgrown hedges. Actions outlined for this area in the Landscape Assessment of Kent (LAK) (Kent County Council, 2004) include reinforcing the ecology of the area by replanting woodland and hedges, and the sensitive management of this woodland and its understorey to develop its ecological interest.

The site for Comfort's Wood was acquired and planted by the Woodland Trust in 1990, as 11.25 ha of commercial orchard and arable land. The soil across the site is classed as Wickham 1 – slowly permeable, seasonally waterlogged fine silts and loams over clay. It is bordered on its northern side by a 3.55 ha belt of ancient semi-natural woodland. A shallow wooded gill with a seasonally wet stream extends south east into Comfort's Wood for approximately 180 m, occupying 0.28 ha. The ancient woodland is characterised by oak standards with hornbeam coppice, and is classified as the wood anemone sub-community of ash-field maple-dog's mercury woodland (W8b). It will provide a rich source of woodland plants for the new woodland: at least eighteen ancient woodland vascular plants (indicator species) occur here. The new woodland contains a seasonally wet pond in the former orchard area, retaining alder coppice with oak standards, plus a remnant ancient woodland flora. The surrounding land has traditionally been managed for fruit and cereal production. Overall, this site is a very good location for new woodland.

© Tony Hamblin

LEFT **Two nightingales held territories in Comfort's Wood in 2004.**

RIGHT **Rides and open spaces contain a good variety of open ground flora including abundant nectar plants for invertebrates.**

LEFT **Ringlet was one of 18 species of butterfly recorded in Comfort's Wood in 2004.**

RIGHT **The new woodland (right) is planted too close (5 m) to the ancient woodland along its entire border: shading is likely to have a significant detrimental affect on the ancient woodland edge.**

LEFT **The direct seeding compartment in Comfort's Wood is dense, supporting few birds.**

RIGHT **Many trees failed on this very wet part of the site, leaving a valuable 'open' habitat for wildlife: lesser whitethroat and yellowhammer were recorded here during the breeding season.**

Summary of landscape character and site description

Criteria	Key Issues; Merits for creating new woodland for wildlife (poor ★ – very good ★★★★★)	
Landscape character assessment		
Landscape context	Cranbrook: Kentish High Weald local character area; site adjacent to narrow belt of ancient woodland; woodland within 1 km SE of site, but little other woodland in the vicinity; replanting woodland and ecosystem development are LAK landscape actions for this area	★★★★★
Classification of nearby woodland (NVC)	Ancient woodland (W8b ash-maple type) immediately adjacent	★★★★★
Classification of nearby grassland (NVC)	Improved agricultural pasture	
Site description		
Site topography and elevation	Flat; 100 m asl	★★★★
Soil type	Slowly permeable, seasonally waterlogged fine silts and loams over clay; likely to be moderate pH (5–6) and nutrient rich (no survey data)	★★★
Original site vegetation	No survey data	
Other natural features such as ponds etc	Seasonal pond retaining alder coppice, oak standards and remnant ancient woodland flora	★★★★
Size and shape	11.25 ha	★★★★
Previous land use	Orchard and arable; satisfactory for new woodland	★★★
Adjacent habitat	Bordered to north by belt of ancient woodland, which extends 180 m into site in form of shallow wooded gill; orchards and arable land to E and W	★★★★
Quality assessment	Prime site for creating new woodland for wildlife	★★★★★

5.1.2 Woodland design and conservation value

Comfort's Wood is divided into three compartments, with a network of rides crossing the site; a narrow ride around the northern periphery separates the new planting from ancient woodland.

Flora

Compartment 1a: trees here have closed canopy, and comprise oak (40%), ash (30%), hornbeam (10%), field maple (10%) and 10% shrubs (hazel, guelder-rose, holly and goat willow). Trees are planted in single species groups, with an edge mix of shrubs. Bracken, bramble and rosebay are common. The new woodland edge adjacent to ancient woodland contains occasional colonists: moschatel, lords-and-ladies, pendulous sedge, enchanter's-nightshade, wavy hair-grass, male-fern, wood avens, bluebell, honeysuckle, three-nerved sandwort, wood dock and thyme-leaved speedwell. The remnant woodland flora around the pond includes bluebell, common hemp-nettle, lesser celandine, ramsons, enchanter's-nightshade and lords-and-ladies. Birch and ash regeneration is common.

Compartment 2a: characterised by poor growth of ash (30% of planting), together with slow canopy development of the remaining components (oak (35%), hornbeam (10%), field maple (10%), sweet chestnut (5%), shrubs (10%)). The canopy is more open than compartment 1a, with a grassy understorey dominated by common bent, common couch, cow parsley, Yorkshire-fog, rough meadow-grass and bramble.

Compartment 2b: direct-seeded with oak (35%), ash (30%), hornbeam (10%), sweet chestnut (5%), field maple (10%) and shrubs (10 %). This is now dominated by oak, with occasional guelder-rose, hazel and hornbeam, plus regeneration of goat willow and ash. The understorey has occasional common couch, common fleabane and cow parsley.

Compartment 2c: most sweet chestnut (75% original planting) failed on this very wet part of the site, resulting in open scrub, and ground vegetation very similar to the rides.

With the exception of sweet chestnut, the trees and shrubs chosen were appropriate for the site. However, the mixes included more oak and substantially less hornbeam than the adjacent ancient woodland; no beech was planted, despite its prominence in the gill woodland; sweet chestnut is not found in the adjacent woodland, and planting it on wet ground resulted in a high failure rate, which has benefited the diversity of the woodland structure and its wildlife. Just five understorey and woodland edge species were planted, which limits fruit resources for woodland birds, mammals and invertebrates. Fifty herbs and grasses were found, including a number of shade plants, and seven ancient woodland vascular plants along the plantation edges.

Rides: The ride layout is good, with the exception of the perimeter ride, which is too narrow, and will eventually shade the natural ancient woodland edge, with the loss of much of its wildlife. Some of the central rides have a well developed grassland flora, particularly along the uncut edges. The wetter areas resemble wet mesotrophic grassland (MG9 and MG10), but lack a number of constant species, probably due to previous agricultural improvement. The better-drained areas are similarly degraded and represent a transition from less base-rich grassland communities to mesotrophic grassland communities (MG5 and MG6): the most appropriate community designation for this area would be a neutral, species-rich grassland (MG5). Fifty-three herbs and grasses were found in the ride ground flora (69 species on site in total). The vegetation is dominated by grasses; common bent, glaucous sedge, Yorkshire-fog and rough meadow-grass; with herbs such as angelica, common bird's-foot-trefoil, creeping cinquefoil, common fleabane and creeping buttercup. Wild flowers here provide abundant pollen and nectar sources for invertebrates throughout the spring and summer months, which attracts a diverse bird fauna. Species such as common fleabane, thistles (*Cirsium* spp.), ragworts (*Senecio* spp.) and common knapweed continue to flower well into the autumn. In addition, foodplants of most of the wider countryside butterfly species can be found, which is reflected in a diverse butterfly fauna. A small oversowing programme would benefit the flora and bring it closer to a neutral grassland community characteristic of the landscape (see Section 4.3.2).

Fauna

Comfort's Wood has a relatively rich avifauna; of 37 species recorded in the new planting areas, 24 are likely breeders. Five red-listed, and eight amber-listed woodland species were recorded in 2004/05, including five

Bird recorded (amber and red-listed species highlighted)	
Mallard	Garden warbler*
Kestrel	Blackcap*
Pheasant	Chiffchaff*
Moorhen	Willow warbler*
Woodpigeon*	Goldcrest*
Turtle dove*	Long-tailed tit*
Cuckoo*	Blue tit
Green woodpecker	Great tit
Great spotted woodpecker	Nuthatch
Swallow	Eurasian jay *
Wren*	Magpie*
Dunnock*	Carrion crow
Robin*	Common chaffinch*
Common nightingale*	Greenfinch
Blackbird*	Goldfinch*
Fieldfare	Linnet*
Song thrush*	Bullfinch*
Lesser whitethroat*	Yellowhammer*
Whitethroat*	
* likely breeder	

song thrush territories and two nightingale territories. Three male turtle doves, which breed in woodland but feed outside, were also found. Several species which occur in open canopy woodland or new plantations still occupy the more open areas, including: whitethroat, lesser whitethroat and yellowhammer.

Comfort's Wood also has a high butterfly species richness; of 18 species recorded in 2004/05, 14 were probably breeding. Most sightings of colonising species occurred in the broader central rides through compartment 2a, and between 2a and 2c. With the exception of speckled wood and orange tip, far fewer butterflies occur in the narrower rides through compartment 1a, and the around the northern edge of the wood.

Butterflies recorded (species suffering a decline in abundance are emboldened)

Small skipper*	Red admiral
Large skipper*	Painted lady
Large white	Peacock
Small white	Comma*
Green-veined white	Speckled wood*
Orange tip*	Gatekeeper*
Small copper*	**Meadow brown***
Common blue*	Ringlet*
Holly blue*	**Small heath***

* likely breeder

Summary of woodland design and conservation value

Criteria	Key Issues; Merits for wildlife (poor ★ – very good ★★★★★)	
Woodland design and conservation value		
Position	Good position in the landscape (★★★★), but external edge of new woodland planted too close to ancient woodland (5 m) along its entire border (★): shading likely to have significant detrimental affect on ancient woodland edge	
Layout	Good overall layout	★★★★
High forest species mix	Appropriate species mix, but could have been more closely matched to adjacent ancient woodland.	★★★★
Woodland edge species mix	Appropriate species, but could have been much more diverse	★★
Grassland species mix	No sowing carried out, but interesting flora has developed; oversowing could improve the rides, and create a habitat closer to unimproved neutral grassland	★★★
High forest structure and design	Single species groups with shrub borders; direct seeded compartment dense, supporting very few birds	★★★
Woodland edge structure and design	Good structural diversity developing in places	★★★
Woodland ground flora	None introduced, but seven ancient woodland vascular plants already colonised	★★★★★
Ride vegetation structure	Good ride network with variable sward heights maintained by mowing; other valuable open areas resulting from death of trees	★★★★
Ride flora	53 herbs and grasses present in rides and open spaces; good variety of open ground flora including abundant nectar plants for invertebrates	★★★★
Woodland fauna	Excellent diversity of woodland birds; supports large proportion of the common woodland and wider countryside butterflies of Kent	★★★★★
Contribution to local BAPs	5 nationally red-listed and 8 amber-listed birds; 4 butterflies suffering decline in abundance; no survey data on mammals and other invertebrates	★★★★★
Conclusion		
	Excellent example of new woodland already rich in wildlife just 15 years after planting	★★★★

5.2 Chalket Farm Wood

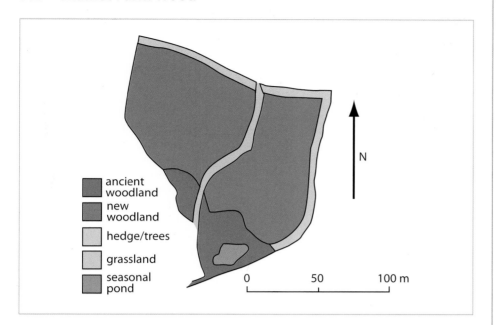

Map of Chalket Farm Wood

Legend:
- ancient woodland
- new woodland
- hedge/trees
- grassland
- seasonal pond

N

0   50   100 m

Chalket Farm Wood is situated in a landscape of rolling hillside pasture with large patches of woodland linked by hedges.

LEFT **Cattle grazing has damaged the ground flora throughout the wood.**

RIGHT **Poor vegetation structure and species diversity characterise the central ride and woodland edge.**

LEFT **Old anthills under the planted trees indicate that the site was formerly unimproved grassland, which should have been conserved.**

RIGHT **The ground flora under the planted trees retains elements of a neutral, species-rich grassland: creeping cinquefoil is one example.**

117

5.2.1 Landscape character and site description

Chalket Farm is in the Bayham: Central High Weald local character area, which is part of the High Weald character area and the High Weald Area of Outstanding Natural Beauty. The High Weald is a well-wooded, mixed farming landscape; the Bayham local character area is characterised by rolling hills, with grazing on lower pastures, dense hedges and extensive deciduous woodland on the hillsides.

Chalket Farm Wood occupies 1.1 ha, and was planted in 1993/94, in part on unimproved grassland. The soil across the site is classed as Wickham 1 – free draining slightly acid but base-rich. It is bordered on its northern and eastern boundaries by an existing hedgerow comprising mainly hazel and hawthorn, with ash, pedunculate oak, holly and occasional elder. The southern edge of the wood borders a 0.35 ha fragment of degraded ancient woodland containing a pond. This was formerly the north eastern corner of the much more extensive Park Wood. This wood was cleared sometime in the last 120 years, although its boundaries are still visible on aerial photographs of the surrounding fields. Woodland shade plants are still present in this fragment, including five ancient woodland vascular plants, which may eventually colonise the new wood. Species present include pignut, bluebell, three-nerved sandwort, primrose and common figwort. Two ancient woods, Chalket Wood and the larger Cooper's Rough (10.4 ha) are just 200 m and 300 m west of the site respectively. The surrounding land has traditionally been managed as pasture.

Summary of landscape character and site description

Criteria	Key Issues; Merits for creating new woodland for wildlife (poor ★ – very good ★★★★★)	
Landscape character assessment		
Landscape context	Bayham: Central High Weald local character area: rolling hillside pasture with large patches of woodland linked by hedges; the landscape is in good condition; woodland creation has not been identified as a priority	★★★
Classification of nearby woodland (NVC)	Ancient woodland (W8b ash-maple type) 200–300 m west of site;	★★★
Classification of nearby grassland (NVC)	Improved agricultural pasture; nearest neutral grassland 1 km east (condition unknown)	
Site description		
Site topography and elevation	Gentle south facing slope (10°); 100 m asl	★★★★
Soil type	Wickham 1 – free draining slightly acid but base-rich soil (no survey data)	★★★
Original site vegetation	No survey data, but remnant grassland flora with old anthills indicates unimproved neutral grassland in area planted with trees	★
Other natural features such as ponds etc	None	
Size and shape	1.1 ha; roughly square	★★
Previous land use	Unimproved grassland; unsuitable for new woodland	★
Adjacent habitat	Southern part of site contains remnant fragment of woodland vegetation, pond with seepages; pasture surrounds the wood	★★
Quality assessment	Poor site for creating new woodland for wildlife	★

5.2.2 Woodland design and conservation value

Flora

Trees have closed canopy over much of the site; the species mix is predominately oak and wild cherry, with smaller numbers of ash and alder. This could have been improved by planting a mix which more closely resembles that in the adjacent woodland, or a more typical ash-maple mix (see Section 4.2.2). The trees were planted as an intimate mix, which will affect the survival of slower growing species. There are just four understorey trees and shrubs in the existing hedgerow, and none were planted in the high forest, or new woodland edge. Consequently the overall tree/shrub species diversity and structure of this wood is poor. However, on the eastern side, bramble sheets are forming (especially from hedgerow margins), which will prove invaluable to invertebrates and their prey. The 'woodland' ground flora is also poor, comprising mainly annual meadow-grass and rough meadow-grass, with patches of common bent, cow parsley and common nettle: 21 species were recorded in total. The flora throughout the site is being damaged by grazing cattle that appear to roam freely in the spring and summer months.

The presence of old anthills under the planted trees indicates that much of the site was formerly unimproved grassland; the present flora has elements of a neutral, species-rich grassland (MG5), although crested dog's-tail and common knapweed are absent. Despite the closing canopy and the cattle, a number of grassland species still survive. Prominent amongst these are: common sorrel, sheep's sorrel, creeping cinquefoil, yarrow, selfheal, germander speedwell, field wood-rush, lesser stitchwort, mouse-ear-hawkweed, devil's-bit scabious, common bent, red fescue, sweet vernal grass and meadow foxtail.

The wood possesses a single ride in a north-south orientation. Just 16 herbs and grasses are present in the ride: the dominant species are common bent and Yorkshire-fog, with small patches of creeping buttercup, creeping thistle and marsh thistle. Two large clumps of bramble provide one of the few nectar sources for invertebrates. Removal of the cattle and an oversowing programme with a species-rich neutral grassland mix (see Section 4.3.2) would benefit the flora and bring it closer to a neutral grassland community characteristic of the landscape. However, a more radical management decision would be to remove the trees from the unimproved meadow area, creating new glades. The felled trees could be replaced by planting new trees in the existing ride, where the ground flora is currently poor.

Fauna

Twenty-two bird species were recorded in Chalket Farm Wood, of which 12 are likely breeders. Two red-listed, and two amber-listed woodland species were present in 2004/05, including single pairs of song thrush and dunnock. The small size of Chalket Farm Wood makes it vulnerable to the loss of birds through events such as natural dispersal and predation. Consequently it will always rely to some extent on immigration of birds. Other notable species in 2004 included chiffchaff and blackcap holding territories, but the presence of these and other birds may have been dependent to some extent on the surrounding hedgerow, and the fragment of degraded ancient woodland.

Chalket Farm Wood has a very low butterfly species richness; small numbers of seven species were recorded in 2004/05, of which three were likely breeders on site (in small numbers). All sightings occurred in the broad central ride, and most were nectaring on bramble. Although the wood was planted on unimproved pasture, the presence of grazing cattle is likely to be responsible for the low numbers of butterflies.

Birds recorded (amber and red-listed species highlighted)

Moorhen*
Wood pigeon*
Green woodpecker
Great spotted woodpecker
Swallow
Wren*
Dunnock*
Robin*
Blackbird*
Song thrush*
Blackcap*
Chiffchaff*
Blue tit
Great tit
Eurasian jay
Magpie*
Carrion Crow
Starling
House sparrow
Common chaffinch*
Greenfinch*
Linnet

* likely breeder

Butterflies recorded (species suffering a decline in abundance are emboldened)

Small skipper	Speckled wood*
Green-veined white	Gatekeeper*
Holly blue	**Meadow brown***
Comma	

* likely breeder

Summary of woodland design and conservation value

Criteria	Key Issues; Merits for wildlife (poor ★ – very good ★★★★★)	
Woodland design and conservation value		
Position	Poor due to species-rich pasture	★
Layout	Central ride would have been better for wildlife if located in an east-west orientation	★★
High forest species mix	Predominately oak and wild cherry, with smaller numbers of ash and alder; could have included more ash, and introduced hornbeam to the mix	★★
Woodland edge species mix	Four shrubs in existing hedgerow border; no shrubs planted along central ride, or along western boundary	★
Grassland species mix	Poor species diversity in central ride due partly to cattle grazing and trampling; shade and cattle destroying areas of remnant unimproved grassland flora	★
High forest structure and design	Intimate mix	★★
Woodland edge structure and design	No internal edge structure; eastern boundary hedge and pockets of bramble scrub adjacent to it provide valuable structure	★★
Woodland ground flora	No signs of colonisation from remnant woodland at the southern boundary	
Ride vegetation structure	Sward heavily grazed by cattle; two bramble patches attractive to invertebrates	★★
Ride flora	16 herbs and grasses present in central ride but few nectar plants	★★
Woodland fauna	22 bird species, but numbers low, so species present may fluctuate from year to year; just 3 butterflies likely to breed	★★★
Contribution to local BAPs	2 nationally red-listed and 2 amber-listed birds; one butterfly suffering decline in abundance; no survey data on mammals and other invertebrates	★★★
Conclusion		
	Poorly designed and managed for wildlife; unimproved grassland should have been conserved	★★

5.3 Cavalry Wood

Map of Cavalry Wood

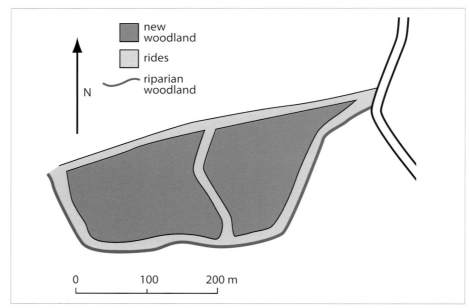

new woodland
rides
riparian woodland

N

0   100   200 m

BOTTOM LEFT **Riparian woodland on the southern boundary, separated from the new woodland by a broad peripheral ride.**

BOTTOM CENTRE **Nearby ancient wood and hedgerows retain some woodland plants, such as primrose.**

BOTTOM RIGHT **Good woodland edge developing: six shrubs were planted along the periphery and central ride.**

Scallop of tall herbs, rich in nectar plants, photographed just after the central ride was mown in mid-August.

www.markhamblin.com

LEFT Willow warblers have been observed in the denser areas of trees and shrubs.

RIGHT Cavalry Wood supports an important colony of marbled white butterflies.

LEFT Brown argus has colonised Cavalry Wood.

RIGHT An inappropriate choice of trees, such as wild cherry, has led to poor survival and establishment on wetter parts of the site.

Alder thickets are naturally regenerating in wetter areas of Cavalry Wood.

5.3.1 Landscape character and site description

Cavalry Wood was planted in the winter of 1992/93 on 5.3 ha of arable land in the Brabourne Vale local character area, which is part of the Wealden Greensand character area. This landscape is characterised by woodland, bushy hedgerows, winter cereals and short term grasslands. Mature woods in the area retain features of very damp, ancient ash-maple woodland with alder. Actions outlined for this area in the Landscape Assessment of Kent (LAK) (Kent County Council, 2004) include reinforcing semi-natural habitats between woodlands (hedges and woodland corridors) and enhancing the ecological interest of wetland corridors.

Cavalry Wood is bordered on its southern boundary by a stream with a fringe of mature trees, which NVC analysis shows most closely resembles alder-nettle woodland (W6), a rare wetland habitat in Kent. This is mainly alder and hawthorn; with mature ash, grey willow, goat willow and white willow; and occasional blackthorn, elder and spindle. Woodland shade plants can still be found in this riparian woodland, including three ancient woodland vascular plants; some of these may eventually colonise the new wood. Species present include pendulous sedge, wood horsetail and giant fescue. A small fragment of ancient woodland (1.5 ha) 150 m north east of the new woodland, consists of ash coppice with some alder along a streamside, containing elements of alder-nettle (W6) and ash-field maple-dog's mercury (W8) communities. Many ancient woodland vascular plants are present here, including yellow archangel, giant fescue, ramsons and herb Paris. This was formerly the south eastern corner of the much larger Coomb Wood. A hedgerow of hazel and field maple, with occasional hawthorn, blackthorn and dogwood runs south from this fragment of ancient wood to within 30 m of the new wood: this supports some woodland plants such as yellow archangel and primrose.

The central and western part of the site was formerly occupied by Coombrough Wood, which was cleared just after the war: its eastern boundary is still visible on aerial photographs of the site. The soil across the site is classed as slowly permeable seasonally wet, acid loam and clay. In winter, the part of the site formerly occupied by Coombrough Wood is waterlogged. Grey heron, little egret and snipe have all been flushed from the 'woodland'. Prior to planting, the site was used as pasture and arable.

Summary of landscape character and site description

Criteria	Key Issues; Merits for creating new woodland for wildlife (poor ★ – very good ★★★★★)	
Landscape character assessment		
Landscape context	Brabourne Vale local character area: gently sloping landscape with winter cereals, short term grasslands, woodlands and bushy hedgerows: reinforcing semi-natural habitats between woodlands is a LAK landscape action for this area	★★★★★
Classification of nearby woodland (NVC)	Wet woodland on southern boundary and small ancient wood (ash-maple type (W8) with alder-nettle (W6)) 150 m north east of site; larger areas of ancient woodland 1.1 km north west	★★★★
Classification of nearby grassland (NVC)	Several areas of neutral grassland 0.7–2 km distant (condition unknown)	
Site description		
Site topography and elevation	Slope 1°; 75 m asl	★★★★
Soil type	Slowly permeable seasonally wet acid loam and clay soil; pH 6.8	★★★
Original site vegetation	Arable	
Other natural features such as ponds etc	Stream along southern boundary	★★★★
Size and shape	5.3 ha; roughly trapezoid	★★★★
Previous land use	Arable; satisfactory for new woodland	★★★
Adjacent habitat	Riparian woodland on southern boundary; nearby hedgerow with ancient hornbeam and field maple pollards; arable land surrounds the new wood	★★★★
Quality assessment	Good site for creation of a wet woodland	★★★★

5.3.2 Woodland design and conservation value

Flora

Despite being planted 15 years ago, there is poor canopy closure over much of the site. The exception is the eastern corner, which is drier in winter, and is also the area that was not part of Coombrough Wood. The high forest areas are predominantly an intimate mix of ash and oak at 3 x 3 m spacing, with a small proportion of hawthorn, rowan, wild cherry and crab apple. Most wild cherry has failed on this seasonally wet site; alder could have been planted instead, although this is naturally colonising the southern 20 m of the site. A distinct woodland edge planting of 4–6 rows of shrubs encircles the whole wood, including the central ride; this includes rowan, hawthorn, dogwood, field maple, crab apple, hazel, blackthorn, buckthorn and hornbeam. This could be further enhanced by introducing late winter fruiting species such as holly, ivy and dog-rose; increasing the density of edge planting in some areas; and pruning the existing edge along the eastern section to provide more structural diversity. This is the only case study wood with a good variety of fruit bearing shrubs planted along the woodland edge. The ground flora along this edge is mostly open ground plants (24 species were recorded). With the exception of the eastern corner, most of the high forest ground flora resembles that of the rides.

The wood possesses a centrally positioned ride in a north-south orientation, and a perimeter ride. Thirty-four plants were found in the ride network (including 11 grasses). The vegetation most closely resembles an open tall herb community deriving from previous arable weed communities, but it is developing into species-poor *Arrenatherum* (false oat-grass) grassland. In the southern perimeter ride, between the new planting and the stream, the dominant grasses are creeping bent, rough meadow-grass, with much lower frequencies of false oat-grass, Yorkshire-fog and smaller cat's-tail; the dominant herbs are creeping buttercup and common fleabane. In the central ride, much of the creeping bent is replaced by Yorkshire-fog, with low frequencies of crested dog's-tail and soft-brome. Wild flowers here provide abundant pollen and nectar sources for invertebrates throughout the spring and summer months. Species such as common fleabane, thistles, ragworts and bristly oxtongue continue to flower well into the autumn. In addition, foodplants of most of the wider countryside butterfly species can be found on the site, and this is reflected in its very diverse butterfly fauna. Just 14 plant species were found in the closely mown northern perimeter ride, which is typical of a rank grassland (MG1) and dominated by creeping bent and false oat-grass.

Fauna

Twenty-one bird species were recorded, just six of which are likely breeders. One red-listed, and five amber-listed species were present in

Birds recorded (amber and red-listed species highlighted)	
Grey heron	Robin*
Little egret	Blackbird*
Snipe	Whitethroat*
Hobby	Blackcap*
Pheasant	Chiffchaff
Wood pigeon	Willow warbler*
Cuckoo	Blue tit
Green woodpecker	Great tit
Great spotted woodpecker	Carrion crow
Skylark	Eurasian jay
Wren*	
*likely breeder	

Butterflies recorded (species suffering a decline in abundance are emboldened)

Small skipper*
Essex skipper
Large skipper*
Brimstone*
Large white
Small white
Green-veined white
Orange tip
Small copper*
Brown Argus*
Common blue*
Painted lady
Small tortoiseshell
Peacock
Speckled wood*
Marbled White*
Gatekeeper*
Meadow brown*
Small heath*

* likely breeder

2004/05, including two male willow warblers, and a juvenile cuckoo which may have been reared on site. The amber-listed little egret and snipe are winter visitors. The open structure of Cavalry Wood over much of its area is not yet conducive to breeding by many woodland species, although it does support several pairs of whitethroat. The presence of the two heron species in winter was surprising, but indicates just how wet the site is at that time. Two species, chiffchaff and great spotted woodpecker, were only observed in the riparian woodland, but both are likely to feed in the new woodland, and chiffchaff will probably breed in the near future.

Nineteen butterflies have been recorded in Cavalry Wood, the highest species richness of all the case study sites. At least 11 of these probably breed on site. Because of the open nature or the wood, butterflies were observed throughout the western part of the wood, together with the central and southern perimeter rides. Few butterflies were observed along the northern perimeter ride, which is regularly mown. A high daily maximum of 24 marbled whites was recorded in July 2004: other notable species included small copper, common blue and small heath, which are suffering declines in abundance within their respective ranges. This is clearly an excellent site for butterflies, which confirms the importance of creating and maintaining open areas of species-rich grassland for these, and other insects. The rides in 2004 were not mown until mid-August. The lack of weed control around the trees has also supported high insect numbers, although in large parts of the site, this may have had a negative impact on the growth rates of trees in the past.

Summary of woodland design and conservation value

Criteria	Key Issues; Merits for wildlife (poor ★ – very good ★★★★★)	
Woodland design and conservation value		
Position	Good position in the landscape	★★★
Layout	Broad north-south ride would have been better for wildlife in the longer term if orientated more east-west; ride around external edge will benefit wildlife if managed appropriately	★★★★
High forest species mix	Predominately ash and oak, with small numbers of rowan, hawthorn and crab apple; wild cherry largely failed due to wet site; missed opportunity to create a wet woodland; could have included alder, birch and more hornbeam in high forest mix	★★
Woodland edge species mix	Good edge planting of six shrubs around periphery and rides: could now be enriched	★★★★
Grassland species mix	No sowing carried out, but good diversity of grasses and wild flowers has developed; oversowing could improve the rides, and create a habitat closer to unimproved neutral grassland	★★★
High forest structure and design	Intimate mix, spaced at 3 x 3 m, has contributed to open nature of the woodland, despite being 14 years old	★★
Woodland edge structure and design	Good structural diversity developing in places; would benefit from pruning and some additional species	★★★
Woodland ground flora	No signs of colonisation from remnant woodland flora along the southern boundary	
Ride vegetation structure	Good ride network; sward heights uniform until autumn mowing, would benefit from a more frequently mown central zone through the central ride and rotational mowing of tall herb areas; other valuable open areas resulting from tree failure	★★★★
Ride flora	34 herbs and grasses present in rides and open spaces; good variety of open ground flora including abundant nectar plants for invertebrates	★★★★
Woodland fauna	Good diversity of birds considering the open nature of the wood is promising for the future; supports large proportion of the common woodland (and wider countryside) butterflies of Kent	★★★★
Contribution to local BAPs	One nationally red-listed and 5 amber-listed birds recorded on site; 4 butterflies suffering declines in abundance; no survey data on mammals and other invertebrates	★★★★
Conclusion		
	Promising new woodland, with some good design features; good woodland edge in places and excellent butterfly fauna; wildlife would benefit at this stage from some carefully targeted management input; wet woodland is rare in Kent, and part of this site could have been used to create this habitat	★★★

5.4   Runham Estate Woods

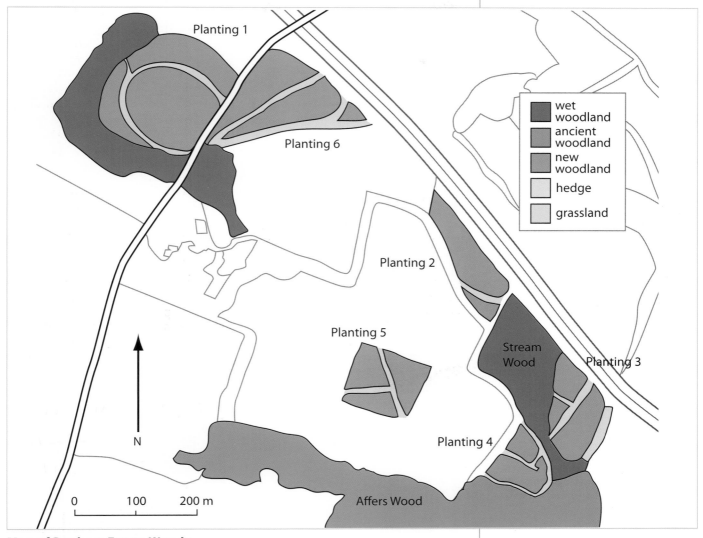

wet woodland
ancient woodland
new woodland
hedge
grassland

Planting 1
Planting 6
Planting 2
Planting 5
Stream Wood
Planting 3
Planting 4
Affers Wood

N

0   100   200 m

Map of Runham Estate Woods

Good canopy closure in Planting 1 has completely shaded-out arable weeds, and provides good habitat for woodland plants.

BELOW **Hybrid common spotted-orchid x southern marsh-orchid (*Dactylorhiza* x *grandis*) growing under the open canopy; protected from mowing by the trees.**

Planting 5 (Square Wood) is located on the site of an original wood, but is isolated from nearby ancient woodland.

LEFT **Exotic mulberry is included in the woodland mixes.**

RIGHT **Trees along the new woodland edge provide an attractive vista, but few opportunities for wildlife which requires edge habitat with a more varied structure.**

LEFT **Regular pruning has had a significant adverse effect on the vegetation structure.**

RIGHT **Rides are mown frequently during the summer, including inter-rows: consequently the habitat is poor for plants and invertebrates.**

The ancient woodland edge (extreme left) will eventually be shaded out by the planted woodland.

5.4.1 Landscape character and site description

Runham Estate is located in the Greensand Fruit Belt-Maidstone and the Leeds-Lenham Farmlands local character areas, both of which are part of the Wealden Greensand character area. Most of the estate is within the Greensand Fruit Belt-Maidstone, which is a landscape of mixed farmlands with a high percentage of orchards, scattered small woodlands and grasslands interspersed with larger arable fields, developed on free draining soils. The farmland is dissected by the River Medway and its tributaries, including the River Len, which crosses the Runham Estate. Actions outlined for this area in the Landscape Assessment of Kent (LAK) (Kent County Council, 2004) include reinforcing the ecological bases within existing woodland and in the river valleys in particular, by the encouragement of replanting and increasing species diversity.

Planting 1 is situated at the eastern end of the Leeds-Lenham Farmlands local character area, which is an undulating rural landscape of narrow lanes of mixed farmland of medium sized arable fields and pastures and small copses, developed on well-drained sandy loams. Networks of semi-natural habitats are physically fragmented – the remaining pockets of woodland and mature trees are vulnerable. Actions outlined for this area in the Landscape Assessment of Kent (2004) include creating a network of semi-natural woodland and heathland habitats.

The planting at Runham comprises six small woods (three of which are described here), ranging in size from 0.6 ha to 2.5 ha. In total, 9,000 trees were planted over 7.1 ha in 1990/91, and they have been carefully managed since. The woods are contained in an area of approximately 35 ha. Planting 1 is bordered to the south and west by 1.7 ha of alder-nettle woodland (W6/W7) – a rare wet woodland habitat in Kent – and to the east by a sunken lane. The canopy of the alder wood is mainly alder, with an understorey of hazel. A rich ground flora found here includes; wood anemone, moschatel, opposite-leaved golden-saxifrage, bluebell, marsh marigold, dog's mercury, cuckooflower and primrose. Similar species occur in the 1.1 ha Stream Wood, which is also an alder-nettle type. This wood borders Plantings 2, 3 and 4. Planting 4 is also bordered on its eastern and southern sides by Affers Wood, a more extensive area of ash-field maple-dog's mercury ancient woodland of the wood anemone sub-community (W8b). Here, the

Summary of landscape character and site description

Criteria	Key Issues; Merits for creating new woodland for wildlife (poor ★ – very good ★★★★★)	
Landscape character assessment		
Landscape context	Wealden Greensand character area: mixed farmlands and small scattered woods; several larger ancient woods to the south and west of the estate; creation of natural woodland ecosystems is a LAK landscape action in this area; screening transport corridors also important for local communities	★★★★★
Classification of nearby woodland (NVC)	Ancient woodland (W8b ash-maple type) and rare wet woodland (W6) immediately adjacent	★★★★★
Classification of nearby grassland (NVC)	Improved agricultural pasture	
Site description		
Site topography and elevation	Gently rolling; 100 m asl	★★★★
Soil type	Well drained sandy loams (no survey data)	★★★
Original site vegetation	No survey data	
Other natural features such as ponds etc	Stream along boundary of two woods	★★★★
Size and shape	Three woods described occupy 4.1 ha (0.6–2.5 ha) of 7.1 ha of new woodland planted	★★★
Previous land use	Arable; satisfactory for new woodland	★★★
Adjacent habitat	Planting 1 and 4 bordered by alder woodland, and the latter by ancient ash-maple woodland	★★★★
Quality assessment	Estate offers good opportunities for new woodland creation for wildlife	★★★★★

canopy is dominated by ash, and the understorey by hazel. The ground flora contains a good variety of woodland plants, such as moschatel, wood anemone, cuckooflower, bluebell, yellow archangel, enchanter's nightshade, broad buckler-fern and honeysuckle. Planting 5 is the only new wood not bordered in part by an area of mature woodland: it is 90 m from Affers Wood and 75 m from Stream Wood. Further afield, there are several large blocks of woodland to the south and west of the estate, the closest being Runham and Gaskin Woods (18 ha), just 0.7 km south west of the farm.

Little unimproved grassland survives in the local landscape. Chilston Park (35 ha) is designated as neutral grassland, and just north of the motorway is an area of acid grassland (2.8 ha), although the condition of these sites in not known.

5.4.2 Woodland design and conservation value

Flora

Planting 1: wild cherry, beech, sweet chestnut, birch and rowan dominate the area adjacent to the alder woodland: inclusion of alder would have been appropriate here. Fifty percent of the shrubs are elder, which is more representative of the mature woodland. Further away from the alder woodland, the planting is dominated by oak (25%), beech (23%), sweet chestnut (20%) and alder (14%), with smaller numbers of white willow, wild cherry and goat willow. Here the soil is much drier, hence less appropriate for alder. Ash and field maple might also have been considered. Occasional hawthorn, hazel, rowan, wayfaring-tree and exotic mulberry have been planted along the ride edges. The woodland floor is dominated by extensive areas of bare ground. However, the ground flora has 18 species, including occasional bugle, lords-and-ladies, wood avens, bluebell and lesser celandine. The ride layout is good, but the structure is poor, as there is no woodland edge zone of shrubs, and the ride is frequently mown and heavily grazed by rabbits, so lacks a tall herb community. As a consequence, the flora, which is dominated by common bent, Yorkshire-fog and creeping buttercup, is species poor, and resembles an open community, presumably derived from previous arable weed communities.

Planting 4: this 0.6 ha wood is the smallest new planting on the estate. The peripheral ride is so narrow, that the new planting will effectively shade the vegetation of the long established ancient woodland edge. The tree mix bares little resemblance to the two adjacent woodland communities. The dominant species in these woods, alder and ash respectively, are only minor components of the new woodland mix. Eight tree species and five understorey species were planted. The dominant tree species are oak (40%) and beech (26%); with smaller numbers of wild cherry, sweet chestnut and alder; and occasional ash, birch and sycamore. Five understorey species (hawthorn, hazel, crab apple, guelder-rose and rowan) are a minor component of the mix: even along the edge they only represent about 20% of the planting. The woodland floor is still dominated by grasses, primarily rough meadow-grass and Yorkshire-fog: 22 open ground species are present. The new woodland edge adjacent to Affers Wood contains wood speedwell, and occasional bluebell and lesser celandine.

A broad central ride lacks a tall herb community through frequent mowing. Mid summer mowing is also carried out between the rows of trees. Consequently, the only area where tall herbs remain is around the base of the trees. The ride vegetation is similar to the 'woodland' ground flora, with creeping buttercup and white clover dominating the ground cover together with the two grasses: just 13 species were found in the rides.

Planting 5 (Square Wood): this 1 ha wood is planted on the site of an old woodland, cleared in the last 100 years. Mature oaks with a few bluebells underneath still mark the corners. Canopy closure is less complete than Planting 1, and consequently there is little bare ground. The dominant tree species is oak, with wild cherry, beech, sweet chestnut and sycamore. Understorey species include crab apple, guelder-rose, hawthorn and hazel. The woodland floor is still dominated by grasses, primarily false oat-grass and creeping soft-grass, with lower frequencies of common bent and Yorkshire-fog: 18 open ground species are present. A broad central ride lacks any structural diversity, and is frequently mown; hence it also lacks a tall herb community. The main components of the vegetation are the same as the 'woodland' ground flora, although just 13 species were found in the rides.

Fauna

The number of birds observed in these woods varied from just five to 13 species. Only three of these, blackbird, blackcap and chiffchaff are likely breeders, all in Planting 1. Several family parties of blue tits and great tits were observed in Planting 1. In total, one red-listed, and four amber-listed woodland species were recorded in 2004/05.

Just 11 butterflies were recorded in the three woods. Numbers varied from just three species in Planting 5 to eight species in Planting 1. Most sightings refer to maximum daily counts of less than four individuals. Five additional species were observed in two of the other new woodlands; small copper,

Birds recorded at Runham Farm Woods (amber- and red-listed species highlighted)

Species	Planting 1	Planting 4	Planting 5
Wood pigeon	*	*	
Green woodpecker		*	
Great spotted woodpecker	*		
Wren			**
Robin	**		
Dunnock	**		
Blackbird	*	*	
Redwing			**
Blackcap	*		
Chiffchaff	*		
Goldcrest	*		**
Blue tit	*	*	**
Great tit	*	*	*
Magpie	*		
Carrion crow	*		
Common chaffinch	*		
Bullfinch			**

* observed in summer
**observed in winter only

Butterflies recorded (species suffering a decline in abundance are emboldened)

Species	Planting 1	Planting 4	Planting 5
Large skipper	*	*	
Small skipper			*
Large white	*	*	
Small white	*		
Green-veined white	*	*	
Orange tip		*	
Red admiral			*
Comma	*		
Speckled wood	*		
Meadow brown	*	*	*
Ringlet*	*	*	

* likely breeder

common blue, gatekeeper, small tortoiseshell and marbled white. Although the new woods offer little habitat for colonising butterflies, the records do indicate that there is a local source of individuals of many species, and given appropriate management, even the small rides could provide valuable breeding habitat for butterflies, and many other invertebrates.

Summary of woodland design and conservation value

Criteria	Key Issues; Merits for wildlife (poor ★ – very good ★★★★★)	
Woodland design and conservation value		
Position	External edge of Planting 4 planted too close to ancient woodland (3 m) along its entire border (★): shading likely to have significant detrimental affect on ancient woodland edge. Planting 5 on site of original copse, but isolated	
Layout	Good overall layout given size restrictions	★★★
High forest species mix	Diverse, but little resemblance to adjacent woodland communities	★★
Woodland edge species mix	Appropriate shrubs included, but much more diversity required, and higher numbers planted along the edge	★★
Grassland species mix	No sowing carried out, and very poor flora has developed due partly to management; oversowing could improve the rides, and create a habitat closer to unimproved neutral grassland	★
High forest structure and design	Intimate mix spaced at 3 x 2 m; good canopy closure in places, open in others	★★★
Woodland edge structure and design	Poor structural diversity due to small numbers of shrubs along edges	★
Woodland ground flora	None introduced, but occasional woodland plants beginning to establish along the edges adjacent to mature woodland	★★★★
Ride vegetation structure	Mowing prevents any structural diversity in sward heights	★
Ride flora	11 to 22 herbs and grasses present in rides and open spaces of the three woods; poor provision of nectar plants for invertebrates	★
Woodland fauna	Low diversity of breeding birds, but position will encourage use during post-breeding dispersal of birds, and by winter feeding flocks; low diversity of butterflies, but potential for considerable improvement	★★
Contribution to local BAPs	One nationally red-listed and 4 amber-listed birds; 1 butterfly suffering decline in abundance; no survey data on mammals and other invertebrates	★★★
Conclusion		
	Good example of new woodland which, through species selection and design, is poor for wildlife, and may adversely affect the wildlife of the ancient woodland edge	★★

5.5   Hastings Spine and Spur roadside

LEFT **Looking south from Crowhurst Road, across a varied habitat of woodland, scrub, meadow and rank grassland.**

RIGHT **Looking north from Crowhurst Road across embankments of rank grassland and scrub towards Marline Valley Woods SSSI.**

LEFT **Ash-field maple-dog's mercury community in the ancient woodland of Marline Valley Woods SSSI, immediately adjacent to the roadside estate.**

RIGHT **Herb-rich flora of Marline meadow, just a few metres from rank grassland on the roadside estate.**

Map of Hastings Spine and Spur Road

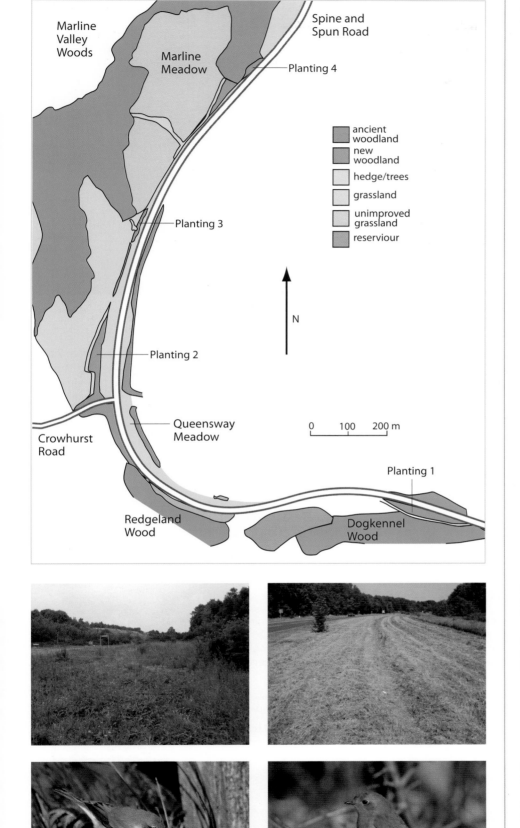

Marline Valley Woods

Marline Meadow

Spine and Spun Road

Planting 4

ancient woodland

new woodland

hedge/trees

grassland

unimproved grassland

reserviour

Planting 3

N

Planting 2

Queensway Meadow

Crowhurst Road

0   100   200 m

Planting 1

Redgeland Wood

Dogkennel Wood

LEFT **Queensway meadow is a valuable grassland community on the roadside estate which already contains 47 plant species.**

RIGHT **Poor management can result in valuable meadows being cut at the wrong time; Queensway meadow was cut in mid July.**

LEFT **Lesser whitethroat is present in the dense hedgerows north of Crowhurst Road.**

RIGHT **Several pairs of robins are likely to breed in the roadside estate.**

Tim Loseby

René Pop

131

ABOVE LEFT **Three reptiles have been recorded on the roadside estate, including grass snake.**

ABOVE RIGHT **Several of the wooded areas are too small (0.1–0.2 ha) to be of conservation value in their own right.**

5.5.1 Landscape character and site description

Hastings Spine and Spur road is within the High Weald character area, but just outside the High Weald Area of Outstanding Natural Beauty. The High Weald is a well-wooded, mixed farming landscape, with characteristic ridges and stream valleys; woods of varying size are interspersed with small, unimproved meadows, bordered by species-rich hedgerows and narrow woodland corridors (shaws). The High Weald landscape assessment (English Nature) states that planting new native woodland should be considered in this area.

The area east of the Hastings Spine and Spur road is mainly built up, although two ancient woodland nature reserves – Church Wood and Robsack Wood – still survive. To the south and west are eight more ancient woods, all within 400 m of the road. Monkham and Redgeland Woods form part of Combe Haven SSSI; Dogkennel Wood and Marline

Summary of landscape character and site description

Criteria	Key Issues; Merits for creating new woodland for wildlife (poor ★ – very good ★★★★★)	
Landscape character assessment		
Landscape context	High Weald character area: well-wooded, mixed farming landscape, with species-rich hedgerows and lowland grassland; woodland creation important in this area	★★★★★
Classification of nearby woodland (NVC)	Typically ash-maple ancient woodland within 400 m of the site, and immediately adjacent to the roadside estate in several places: Marline Valley Woods SSSI dominated by oak-hornbeam woodland	★★★★
Classification of nearby grassland (NVC)	Several areas of neutral grassland: Marline SSSI and Combe Haven SSSI (0.7 km west)	★★★★★
Site description		
Site topography and elevation	Level areas, gentle slopes and steeper embankments; 15–80 m asl	★★★
Soil type	Unknown	
Original site vegetation	Unknown	
Other natural features such as ponds etc	None	
Size and shape	Linear roadside estate, maximum width 72 m; 8.1 ha over 2.1 km	★★★★
Previous land use	Unknown	
Adjacent habitat	Ancient woodland and unimproved grassland to the west of the site	★★★★★
Quality assessment	Prime site for habitat creation, including linear woodland	★★★★★

Valley Woods SSSI border the highway estate. Unimproved neutral grassland is also present in the local landscape: in Marline Valley Woods SSSI; and larger areas of alluvial meadows south east of the road, along the 120 ha Combe Haven Valley.

The spine and spur road was completed in 1983, and runs south west from the A2100 to the junction with Crowhurst Road, where it turns east towards Hastings. Landscaping and planting of approximately 8.1 ha of roadside estate was carried out in 1983/84 over a distance of 2.1 km: it is 72 m at its widest point. Surveys were carried out in 6.2 ha of the roadside estate during 2004/05. The areas of new woodland surveyed varied in size from just 0.1 ha to 0.8 ha, which severely limits the potential for colonisation of these areas by woodland wildlife. Consequently, the areas of tree planting need to be primarily evaluated for the contribution they make to the wildlife of the site as a whole, and that of the wider landscape.

5.5.2 Woodland design and conservation value

Flora

Planting 1 occupies 0.4 ha of roadside embankment, and is separated from Dogkennel Wood by a narrow shaded track. Maps published in the late 19th century show this track as a road or bridleway forming the original northern boundary of the wood, with the area now planted alongside the highway being unwooded. Dogkennel Wood is an ash-field maple-dog's mercury woodland, of the wood anemone sub-community (W8b), with numerous alders. Nearby Redgeland and Monkham Woods are classified as oak-hazel-ash woods (English Nature SSSI citation). Though highly disturbed, Dogkennel Wood has a number of woodland plants such as ramsons, wood anemone, pendulous sedge, opposite-leaved golden-saxifrage and bluebell. Planting 1 is primarily alder – which may have colonised since planting – with occasional ash and hornbeam; understorey species include hazel and field maple. This does not closely reflect the tree communities of Dogkennel Wood or nearby woodland. Planting 1 has a very high percentage of bare ground with a ground flora of just 10 herbs and grasses, although these are woodland species, and include pendulous sedge, broad buckler-fern, bluebell and ivy. Ramsons are just surviving on the track between the woods, but disturbance caused by human traffic (including motorbikes) is hindering colonisation.

Three smaller plantings (0.1–0.2 ha each) were surveyed north of Crowhurst Road, two of which are immediately adjacent to woodland of Marline Valley Woods SSSI. Marline Wood is reported to be dominated by the birch-hazel variant of the nationally uncommon pedunculate oak-hornbeam woodland (Peterken's classification system) (English Nature SSSI citation). However, there is some variation in composition due to local differences in drainage, soil type, slope and management. The areas adjacent to the highway plantings are closer to ash-field maple-dog's mercury woodland, of the wood anemone sub-community (W8b). Typical woodland herbs here include ramsons, wood anemone, pignut, yellow archangel and dog's mercury. The tree mixes in Plantings 3 and 4, which are next to Marline Wood are broadly similar to the communities found in the ancient woodland itself, although Planting 3 does not include hornbeam, which accounted for 90% of the canopy cover in the area of Marline Wood immediately adjacent to it. Canopy closure has resulted in large areas of bare ground in these plantings, although 24 herbs and grasses were found, including woodland species such as: moschatel, lords-and-ladies, herb robert, ivy, bluebell and wood speedwell. Just four species were recorded in the isolated Planting 2, but surprisingly, this included small numbers of lords-and-ladies and bluebell. Native alder would have been more appropriate here than the exotic grey alder (*Alnus incana*) which was planted.

The site has little structured woodland edge, but hedgerows and smaller patches of scrub have been planted north of Crowhurst Road, with hawthorn, blackthorn, elder, guelder-rose, hazel, field maple, holly and goat willow. These species are appropriate for the area, and will provide fruit primarily in the autumn and early winter, with guelder-rose persisting into the new year, and holly through to the spring.

Grassland along the bypass as a whole supports 73 herbs and grasses. The best area is Queensway meadow (1.3 ha), which includes a 'community' of 47 herbs and grasses. NVC analysis showed that this most closely resembles a crested dogstail-common knapweed grassland, of the meadow vetchling sub-community (MG5a). This is the classification of rare unimproved semi-natural neutral grassland in Kent and East Sussex, including nearby Marline Meadow. Wild flowers here provide abundant pollen and nectar sources for invertebrates throughout the spring and summer months. Species such as common knapweed, common fleabane and thistles (*Cirsium* spp.) continue to flower well into the autumn. This is complemented by numerous brambles which constitute the 'woodland edge'. In addition, food plants of many of the wider countryside butterfly species can be found, which is reflected in the diverse butterfly fauna across the site. A small oversowing programme could benefit the flora and bring it even closer to a neutral grassland community (see Section 4.3.2).

West of the carriageway, and north of Crowhurst Road, is a steep embankment of rank grassland and scrub, where only 30 grassland species were recorded. NVC analysis suggests that false oat-grass (MG1) is the most appropriate classification for this community. Far fewer butterflies were recorded here. On the top of the embankment, the flora is impoverished, just 19 herbs and grasses were present, together with valuable areas of bare ground. This may be due to extensive grazing by rabbits. Further north, twenty five grassland plants were found on a rank grassland embankment adjacent to Marline Valley Woods SSSI.

Marline meadow is an unimproved species-rich neutral grassland (English Nature SSSI citation), which our survey confirmed had a reasonable fit with crested dogstail-common knapweed grassland (MG5). Species present include yellow rattle, Dyer's greenweed, sheep's fescue, common knapweed and common spotted-orchid. This meadow could act as a natural source of plants for the roadside grassland and meadows, and should have been considered as a source of seed and/or hay when the road was landscaped. It might still be feasible to harvest seed or hay from this meadow to further enrich the roadside meadows. The rank roadside grassland would even benefit from strewing hay harvested from Queensway meadow.

Fauna

Twenty-three birds were recorded in the roadside estate, 13 of which are likely breeders. Four red-listed and three amber-listed species were recorded in 2004/05, including an estimated three pairs of song thrush and two pairs of bullfinch. Other notable woodland birds which occur here include wren, dunnock, robin, blackcap and chiffchaff. Several pairs of whitethroat and lesser whitethroat occur in the thicker hedgerows and scrub. The site is also used by family feeding parties from nearby woodland: six family parties of blue tits and great tits were recorded on one June morning in the vegetation north of Crowhurst Road. The small size of the woodland and scrub areas make the site vulnerable to the loss of birds through events such as natural dispersal and predation, but this is compensated for by the close proximity of large areas of ancient woodland.

Viviparous lizard, slow worm and grass snake were also found in the grassland areas.

Birds recorded (amber and red-listed species highlighted)

Woodpigeon
Green woodpecker
Wren*
Dunnock*
Robin*
Blackbird*
Song thrush*
Redwing
Mistle thrush
Lesser whitethroat*
Whitethroat*
Blackcap*

Chiffchaff*
Long-tailed tit*
Blue tit
Great tit
Magpie
Carrion crow
House sparrow
Common chaffinch*
Greenfinch*
Linnet
Bullfinch*

* likely breeder

Butterflies recorded (species suffering a decline in abundance are emboldened)

Small skipper*
Essex Skipper
Large skipper*
Large white
Small white
Green-veined white
Orange tip
Holly Blue*
Red admiral
Painted lady
Speckled wood*
Marbled white
Gatekeeper*
Meadow brown*
Ringlet*
Small heath*

* likely breeder

Sixteen butterflies were recorded along the roadside during 2004/05. At least eight of these are likely to be breeding on site. Butterflies were observed throughout the grassland areas, particularly Queensway meadow and the embankment adjacent to Marline meadow. No butterflies were recorded in the new woodland areas, although speckled woods were found along a shady bridleway north of Crowhurst Road, and probably breed. Another notable species was small heath, which is suffering a decline in abundance across most of its range. This is a good area for butterflies, and the species diversity may increase in the next few years. Queensway meadow was almost completely cut early in July 2005, which highlights the problems of roadside management, and must be avoided in future years to protect the developing grassland ecosystem.

Summary of woodland design and conservation value

Criteria	Key Issues; Merits for wildlife (poor ★ – very good ★★★★★)	
Woodland design and conservation value		
Position	Position enforced; Planting 1 successfully buffers Dogkennel Wood	★★★
Layout	Very small woodland areas offer little opportunity for design and are too small to evaluate (0.1–0.4 ha); structured woodland edge planting could have been considered in 'woodland' areas	★★★
High forest species mix	Variable: Planting 3 & 4 have appropriate species (★★★★); Planting 2 near Crowhurst Road includes an exotic alder and may have been better designed as scrub or a hedge (★★★); Planting 1 has too many alders, too few ash and hornbeam (★★)	
Woodland edge species mix	Small patches of scrub and longer lengths of hedgerow include 8 species: would benefit from enrichment	★★★
Grassland species mix	No sowing carried out, but good diversity of grasses and wild flowers in certain areas; oversowing or hay strewing could improve all grassland areas and create a habitat closer to unimproved neutral grassland	★★★★
High forest structure and design	Intimate mix spaced at 1.5 m	★★
Woodland edge structure and design	No structured woodland edge created, but scrub compensates to some extent	★★★
Woodland ground flora	None introduced, but six ancient woodland vascular plants already colonised	★★★★
Ride vegetation structure	Bridleway along embankment is largely overgrown by bramble. Grassland present in open meadows and along embankments; sward heights uniform; managed mowing regime urgently required	★★
Ride flora	Grassland supports 73 herbs and grasses; 47 in Queensway meadow which has the appearance of a more natural grassland community; nectar plants plentiful in some areas; good variety of open ground plants for invertebrates	★★★★
Woodland fauna	Habitat mosaic is good for birds, which move between scrub, woodland planting and ancient woodland; open areas support many of the common woodland butterflies of East Sussex; viviparous lizard, grass snake and slow worm also recorded	★★★★
Contribution to local BAPs	Four nationally red-listed and 3 amber-listed birds recorded on site; 2 butterflies suffering decline in abundance; no survey data on mammals and other invertebrates	★★★★
Conclusion		
	Habitat mosaic has considerable potential; active management required at this stage to improve the diversity of scrub and grassland species; opportunity to introduce plants from nearby Marline meadow, and even to use hay from Queensway meadow to enrich the rank grassland embankments	★★★

5.6 Robertsbridge Bypass

Map of Robertsbridge Bypass

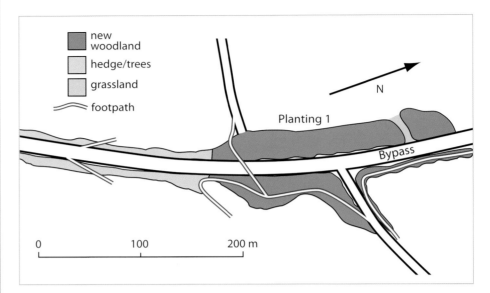

new woodland

hedge/trees

grassland

footpath

Planting 1

Bypass

N

0   100   200 m

The bypass is situated in a well-wooded, mixed farming landscape where woodland creation is important; the ancient woodland of Park Wood is just 160 m east of the bypass.

BELOW LEFT **The flora of Robertsbridge bypass is the most diverse of all the case study sites; 96 species were recorded, including several ancient woodland species such as common spotted-orchid.**

BELOW RIGHT **Thirty-two herbs and grasses grow under the trees at Poppinghole Lane, including good colonies of early-purple orchid and cuckooflower.**

www.markhamblin.com

LEFT **Dunnock occurs along the roadside and may have bred.**

RIGHT **This block of woodland (left of carriageway) occupies just 0.7 ha; it is 30 m at its widest point, and isolated, offering little opportunity for colonisation by woodland flora and fauna; its close proximity to the carriageway may cause problems in future years.**

LEFT **The hedgerow planting on this site is more appropriate, but species-poor; it is dominated by birch, field maple and bramble, with small numbers of oak and guelder-rose.**

RIGHT **Frequent mowing at Poppinghole Lane to improve line-of-sight prevents the growth of grassland containing species such as early-purple orchid and cuckooflower.**

5.6.1 Landscape character and site description

Robertsbridge bypass is within the High Weald character area, and the High Weald Area of Outstanding Natural Beauty. This is a well-wooded, mixed farming landscape, with characteristic ridges and stream valleys; woods of varying size are interspersed with small, unimproved meadows, bordered by species-rich hedgerows and shaws. The area immediately west of the bypass is occupied by lowland grazing marsh, pasture and the built up areas of Robertsbridge. Beyond the town, approximately 1.5 km west of the bypass, there are extensive areas of ancient woodland. The area to the north, south and east of the bypass is mainly farmland and woodland. The ancient woodland of Park Wood and Maynard's Wood (24.3 ha) is just 160 m east of the bypass. Birching Wood, which is also an ancient wood, lies 0.8 km to the south, close to roadside planting at Poppinghole Lane. There are no records of unimproved neutral grassland in the vicinity of the bypass.

Summary of landscape character and site description		
Criteria	**Key Issues; Merits for creating new woodland for wildlife (poor ★ – very good ★★★★★)**	
Landscape character assessment		
Landscape context	High Weald character area: well-wooded, mixed farming landscape, with species-rich hedgerows and lowland grassland; woodland creation important in this area	★★★★★
Classification of nearby woodland (NVC)	Extensive areas of ancient woodland, typically ash-maple communities, within 1.5 km of the bypass	★★★★
Classification of nearby grassland (NVC)	Lowland grazing marsh adjacent (condition unknown); no known unimproved neutral grassland in the immediate vicinity	
Site description		
Site topography and elevation	Level areas, gentle slopes and steeper embankments; 20–50 m asl	★★★
Soil type	Unknown	
Original site vegetation	Unknown	
Other natural features such as ponds etc	None	
Size and shape	Linear roadside estate, maximum width 30 m; 1.6 ha over 0.5 km of main bypass; 0.2 ha at Poppinghole Lane	★★★
Previous land use	Unknown	
Adjacent habitat	Farmland and suburban gardens border the main bypass; ancient woodland immediately across the road from Poppinghole Lane planting	★★
Quality assessment	Poor site for woodland creation; better for grassland, hedge/scrub	★★

The bypass is 1.2 km in length, of which 0.5 km was surveyed in 2005; the roadside estate along this stretch of road occupies 1.6 ha, and is 30 m at its widest point. The planting of this area was carried out in 1989/90. The woodland planted along the main bypass occupies 0.7 ha of embankment, with an access track at the northern end creating a very small ride; other planting is better defined as hedgerow, scrub or shaw. Surveys were also carried out at Poppinghole Lane, 0.8 km south of the bypass, where just 0.2 ha was landscaped and planted in 1989/90.

5.6.2 Woodland design and conservation value

Flora

In total, 96 plant species were recorded at this site, which is the highest of any of the case study sites, despite being one of the smallest. Planting 1 is primarily wild cherry and oak, with smaller numbers of hornbeam and ash. Understorey species, which account for 20% of the mix, include maple, hazel and spindle. Although there were considerable areas of bare ground, 31 herbs and grasses were recorded, including woodland species such as hedge woundwort, lords-and-ladies, lesser celandine and ivy; two ancient woodland vascular plants, pendulous sedge and pignut were also found. Across the road, the woody vegetation is dominated by birch and bramble, with small numbers of field maple, oak and guelder-rose. Nineteen plants were found here, including two ancient woodland plants; common spotted-orchid and bluebell. The area planted at Poppinghole Lane is just across the road from Birching Wood, which is an ash-field maple-dog's mercury wood of the wood anemone sub-community (W8b). The roadside planting is essentially a hedgerow, dominated by field maple, with a small number of birch and occasional hawthorn and gorse. Thirty-two herbs and grasses were found, including good colonies of early-purple orchid and cuckooflower.

Grassland verges, no more than 2 m wide in most places, support 59 herbs and grasses. NVC analysis of the verges along the main bypass suggests that the 'floristically dull' Yorkshire-fog-tufted hair-grass community (MG9) is the most appropriate classification. Some wild flowers here provide pollen and nectar sources for invertebrates throughout the spring and summer months, although insects will be disturbed by the proximity of fast-moving traffic. Frequent mowing at the junction with Poppinghole Lane to improve line-of-sight, reduces the area of rank grassland (MG1) which has a number of interesting wild flowers, including colonies of early-purple orchid and cuckooflower.

Fauna

The bird community along the bypass is characteristic of hedgerows and open countryside. Seventeen birds were recorded, including four red-listed and one amber-listed species. Song thrush and bullfinch were amongst

Birds recorded (amber and red-listed species highlighted)	
Wood pigeon	Blue tit
Great spotted woodpecker	Great tit
Wren*	Magpie
Dunnock*	House sparrow
Robin*	Common chaffinch*
Blackbird*	Greenfinch
Song thrush*	Bullfinch*
Lesser whitethroat*	Yellowhammer
Blackcap*	
* likely breeder	

nine species which may have bred. Notable woodland birds included wren, dunnock, robin and blackcap, although few birds were observed in Planting 1. Species of hedgerows, scrub or very open woodland included lesser whitethroat and yellowhammer. The site is also used by family feeding parties from nearby woodland or suburban gardens: four family parties of blue and great tits were recorded in June.

This is a poor site for butterflies, due to the narrow grassland verges, frequent mowing, and the close proximity of traffic. It is interesting that speckled wood and ringlet were found, both of which prefer shade. Just six species have been recorded, mainly along the very small access track at the northern end of the survey area. It is possible that all may breed at the site.

Butterflies recorded (species suffering a decline in abundance are emboldened)

Small skipper*
Large skipper*
Speckled wood*
Gatekeeper*
Meadow brown*
Ringlet*

* likely breeder

Summary of woodland design and conservation value

Criteria	Key Issues; Merits for wildlife (poor ★ – very good ★★★★★)	
Woodland design and conservation value		
Position	Planting 1 will screen houses, but trees planted within 2 m of the road may cause problems on the carriageway in future years	★★
Layout	Planting 1 is just 222 m x 30 m (0.7 ha), which offers little opportunity for design, although an access track at the northern end effectively creates a small ride; scrub planted in other areas is more appropriate for this narrow roadside corridor	★★★
High forest species mix	Balance between canopy and understorey species in Planting 1 is good, but dominance of wild cherry is uncharacteristic of local woodland	★★★
Woodland edge species mix	Hedgerow/scrub planting are species-poor, and would benefit from enrichment	★★
Grassland species mix	No sowing carried out, but good diversity of grasses and wild flowers across the site	★★★★
High forest structure and design	Intimate mix	★★
Woodland edge structure and design	No structured woodland edge	
Woodland ground flora	None introduced, but several woodland shade plants including 2 ancient woodland vascular plants present	★★★
Ride vegetation structure	No ride network, narrow verges; revised mowing regime would be beneficial at Poppinghole Lane	★★
Ride flora	Very small area of roadside verge supports a diverse 'grassland community' of 59 herbs and grasses;	★★★★
Woodland fauna	Habitat is generally good for birds (★★★), although woodland is small and lacks structural diversity (★); limited open areas support small numbers of butterflies (★)	
Contribution to local BAPs	4 nationally red-listed and 1 amber-listed birds recorded on site; few butterflies; no survey data on mammals and other invertebrates	★★★
Conclusion		
	Hedgerow/scrub planting appropriate for site, but could be enriched; small pockets of grassland support a diverse flora; even the very small access track supports some butterflies; Planting 1 provides a screen for neighbouring houses, but is too small to support a diverse woodland ecosystem, and may create problems in future due to proximity of trees to carriageway; might have been better with a wider grass verge and hedgerow planting	★★

REFERENCES

Agate, E. (ed.) 2000. *Tree planting and aftercare a practical handbook*. BTCV.

Agate, E. (ed.) 2002. *Woodlands a practical handbook*. BTCV.

Asher, J, Warren, M, Fox, R, Harding, P, Jeffcoate, G and Jeffcoate, S. 2001. *The millennium atlas of butterflies in Britain and Ireland*. Oxford University Press, Oxford.

Bossuyt, B, Heyn, M and Hermy, M. 2002. Seed bank and vegetation composition of forest stands of varying ages in central Belgium: consequences for regeneration of ancient forest vegetation. *Plant Ecology* 162, 33–48.

Bourn, N, Thomas, J, Stewart, K and Clarke, R. 2002. Importance of habitat quality and isolation. Implications for the management of butterflies in fragmented landscapes. *British Wildlife* 13, 398–403.

Brenchley, WE and Adam, H. 1915. Recolonisation of cultivated land allowed to revert to natural conditions. *Journal of Ecology* 3, 193–210.

Broadmeadow, MSJ, Ray, D and Samuel, CJS. 2005. Climate change and the future for broadleaved tree species in Britain. *Forestry* 78, 145–161.

Broadmeadow, MSJ, Ray, D, Sing, L and Samuel, CJS. 2004. Climate change and British woodland: what does the future hold? Forest Research Annual Report and Accounts 2002–2003.

Central Science Laboratory. 2003. Maximising the biodiversity value of farm woodlands to the agri-environment. Defra Final Project Report WD0129.

Countryside Agency. 1999. *Countryside Character. Volume 7 South East and London*. CA13. Countryside Agency, Cheltenham.

Countryside Commission and the Forestry Commission. 1997. Woodland creation: needs and opportunities in the English countryside: responses to a discussion paper.

Crafer, T. 2005. *Foodplant list for the caterpillars of Britain's butterflies and larger moths*. Atropos Publishing.

Day, J, Symes, N and Robertson, P. 2003. *The scrub management handbook: guidance on the management of scrub on nature conservation sites*. FACT, English Nature, Peterborough.

Defra. 2004. Farm Woodland Premium Scheme Statistics.

Elton, CS. 1966. *The pattern of animal communities*. Methuen, London.

Ferris, R and Carter, C. 2000. Managing rides, roadsides and edge habitats in lowland forests. *Bulletin* 123, Forestry Commission, Edinburgh.

Ford, HA. 1987. Bird communities on habitat islands in England. *Bird Study* 34, 205–218.

Forestry Commission. 1998a. *England Forestry Strategy: a new focus for England's woodlands, strategic priorities and programmes*. Forestry Commission, Cambridge.

Forestry Commission. 1998b. *The UK Forestry Standard*. Forestry Commission, Cambridge.

Forestry Commission and Defra. 2005. *Keepers of time: a statement of policy for England's ancient and native woodland*. Forestry Commission and Defra.

Fraser, S and Buckley, GP. 2000. *The Farm Woodland Premium Scheme in England, with particular reference to participants in Kent and East Sussex*. In Yoshimoto, A (ed.). *Optimal management in farm woodlands*. Miyazaki University, Japan.

Fuller, RJ. 1982. *Bird habitats in Britain*. Calton: Poyser.

Fuller, RJ. 1995. *Bird life of woodland and forest*. Cambridge University Press, Cambridge.

Fuller, RJ, Noble, DG, Smith, KW and Vanhinsbergh, D. 2005. Recent declines in populations of woodland birds in Britain: a review of possible causes. *British Birds* 98, 116–143.

Fuller, RJ and Warren, MS. 1991. *Conservation management in ancient and modern woodlands: responses of fauna to edges and rotations*. In Spellerberg, IF, Goldsmith, FB and Morris, MG (eds). *The scientific management of temperate communities for conservation. British Ecological Society 31st Symposium*. Blackwell, Oxford. Pp. 445–471.

Gibbons, DW, Avery, MI, Baillie, SR, Gregory, RD, Kirby, J, Porter, RF, Tucker, GM and Williams, G. 1996. Bird species of conservation concern in the United Kingdom, Channel Islands and Isle of Man: revising the Red Data List. *RSPB Conservation Review* 10, 7–18.

Gregory, RD, Wilkinson, NI, Noble, DG, Robinson, JA, Brown, AF, Hughes, J, Gibbons, DW and Galbraith, CA. 2002. The population status of birds in the United Kingdom, Channel Islands and the Isle of Man: an analysis of conservation concern 2002–2007. *British Birds* 95, 410–450.

Griffith, GW, Bratton, JH and Easton, G. 2004. Charismatic megafungi – the conservation of waxcap grasslands. *British Wildlife* 16, 31–43.

Grime, JP, Hidgson, JG and Hunt, R. 1990. *The abridged comparative plant ecology*. Unwin Hyman Ltd. London.

Hall, JE, Kirby, KJ and Whitbread, AM. 2004. *National Vegetation Classification: field guide to woodland*. Joint Nature Conservation Committee, Peterborough.

Harmer, R, Peterken, G, Kerr, G and Poulton, P. 2001. Vegetation changes during 100 years of development of two secondary woodlands on abandoned arable land. *Biological Conservation* 101, 291–304.

Harris, S, Morris, P, Wray, S, and Yalden, DW. 1995. *A review of British mammals: population estimates and conservation status of British mammals other than cetaceans*. Joint Nature Conservation Committee, Peterborough. HMSO.

Hermy, M, Honnay, O, Firbank, L, Grashof-Bokdam, CJ and Lawesson, JE. 1999. An ecological comparison between ancient and other forest plant species of Europe, and the implications for forest conservation. *Biological Conservation* 91, 9–22.

Hill, MO, Mountford, JO, Roy, DB and Bunce, RGH. 1999. *Ellenberg's indicator values for British plants. ECOFACT Volume 2A, Technical Annex*. ITE Monkswood, Huntingdon. DETR.

Hill, MO. 1996. TABLEFIT Version 1.0, For Identification of Vegetation Types. Institute of Terrestrial Ecology, Huntingdon.

HMSO. 1995. *Biodiversity: the UK Steering Group report. Volume 2: Action Plans*. London, HMSO.

Hodder, KH, Bullock, JM, Buckland, PC and Kirby, KJ. 2005. Large herbivores in the wildwood and modern naturalistic grazing systems. English Nature Research Report no. 648.

Honnay, O, Bossuyt, B, Verheyen, K, Butaye, J, Jacquemyn, H and Hermy, M. 2002. Ecological perspectives for the restoration of plant communities in European temperate forests. *Biodiversity and Conservation* 11, 213–242.

Honnay, O, Hermy, M and Coppin, P. 1999. Impact of habitat quality on forest plant species colonisation. *Forest Ecology and Management* 115, 157–170.

Hulme, M, Jenkins, G and Lu, X. 2002. Climate change scenarios for the United Kingdom. The UKCIP02 scientific report.

Huntley, B and Birks, HJB. 1983. *An atlas of past and present pollen maps Europe: 0–13000 years ago*. Cambridge University Press, Cambridge.

Hutson, AM. 1993. *Action plan for the conservation of bats in the United Kingdom*. Bat Conservation Trust, London.

de Keersmaeker, L, Martens, L, Verheyen, K, Hermy, M, de Schrijver, A and Lust, N. 2004. Impact of soil fertility and insolation on diversity of herbaceous woodland species colonising afforestation in Muizen forest (Belgium). *Forest Ecology and Management* 188, 291–304.

Kent Biodiversity Action Plan Steering Group. 1997. The Kent Biodiversity Action Plan. A framework for the future of Kent's wildlife.

Kent County Council. 1998. *North East Kent landscape assessment and guidelines.*

Kent County Council. 2004. *The landscape assessment of Kent.*

Kent Habitat Survey Partnership. 2003. Kent habitat survey.

Key, R. 2000. Bare ground and the conservation of invertebrates. *British Wildlife* 11, 183–191.

Kirby, K, Saunders, G and Whitbread, A. 1991. The National Vegetation Classification in nature conservation surveys – a guide to the use of the woodland section. *British Wildlife* 3, 70–80.

La Dell, TFG. 1983. An introduction to tree and shrub seeding. *Landscape Design* 144, 27–31.

Liley, D, Brereton, T and Roy, D. 2004. The current level of butterfly monitoring in UK woodlands and potential use of the data as a biodiversity indicator to inform sustainable forestry. Butterfly Conservation Report to the Forestry Commission. Report no. SO4–35.

MAFF, (1988, 1998). *Farm Woodland Premium Scheme rules and procedures.* MAFF, London.

Matlack, GR. 1994. Plant species migration in a mixed-history forest landscape in eastern North America. *Ecology* 75, 1491–1502.

Mountford, E, Peterken, GF, Edwards, PJ and Manners, JG. 1999. Long-term change in growth, mortality and regeneration of trees in Denny Wood, an old-growth wood-pasture in the New Forest (UK). *Perspectives in Plant Ecology, Evolution and Systematics* 2, 223–272.

Nature Conservancy Council. 2004. *Handbook for Phase I habitat survey – a technique for environmental audit.* Joint Nature Conservation Committee, Peterborough.

Oates, M. 2004. The ecology of the Pearl-bordered Fritillary in woodland. *British Wildlife* 15, 229–236.

Oliver, CD. 1981. Forest development in North America following major disturbances. *Forest Ecology and Management* 3, 153–168.

Pepper, H. 1999. Recommendations for fallow, roe and muntjac deer fencing: new proposals for temporary and reusable fencing. Forestry Commission Practice Note 9. Forestry Commission, Edinburgh.

Peterken, GF. 1981. *Woodland conservation and management.* Chapman and Hall, London.

Peterken, GF. 2000. Identifying ancient woodland using vascular plant indicators. *British Wildlife* 11, 153–158.

Peterken, GF and Francis, JL. 1999. Open space as habitats for vascular ground flora species in the woods of central Lincolnshire, UK. *Biological Conservation* 91, 55–72.

Peterken, GF and Game, M. 1984. Historical factors affecting the number and distribution of vascular plant species in the woodlands of central Lincolnshire. *Journal of Ecology* 72, 155–182.

Peterken, GF and Mountford, EP. 1995. Lady Park Wood: the first fifty years. *British Wildlife* 6, 206–213.

Pyatt, DG, Ray, D and Fletcher, J. 2001. An ecological site classification for forestry in Great Britain. *Bulletin* 124. Forestry Commission.

Rackham, O. 1990. *Trees and woodland in the British landscape.* Dent, London.

Rackham, O. 2003. *Ancient woodland its history, vegetation and uses in England,* New edition. Castlepoint Press, Scotland.

Rodwell, JS (ed.). 1991. *British Plant Communities Volume 1. Woodlands and Scrub.* Cambridge University Press, Cambridge.

Rodwell, JS (ed.). 1992. *British Plant Communities Volume 3. Grasslands and Montane Communities.* Cambridge University Press, Cambridge.

Rose, F. 1999. Indicators of ancient woodland – the use of vascular plants in evaluating ancient woods for conservation. *British Wildlife* 10, 241–251.

Smith, S. 2001 *The national inventory of woodland and trees.* Forestry Commission, Edinburgh.

Snow, B and Snow, D. 1988. *Birds and berries.* T & AD Poyser, England.

Stebbings, RE. 1988. *Conservation of European bats.* Christopher Helm Publishers Ltd.

Sussex Biodiversity Partnership. 2001. *A Biodiversity Action Plan for Sussex.*

Swanwick, C. 2002. *Landscape character assessment. Guidance for England and Scotland.* Countryside Agency and Scottish Heritage.

Tansley, AG. 1939. *The British Isles and their vegetation.* Cambridge University Press, Cambridge.

Thomas, JA, Telfer, MG, Roy, DB, Preston, CD, Greenwood, JJD, Asher, J, Fox, R, Clarke, RT and Lawton, JH. 2004. Comparative losses of British butterflies, birds, and plants and the global extinction crisis. *Science,* 303, 1879–1881.

Thompsom, K, Bakker, J and Bekker, RM. 1997. *The soil seed banks of north west Europe: methodology, density and longevity.* Cambridge University Press, Cambridge.

Turner, J. 1962. The *Tilia* decline: an anthropogenic interpretation. *New Phytologist* 61, 328–341.

Vera, FWM. 2000. *Grazing ecology and forest history.* CABI Publishing, UK.

Verheyen, K and Hermy, M. 2001. The relative importance of dispersal limitation of vascular plants in secondary forest succession in Muizen Forest, Belgium. *Journal of Ecology* 89, 829–840.

Ward, LK and Spalding, DF. 1993. Phytophagous British insects and mites and their food-plant families: total numbers and polyphagy. *Biological Society of the Linnean Society* 49, 257–276.

Warren, MS and Fuller, RJ. 1993. *Woodland rides and glades: their management for wildlife.* Joint Nature Conservation Committee, Peterborough.

Watson, JW. 1996. Establishment of broadleaf woodland by direct seeding with arable crops: ecology of the Temperate Taungya method. *Aspects of Applied Biology* 44, 117–119.

Whitbread, AM and Kirby, KJ. 1992. *Summary of National Vegetation Classification woodland descriptions.* UK Nature Conservation Report 4, Joint Nature Conservation Committee, Peterborough.

Williamson, DR. 1992. *Establishing farm woodlands.* Forestry Commission Handbook 8.

Willoughby, I, Jinks, R, Gosling, P and Kerr, G. 2004. *Creating new broadleaved woodland by direct seeding.* Forestry Commission Practice Guide. Forestry Commission, Edinburgh.

Woolhouse, MEJ. 1983. The theory and practice of the species-area effect applied to the breeding birds of British woods. *Biological Conservation* 63, 23–30.

Worrell, R, Pryor, SN, Scott, A, Peterken, GF, Taylor, K, Knightbridge, R and Brown, N. 2002. *New wildwoods in Britain: the potential for developing new landscape-scale native woodlands.* Report produced for the Land Use Policy Group.

FURTHER READING

Armstrong, H, Gill, R, Mayle, B and Trout, R. 2003. Protecting trees from deer: an overview of current knowledge and future work. Forest Research Annual Report and Accounts 2001–2002. Pp 29–39.

Boyce, P and Dietz, M. 2005. *Development of good practice guidelines for woodland management for bats*. English Nature Research Report no. 661.

Broad, K. 1998. *Caring for small woods*. Earthscan Publications Ltd., London

Buckley, GP (ed.) 1989. *Biological Habitat Reconstruction*. Belhaven Press, London.

Crofts, A. and Jefferson, RG. 1999. *Lowland grassland management handbook*. English Nature/The Wildlife Trusts, Peterborough.

Defra. 2002. *Working within the grain of nature. A biodiversity strategy for England*. Defra Publications, London.

Ferris-Kaan, R (ed.). 1995. *The ecology of woodland creation*. John Wiley, Chichester.

Forestry Commission. 2002. *National Inventory of Woodland Trees England: Regional Report for the South East*. Forestry Commission, Edinburgh.

Harmer, R. 1999. Creating new native woodlands: turning ideas into reality. *FCIN* 15. Forestry Commission, Edinburgh.

Harmer, R. 1999. Using natural colonisation to create or expand new woodlands. *FCIN* 23. Forestry Commission, Edinburgh.

Harmer, R and Gill, R. 2000. Natural regeneration in broadleaved woodlands: deer browsing and the establishment of advance regeneration. *FCIN* 35. Forestry Commission, Edinburgh.

Herbert, R, Samuel, S and Patterson, G. 1999. Using local stock for planting native trees. *FCPN* 8. Forestry Commission, Edinburgh.

Highways Agency. 1999. Towards a balance with nature: Highways Agency Environmental Strategic Plan. Highways Agency.

Hill, D. 2001. *Highways and birds*. Highways Agency.

Humphrey, J, Newton, A, Latham, J, Gray, H, Kirby, K, Poulsom, E, and Quine, C (eds). 2003. *The restoration of wooded landscapes*. Forestry Commission, Edinburgh.

Kerr, G and Williams, HV. 1999. Woodland creation experience from the National Forest. *Forestry Commission Technical Paper* 27. Forestry Commission, Edinburgh.

Kirby, P. 2001. *Habitat management of invertebrates: a practical handbook*. The RSPB, Sandy.

Kent Partnership. 2003. Kent Environment Strategy. Kent County Council.

MAFF. 1999. The environmental benefits of farm woodlands planted under the Farm Woodland Scheme and Farm Woodland Premium Scheme. WD0121. Cranfield University.

McColin, D, Jackson, JI, Bunce, RGH, Barr, CJ and Stuart, R. 2000. Hedgerows as habitat for woodland plants. *Journal of Environmental Management* 60, 77–90.

Mitchley, J, Burch, F, Buckley, P and Watt, T. 2000. *Habitat restoration monitoring handbook*. English Nature Research Report no 378.

Mortimer, SR, Turner, AJ, Brown, VK, Fuller, RJ, Good, JEG, Bell, SA, Stevens, PA, Norris, D, Bayfield, N and Ward, LK. 2000. The nature conservation value of scrub in Britain, JNCC Report No. 308, Joint Nature Conservation Committee, Peterborough.

Porley, R and Hodgetts, N. 2005. *Mosses and liverworts*. The New Naturalist Library, HarperCollins, London.

Read, H and Frater, M. 1999. *Woodland habitats*. Routledge, London.

Rodwell, J and Patterson, G. 1994. Creating new native woodlands. *Forestry Commission Bulletin* 112. HMSO, London.

Smart, SM, Bunce, RGH, Black, HJ, Ray, N, Bunce, F, Kirby, K, Watson, R and Singleton, D. 2001. Measuring long term ecological change in British woodlands. English Nature Research Report no. 461.

Spooner, B and Roberts, P. 2005. *Fungi*. The New Naturalist Library, HarperCollins, London.

Symes, N and Currie, F. 2005. *Woodland management for birds: a guide to managing for declining woodland birds in England*. The RSPB, Sandy and Forestry Commission England, Cambridge.

Trueman, I and Millett, P. 2003. Creating wild-flower meadows by strewing green hay. *British Wildlife* 15, 37–44.

Usher, MB, Brown, AC and Bedford, SE. 1992. Plant species richness in farm woodlands. *Forestry* 65, 1–13.

Waite, A. 2000. *The Kent Red Data Book. A provisional guide to the rare and threatened flora and fauna of Kent*. Kent County Council.

Winspear, R and Davies, G. 2005. *A management guide to birds of lowland farmland*. The RSPB, Sandy.